Stress Management for Teachers

The Guilford Practical Intervention in the Schools Series

Kenneth W. Merrell, Founding Editor
T. Chris Riley-Tillman, Series Editor

www.guilford.com/practical

This series presents the most reader-friendly resources available in key areas of evidence-based practice in school settings. Practitioners will find trustworthy guides on effective behavioral, mental health, and academic interventions, and assessment and measurement approaches. Covering all aspects of planning, implementing, and evaluating high-quality services for students, books in the series are carefully crafted for everyday utility. Features include ready-to-use reproducibles, lay-flat binding to facilitate photocopying, appealing visual elements, and an oversized format. Recent titles have companion Web pages where purchasers can download and print the reproducible materials.

Recent Volumes

RTI Team Building: Effective Collaboration and Data-Based Decision Making
Kelly Broxterman and Angela J. Whalen

RTI Applications, Volume 2: Assessment, Analysis, and Decision Making
T. Chris Riley-Tillman, Matthew K. Burns, and Kimberly Gibbons

Daily Behavior Report Cards: An Evidence-Based System of Assessment and Intervention
Robert J. Volpe and Gregory A. Fabiano

Assessing Intelligence in Children and Adolescents:
A Practical Guide
John H. Kranzler and Randy G. Floyd

The RTI Approach to Evaluating Learning Disabilities
Joseph F. Kovaleski, Amanda M. VanDerHeyden, and Edward S. Shapiro

Resilient Classrooms, Second Edition: Creating Healthy Environments for Learning
Beth Doll, Katherine Brehm, and Steven Zucker

The ABCs of Curriculum-Based Evaluation: A Practical Guide
to Effective Decision Making
John L. Hosp, Michelle K. Hosp, Kenneth W. Howell, and Randy Allison

Curriculum-Based Assessment for Instructional Design:
Using Data to Individualize Instruction
Matthew K. Burns and David C. Parker

Dropout Prevention
C. Lee Goss and Kristina J. Andren

Stress Management for Teachers: A Proactive Guide
Keith C. Herman and Wendy M. Reinke

Interventions for Reading Problems, Second Edition:
Designing and Evaluating Effective Strategies
*Edward J. Daly III, Sabina Neugebauer, Sandra Chafouleas,
and Christopher H. Skinner*

Classwide Positive Behavior Interventions and Supports:
A Guide to Proactive Classroom Management
Brandi Simonsen and Diane Myers

Stress Management for Teachers

A Proactive Guide

KEITH C. HERMAN
WENDY M. REINKE

THE GUILFORD PRESS
New York   London

© 2015 The Guilford Press
A Division of Guilford Publications, Inc.
370 Seventh Avenue, Suite 1200, New York, NY 10001
www.guilford.com

All rights reserved

Except as indicated, no part of this book may be reproduced, translated, stored in a retrieval system, or transmitted, in any form or by any means, electronic, mechanical, photocopying, microfilming, recording, or otherwise, without written permission from the publisher.

Printed in the United States of America

This book is printed on acid-free paper.

Last digit is print number: 9 8 7 6 5 4 3 2

LIMITED PHOTOCOPY LICENSE

These materials are intended for use only by qualified professionals.

The publisher grants to individual purchasers of this book nonassignable permission to reproduce all handouts for which photocopying permission is specifically granted in a footnote. This license is limited to you, the individual purchaser, for personal use. This license does not grant the right to reproduce these materials for resale, redistribution, electronic display, or any other purposes (including but not limited to books, pamphlets, articles, video- or audiotapes, blogs, file-sharing sites, Internet or intranet sites, and handouts or slides for lectures, workshops, or webinars, whether or not a fee is charged). Permission to reproduce these materials for these and any other purposes must be obtained in writing from the Permissions Department of Guilford Publications.

Library of Congress Cataloging-in-Publication Data

Herman, Keith C.
  Stress management for teachers : a proactive guide / Keith C. Herman and Wendy M. Reinke.
    pages cm. — (The Guilford practical intervention in the schools series)
  Includes bibliographical references and index.
  ISBN 978-1-4625-1798-5 (pbk. : alk. paper)
  1. Teachers—Job stress. 2. Teachers—Job stress—Prevention. I. Reinke, Wendy M.
II. Title.
  LB2840.2.H37 2015
  371.1001'9—dc23

2014026327

About the Authors

Keith C. Herman, PhD, is Professor in Counseling Psychology at the University of Missouri and Co-Director of the Missouri Prevention Center. Much of his work focuses on working with teachers and families to promote effective environments for children. He presents nationally and has published more than 80 peer-reviewed articles and chapters and four books on effective practices in schools.

Wendy M. Reinke, PhD, is Associate Professor in School Psychology at the University of Missouri and Co-Director of the Missouri Prevention Center. She developed the Classroom Check-Up, an assessment-based, classwide teacher consultation model. Her research focuses on preventing disruptive behavior problems in children and increasing school-based implementation of evidence-based practices. Dr. Reinke presents nationally, has published more than 50 peer-reviewed articles, and has coauthored four books on teacher consultation and effective practices in school.

Acknowledgements

We would like to thank the scores of dedicated teachers who have granted us the privilege of working with them over the years and inspired us to write this book. We would also like to acknowledge the following Missouri Prevention Center team members for their assistance in editing chapters of the book as it developed: Angela Colletta, Melinda Gross, Tracey Latimore, Marcus Petree, Dan Cohen, Sarah Owens, Lisa Aguilar, Rebecca Leaf, and Ryan Bahr.

Contents

List of Handouts   xv

PART I. OVERVIEW OF STRESS AND COPING

1. Background and Rationale   3

Assault on Teachers: Stories of Teachers in the Accountability Era   3
Challenges and Ironies   4
What's a Teacher to Do?   5
An Overview of This Book   6
Potential Applications of This Book   7
Special Features   8
Who Should Read This Book?   8
What Does the Research Say?   9

2. Stress: The Good, the Bad, and the Lion   11

Stress: The Basics   11
    What Is Stress?   11
    Common Stress Reactions   12
    Stress and Illness   12
    Physiology of Stress   13
The Purpose of Stress   14
    The Good   14
    The Bad   15
    Take-Home Message   16
Sources of Teacher Stress   16
    Work-Related Stressors   17
    Life Stress   22
Ineffective Coping Strategies   22
Reflecting on Your Own Stress and Coping Response   23
    Self-Assessments   23
    Your Stress and Coping   24
Building Commitment to Change   25
Summary   26

3. The Teacher Coping Model — 30

A Good Theory about Stress   30
  Interrelations   32
  A Negative Cycle   33
  Creating a Positive Cycle   34
  Which One Is Most Difficult to Control?   35
  The Big Idea   36
The TCM   36
The TCM Building Blocks and Getting to Good   37
  Awareness   37
  Adaptive Thoughts   38
  Adaptive Behaviors   39
  Beyond Survival   41
Self-Assessments   41
  Thinking Habits   41
  Behavior Patterns   41
  Other Symptoms and Problem Areas   42
Summary   43

PART II. COPING STRATEGIES

4. Awareness — 49

Mood Monitoring   49
Feelings Journal   51
Deep Breathing   52
Goal Setting   53
Problem Solving   54
Summary   57

5. Adaptive Thinking I: The Positive/Negative Thoughts Method — 62

Becoming an Expert on Your Thoughts   62
Disclaimer: Adaptive Thinking, Not Rose-Colored Glasses   64
Self-Assessment   64
Positive/Negative Thoughts Method: Planting Positive Thoughts
    and Reducing Negative Thoughts   65
  Tracking Your Positive and Negative Thoughts   66
  Strategies for Generating Positive Thoughts   66
  Strategies for Reducing Negative Thoughts   71
Using the Method   72
  Goal Setting   72
Summary   72

6. Adaptive Thinking II: The ABC Method — 83

Self-Assessment   84
Self-Monitoring: ABC   84
  The ABC Worksheet   84
  Identifying Your Beliefs   87
  Digging Deeper: The Funnel Technique   91

Contents   xi

    Common Thinking Errors   91
    Which Thinking Errors Do You Make?   94
    Identifying Core Beliefs   94
  Challenging Maladaptive Thinking: ABCDE   95
    The ABCDE Worksheet   96
  Summary   99

7. Adaptive Behaviors   109

  Increasing Your Positive-to-Negative Ratio   110
    In the Classroom   111
    In Your Friendships   111
    At Home   111
  Pleasant Activities   112
    Fun in the Classroom   113
    Reward Yourself   113
  Effective Communication and Social Problem Solving   114
    Social Support and Expressing Your Feelings   114
    Connecting with Other Teachers   115
    Assertive Communication   116
  Relaxation Skills   119
    Deep Breathing   119
    Progressive Muscle Relaxation   120
    Mini-Muscle Relaxations   121
    Autogenic Relaxation   121
    Guided Imagery   122
    Relaxation Tapes   122
  Healthy Eating and Exercise   123
  Minimal Interventions   124
    Written Self-Disclosure   124
    Plants and Nature   125
  Summary   126

8. Competence and Self-Efficacy   140

  Classroom Management and Challenging Student Behaviors   141
    Authentic Relationships with Students   141
    Using Proactive Classroom Management Strategies   142
  Students with Challenging Behaviors   159
  Professional Development   164
    Consultation and Coaching   164
    Peer Coaching   164
    Goal Setting   165
  Summary   167
  Resources   167

9. Beyond Survival: Getting to Good   175

  Getting to Good   175
  Mindfulness   177
    Paradox   178
    Mindful Breathing   179
    Aspects of Mindfulness   179
    Practicing Mindfulness   180

Values, Virtues, and Affirmations 181
   Values Card Sort 181
   Exploring Your Virtues 182
   Values and Virtues Affirmations 182
Gratitude and Generosity 183
Using Stories 183
Summary 185
Resources 185

PART III. APPLICATIONS AND EXTENSIONS

10. Specific Applications   189

Administrative Pressures 189
   Adaptive Behaviors 190
   Adaptive Thoughts 190
   Practice 191
Peer Conflicts 192
   Gossip 193
   Bullying 193
Working with Parents 195
Work–Life Balance 201
   My Life Pie 201
   Taking Care of Yourself 202
Summary 203

11. Coping with Serious Symptoms   207

Anxiety 207
   A Caveat 208
   Self-Assessment 208
   Understanding and Treating Anxiety Symptoms and Disorders 209
Depression 210
   Self-Assessment 210
   Understanding and Treating Depression Symptoms and Disorders 211
Anger 212
Substance Abuse 212
Seeking Professional Help 213
Summary 214

12. For School Administrators and Other School Professionals   215

Awareness 215
   Assessing Current Perceptions 216
   Adaptive Behaviors 218
   Positive-to-Negative Ratio 219
   Delivering Negative Feedback 220
Talking with Teachers about Stress and Coping 223
   Tips for Talking with Teachers and Supporting Wellness 223
   What If the Person Doesn't See the Problem? 224
Using the TCM for Administrator Stressors 225
Summary 228

13. Setting Up a TCM Study Group   232

Developing a Plan and Timeline   232
Establishing Group Ground Rules   234
Group Facilitation   234
   OARS   235
   Structure of the Group   235
Tips for Successful Groups   236
Summary   238

14. Your Personal Development Plan and Broader Systems Change   240

Personal Development Plan   240
Creating Systems Change   240
   Big Ideas of PBIS   241
Summary   242

References   247

Index   252

Purchasers of this book can download
and print additional copies of the handouts
from *www.guilford.com/herman-forms*.

List of Handouts

HANDOUT 2.1.	Life Events Questionnaire	27
HANDOUT 2.2.	Perceived Stress Scale	28
HANDOUT 2.3.	Building Commitment	29
HANDOUT 3.1.	Thinking Habits	44
HANDOUT 3.2.	Behaviors Related to Stress and Coping Screening	45
HANDOUT 3.3.	Classroom and Teaching Screening	46
HANDOUT 4.1.	Basic Mood Monitoring Form	58
HANDOUT 4.2.	Mood Monitoring Form with Three Feelings	59
HANDOUT 4.3.	Goal-Setting Sheet	60
HANDOUT 4.4.	Problem-Solving Sheet	61
HANDOUT 5.1.	Dysfunctional Attitude Scale	74
HANDOUT 5.2.	Common Negative Thoughts and Their Positive Replacements	77
HANDOUT 5.3.	Tracking Positive and Negative Thoughts	78
HANDOUT 5.4.	Why I Became a Teacher	79
HANDOUT 5.5.	What I Like Most about Being a Teacher	80
HANDOUT 5.6.	My Coping Thoughts	81
HANDOUT 5.7.	Positive and Negative Method Goal Setting	82
HANDOUT 6.1.	List of Common Challenging Areas	101

HANDOUT 6.2.	ABC Worksheet (with Instructions)	102
HANDOUT 6.3.	ABC Worksheet (without Instructions)	103
HANDOUT 6.4.	Complete Mr. Caldera's ABC Worksheet	104
HANDOUT 6.5.	Complete Ms. Simone's ABC Worksheet	105
HANDOUT 6.6.	The Funnel Method	106
HANDOUT 6.7.	ABCDE Worksheet (with Instructions)	107
HANDOUT 6.8.	ABCDE Worksheet (without Instructions)	108
HANDOUT 7.1.	Pleasant Events Schedule	127
HANDOUT 7.2.	Pleasant Events I Want to Try	135
HANDOUT 7.3.	Pleasant Events Goals and Weekly Schedule	136
HANDOUT 7.4.	Adding Fun to My Classroom	137
HANDOUT 7.5.	Incentives for Me	138
HANDOUT 7.6.	Interpersonal Support Evaluation List	139
HANDOUT 8.1.	Assessment of Teacher–Student Relationships	169
HANDOUT 8.2.	Plan for Teaching Classroom Rules	171
HANDOUT 8.3.	Plan for Teaching Classroom Routines and Tasks	172
HANDOUT 8.4.	Step-by-Step Guide for Determining the Function of Student Behavior	173
HANDOUT 9.1.	Self-Affirmation Manipulations to Encourage Adaptive Functioning	186
HANDOUT 10.1.	Parent–Teacher Conference Feedback Form	204
HANDOUT 10.2.	My Life Pie	205
HANDOUT 10.3.	Taking Care of Myself Worksheet	206
HANDOUT 12.1.	Questions to Guide an Effective Problem-Solving Framework	229
HANDOUT 12.2.	Complete Mr. Ellison's ABC Worksheet	230
HANDOUT 12.3.	Complete Mr. Ellison's ABCDE Worksheet	231
HANDOUT 13.1.	Summary Session Form	239
HANDOUT 14.1.	Personal Development Plan	243
HANDOUT 14.2.	Changing the School Environment	245

PART I

OVERVIEW OF STRESS AND COPING

CHAPTER 1

Background and Rationale

What causes people to experience negative emotions like stress, sadness, or anger? Do events cause emotions? That is, are emotions caused by what happens to us? The answer may surprise you and is the foundation for understanding how to manage our emotional experiences. Before we provide an answer, consider the following scenario:

> At a faculty meeting at Riley Elementary School, the principal announces that she will make weekly observations in every teacher's classroom for the remainder of the school year. Three teachers at the school have very different emotional reactions to the news. Ms. Malcolm feels inspired and excited about the announcement, Mr. Gonzalez feels anxious, and Ms. Phipps feels angry. They all experienced the exact same event, yet their emotional reactions were completely different.

Do events, or the things that happen to us, cause our feelings? The short answer is no. Events can trigger a series of reactions, but they do not, in themselves, cause us to feel certain ways. The same event can lead to a range of reactions in different people. Something more immediate determines our emotional reaction. This is good news, because if our emotional lives were solely determined by events we would all be at the mercy of every event that occurs.

So if not events, what has a more direct impact on how we feel? And equally important, is it something we can control? The short answer is yes. We describe the long answer in the remainder of this book.

ASSAULT ON TEACHERS: STORIES OF TEACHERS IN THE ACCOUNTABILITY ERA

Teaching can be a stressful profession. Nearly half of all new teachers leave the field within five years of receiving their degrees, many citing the reason for leaving as ongoing challenges and stressors in the school environment (Ingersoll, 2002). Teachers often bear the brunt of the burden created by the growing emphasis on accountability, where the focus is on student outcomes, leaving little time or attention for teacher well-being. At the same time, it is clear that stress interferes with teacher performance, thus making positive outcomes less likely in classrooms where teachers do not cope well.

> **Teachers often bear the brunt of the burden created by the growing emphasis on accountability where the focus is on student outcomes, leaving little time or attention for teacher well-being.**

"Every day I feel under attack. Sometimes it feels like nobody respects teachers anymore. At work, many students and parents don't seem to respect us. Even worse, it seems like every time I pick up a paper or turn on the news there is a story about what's wrong with teachers. It's as if society expects us to solve all the world's problems and blames us when we don't." —Eighth-Grade Teacher

We have had the privilege to work with hundreds of teachers over the years and to listen to their stories. It seems that regardless of the purpose of our visits or workshops, conversations always seem to drift to the topic of teacher stress and coping. We have been struck by how powerful and consistent these stories are, and how most teachers have experienced mounting pressure and lessening support over the past decade. Throughout the book we return to these stories to guide our examples of teacher work-related stress.

CHALLENGES AND IRONIES

The irony is that these experiences of teachers, and the high pressure society puts on them, undermine the qualities that teachers need to be effective. Teaching has always been a challenging job, only more so recently. With any challenging job, it is essential to have time to focus, relax, and reflect. This is especially true for teachers, because their daily interactions can have profound effects on the children in their classroom. Teachers may project their stress onto their students, making it more likely that students will experience stress themselves, and, thereby less likely they will be open to learning.

> **When teachers are stressed, they are less able to provide the types of environments we know are conducive to learning and to support children's social and emotional development.**

There is a wealth of literature that has documented the importance of positive teaching (see Reinke, Herman, & Sprick, 2011). Effective classroom management begins with a calm, warm, and affirming teacher who can deliver high rates of positive attention to students when they are meeting expectations and composed, brief redirections when needed. When teachers are stressed, they are less able to provide the type of environment we know is conducive to learning and to support children's social and emotional development.

WHAT'S A TEACHER TO DO?

Based on the climate of education in the United States and the challenges many teachers encounter, it is tempting to conclude that excessive teacher stress is inevitable and that teachers are helpless to reduce it. If that were true, this would turn out to be a very boring and impractical book. The reality is that despite all the changes in education and the daily stressors and hassles teachers experience, there remains great variability in how well a teacher will function and cope. Some teachers continue to flourish, even in this challenging environment, while others feel overwhelmed.

> **We all possess tendencies to act and think in certain ways, but we can learn to adapt how we act and think.**

Let us return to the example from the beginning of this chapter. Recall that three teachers had very different reactions to the announcement that they would be subject to weekly performance evaluations. Same event, three diverse stress experiences; so the event by itself cannot explain why people feel a particular way. If not the event, then what accounts for different emotional reactions? Think for a moment why Ms. Malcolm might be feeling inspired and excited about having weekly performance observations. Why does Mr. Gonzalez feel anxious about this news? What could explain why Ms. Phipps feels angry?

If you answered these questions with some version of "because of the way he or she was thinking about the observations," we like the way you are thinking! Ms. Malcolm feels excited about the prospect of being observed in her classroom because she is viewing it as an opportunity, perhaps to learn more about herself, to improve her teaching, or simply to have more interaction with her principal. She is thinking about the event in a positive way.

In contrast, Mr. Gonzalez and Ms. Phipps are clearly thinking about the event (the announcement of weekly observations) in a negative manner, but in slightly different ways. We know this because they have different negative emotions to the same event. This is important to notice because our specific emotional reactions are always tied to the very particular way we are thinking about events in our lives. Mr. Gonzalez is feeling anxious about the news, so he is focusing his thoughts on some aspect of the event that makes him feel vulnerable. Perhaps he thinks that his principal will discover his flaws as a teacher, give him a poor evaluation and recommend a remediation plan, or even that the observations may ultimately lead to his being fired. The more serious the worry in his head, the more intensely he will experience the feeling. For instance, if at his core he believes he is a defective teacher, an imposter who is at risk of being fired, he will likely experience very intense anxiety in response this announcement. Only Mr. Gonzalez knows for sure which thoughts most trouble him, and he will only realize this if he takes time to reflect on his thoughts in ways that we teach you in this book. Based on our impressions of how he is feeling, though, we can guess the types of thoughts he is likely to have.

Finally, Ms. Malcolm is angry, so her most immediate thoughts are not about her vulnerability but rather about feeling bothered or attacked by the news. Some thoughts that might go along with her anger could be that she is annoyed that the principal is inconveniencing her with visits to her class, or perhaps she does not respect her principal and believes she has no right to judge the quality of her teaching. Again, only Ms. Malcom knows for sure, but the nature of her emotional response gives her clues as to the type of thoughts that go along with those emotions.

In summary, we have three people experiencing three very different emotions related to the same event, and these emotions arise and persist largely because of how each of them thinks about the event. Now the question is, are they all at the mercy of their thoughts? Are they just hardwired to think in these ways with no hope of altering their thinking and, in turn, their emotions? Fortunately, no. We all possess tendencies to act and think in certain ways, but we can learn to adapt how we act and think. Decades of research has demonstrated this fact (Butler, Chapman, Forman, & Beck, 2006; Clark & Beck, 2010).

The skills described in this book teach you new ways of thinking and acting that make it more likely for you to manage stress at work and in life better. The key skill to focus on is the ability first to be aware of your feelings, thoughts, and actions. Once you are conscious of those, you will have a greater capacity to adapt to the stressors you face on a daily basis. The skills required to think about events differently or to choose different courses of action naturally follow from this type of self-awareness.

AN OVERVIEW OF THIS BOOK

This book is designed to provide a framework for understanding common stressors in schools and practical strategies for coping with these stressors. The goal is to describe practical strategies to bolster effective coping responses of teachers. A secondary goal is to provide a framework for administrators, school mental professionals, and even teachers to create an environment for promoting effective coping of school professionals.

Part I provides a background and rationale for the book including definitions of key terms (stress, coping) and an overarching model for understanding the strategies that we present in subsequent chapters. This section briefly reviews the theory and research that underlies all the strategies in the book. In addition, it presents stories in the voice of teachers of how they experience unparalleled stressors in their work. Embedded throughout the text, these stories provide real-life examples of teachers and their efforts to cope with the demands of their job.

Part II provides specific coping strategies within each area of the model. It starts with a focus on mood monitoring, as this is the most accessible skill for developing awareness needed to interrupt the stress cycle. The next three chapters discuss coping responses within two categories: cognitive coping and adaptive behaviors. Throughout this section, we provide real examples of teachers who use these methods to reduce their stressors and then suggest specific application exercises for the reader to practice the skills. In addition, Part II builds on these basic skills in order to encourage readers to go beyond stress reduction and build toward even more positive outcomes (e.g., the absence of illness is not the same thing as health). Chapter 8, Competence and Self-Efficacy, focuses on improving the teacher's effectiveness in the classroom, a critical aspect of stress reduction. We show the connection between teaching competence, self-beliefs, and stress, and then highlight critical areas of competence for all teachers to improve on. In addition, we describe strategies and resources for improving teaching competence (including topics discussed in other books in the Practical Interventions for Schools Series). The section ends with a chapter on facilitating even more positive outcomes, including happiness, satisfaction, and mindfulness.

Part III extends the core concepts of the model to include other applications and the broader school context. For instance, Chapter 11 focuses on more serious problems (depression, substance abuse) that go beyond the primary focus of the book but are common consequences of persistent stressors. Chapter 12 focuses on other school personnel (administrators and other school staff) and how they can promote a positive coping environment. Because these skills lend themselves to social discussion, Chapter 13 discusses how to set up a reading group with colleagues and strategies for making such a group successful. Chapter 14 focuses on broader systems change and acknowledges that individual coping is important, but it is always situated within broader contexts that influence these responses.

In this book we intend to produce five primary outcomes:

1. Provide a rationale for promoting effective coping in teachers.
2. Provide a practical model for supporting teacher use of effective coping strategies.
3. Describe specific cognitive and behavioral strategies for improving teacher coping.
4. Extend the model and strategies to include promoting broader outcomes beyond stress reduction, including happiness and well-being.
5. Provide suggestions for administrators and other school personnel to support teachers and promote an effective coping environment.

POTENTIAL APPLICATIONS OF THIS BOOK

We wrote this book with a range of applications in mind. Our overarching goal is to provide teachers and their colleagues with a well-established framework for improving their coping and problem-solving skills and, therefore, improve their ability to manage the inevitable stressors of their jobs. Within this goal we anticipate at least four potential ways to use the book. First, we intend the book to be a resource for any K–12 (possibly even PreK) inservice and preservice teacher to use as a self-improvement guide. The strategies we describe have been used and described in other self-improvement-oriented books for other audiences (David Burns's bestseller *Feeling Good* [1999] is an excellent example). Research shows that individuals can use these skills described in such books to reduce stress, anxiety, and depression (e.g., see Cuijpers, 1997, 1998). A second use of the book is in groups of teachers in such formats as teacher book clubs, resource meetings, or workshops led by professionals within the school (school psychologists, school counselors) or by teachers themselves. Third, the book is a resource for other professionals in schools who interact with teachers and whose role, at least in part, is to support teachers. These individuals include administrators who seek strategies to foster a less stressful work environment and effective interactions with teachers, as well as other teachers, school psychologists, and special educators who struggle with how best to support teachers who are stressed and/or burned out by their jobs. Fourth, we see the potential to use the book in preservice courses for teachers. The book is a helpful supplemental reading for practicum and other training encounters in which preservice teachers may experience high levels of stress.

SPECIAL FEATURES

We have included two special features to the book to help you get the most out of it. First, in each chapter we have a section called "If You Do Only One Thing." We recognize that you are busy and that you may be reluctant to commit to doing all of the activities in each chapter. Although we hope that you do all activities, we wanted to be sure to highlight one activity in each chapter that will give you the biggest bang for your buck. The activities described in the "If You Do Only One Thing" sections are proven methods for giving a positive boost to your mood. As with any skill, the benefits will only last as long as you use the method. But we hope by showing you the power of these tools that it will catch your attention and motivate you to return to the book for more exercise and practice.

Second, for those of you who choose to use the book as part of a class or a study group, we have a section in each chapter called "Group Activities." These are special adaptations of the methods for groups to capitalize on the power of group process. At the end of the book, we give special focus to planning study groups and helping ensure their success, so if you are going to use the book in a study group, this chapter might be a good place to start.

WHO SHOULD READ THIS BOOK?

How do you know whether this book is for you, and how can you best use it to maximize your potential? As we note, if you are a school professional who works with colleagues who are stressed and you would like to provide support, you can use the resources presented in this book. If you are a school professional who experiences stress and would like help reducing it, then this book can be useful for you.

Teachers who fit a profile of high stress and low coping not only suffer inside because of their stress, but it shows in their classrooms.

A helpful starting point is to complete a quick self-assessment about your current levels of stress and coping. We'll start with a simple one in this chapter and will include several more detailed assessments in subsequent chapters. To start, answer the following two questions about your current level of stress and coping.

1. How stressful is your job?

   0   1   2   3   4   5   6   7   8   9   10

   Not Stressful   Very Stressful

2. How well are you coping with the stress of your job right now?

    0   1   2   3   4   5   6   7   8   9   10

Not Well   *Very Well*

We recently asked 121 teachers these same questions and then compared their answers to other survey results they provided about topics like burnout and self-efficacy (Hickmon, Reinke, & Herman, 2013). We also collected objective ratings of disruptive behaviors and academic achievement of students in their classrooms. Based on these data, we were able to conclude something that probably will not surprise you. The vast majority of teachers report high levels of work-related stress. Only 7% of teachers fit a profile characterized by low levels of stress and high levels of positive coping. The rest were characterized by above-average stress ratings (scores of 6 or higher). Compared to teachers in the low-stress group, teachers who fell into any group with above-average stress scores reported lower levels of self-efficacy and confidence in their teaching and higher levels of burnout.

Based on our findings, if you answered question 1 with a rating of 6 or higher, we are confident that some of the skills and strategies in this book can help you. Depending on how stressed you feel, you may be able to pick and choose certain skills throughout the book that better fit your needs. If you rated yourself lower than a 6, that's great! Take time to complete some of the more detailed assessments in Chapters 2 and 3 to get a better sense of your overall stress and coping as well as related symptoms and vulnerabilities. These allow you to assess the parts of the book that apply to your needs.

The second question is helpful in further distinguishing the impact of teachers' stress on their job performance. Teachers who fit a profile of high stress and low coping not only suffer inside because of their stress, but also it shows in their classrooms. These teachers report the lowest ratings of confidence and efficacy in the classroom, the highest rates of student disruptive behaviors, and the lowest rates of student adaptive behaviors. Perhaps most concerning, this translates into worse academic performance for their students on standardized achievement tests. Based on these findings, if you answered question 2 with a rating of 6 or lower, the skills throughout the book are especially relevant to you. In order to determine your specific needs and areas for skill development, you should read each chapter and complete each self-assessment.

WHAT DOES THE RESEARCH SAY?

Now that you have a sense of the areas and topics in this book that best fit you and you have a plan for moving forward, you probably would like to know, "Will it work?" Can reading a book actually help you learn new skills and reduce your stress or improve your mood? We can answer with a confident absolutely! Many studies have examined this question about whether bibliotherapy, as it is called in research articles, works. Several studies show that bibliotherapy works for a variety of problems and topics. For instance, one line of research shows that bibliotherapy is an effective treatment for mild to moderate depression and anxiety (Cuijpers, 1997, 1998). Other research has shown that people can use the tools in books to reduce their stress and increase coping behaviors.

Of course, not all books are created equal, and not all books are based on the science that led to these discoveries. We wrote this book based on the established science in bibliotherapy, using the theories and strategies that prior studies found most helpful in producing positive changes for readers.

An important detail to mention is that in order to achieve the results found in these studies, a couple things need to happen. First, you actually need to read the book. Simply owning or possessing it does not have any benefit to you unless you actively read it. Second, information alone is probably not enough to create lasting change for you. You need to complete some exercises and activities to learn the strategies and apply them in your life. Like any new skill, learning new ways to think or act requires practice. As they say, the more you put into it, the more you will get out of it. Finally, approach the book and the activities in it like a scientist. Not everything will work for you, but some things will. Undoubtedly, you will already be good at some skills described in the book. That's great. Pay attention to these as your skills and resources to build upon. Your job is to find which new skills are most important for you to adopt in order to become even more effective at coping with stress. Try them, test your hypotheses as whether they are helpful or not, be open to what you will find, and then monitor what works. At the end of the book, you will have several new skills that you can use in the future.

CHAPTER 2

Stress
The Good, the Bad, and the Lion

To better manage stress, it is helpful to understand why stress exists in the first place. Stress has a bad reputation, but as you probably know, it serves a purpose. In this chapter, we review the basics of stress, what it is, how and why we experience it, and how our bodies react to it. This information is important to understand as you develop a plan to better manage your stress. Understanding the physiology of stress provides you with insights about how your body works and how you can better make it work for you. Next, we examine common stressors teachers experience in the accountability era of education. We identify several categories of stressors reported to us by teachers and describe how these stressors relate to the physiological basis of stress described in the outset of the chapter. Finally, we conclude with some self-assessments and self-reflection exercises to prepare you for future chapters.

STRESS: THE BASICS

What Is Stress?

Stress refers to our response to a stressor. One of the most influential stress scientists, Hans Selye (1974) defined stress as "the nonspecific response of the body to any demand made upon it" (p. 27). More recently, famed neuroendocrinologist Robert Sapolsky (2004), defined a stressor as "anything in the outside world that knocks you out of homeostatic balance" and the stress response as "what your body does to reestablish homeostatic balance" (p. 6). Viewed this way, stress and stressors are neither good nor bad in themselves. What determines how they affect us, favorably or not, is how we interpret and respond to them.

> **Psychological and social stressors are the daily hassles that so often undermine our productivity, well-being, and happiness.**

In his popular book, *Why Zebras Don't Get Ulcers*, Sapolsky (2004) identified three broad categories of stress: acute physical stress (life-and-death circumstances), chronic physical stressors (e.g., lack of food and shelter), and psychological and social stressors. This third category is the focus of this book. Psychological and social stressors are the daily hassles that so often undermine our productivity, well-being, and happiness.

Common Stress Reactions

How do you experience stress? What does it feel like? How do you know when you are stressed? Stress is associated with a range of physical, behavioral, and emotional experiences. Many people answer these questions by referring to their bodies in some way.

"I feel tension in my shoulders."
"I have a knot in my stomach."
"I get restless and fidgety."
"I pick my nails."
"I get headaches."

Often people also refer to their thoughts:

"I worry more."
"I can't think clearly."
"I can't focus."
"I expect the worst."
"I think things won't get any better."

Stress is also experienced as a range of emotions:

"I feel anxious."
"I feel tired and worn out."
"I feel overwhelmed."
"I feel tense."
"I get irritable."

These responses illustrate how intertwined the stress experience is with our mind and body, which are really one and the same (more about that later).

Stress and Illness

One of the reasons physicians and psychologists are so interested in stress is because of its possible connection to illness. Can stress make us more vulnerable to disease? The answer is yes. Selye did some of the original work in this regard and found that chronic stress resulted in what he termed the general adaptation system, later called the stress response.

Our bodies have immediate and predictable responses to stress. There is nothing wrong with or damaging about our stress response by itself. However, Selye found that if the stress response persists for too long, our bodies adapt to these chronic circumstances, often with devastating consequences. At some point, with chronic stress activation, our bodies wear down and become vulnerable to illness.

Physiologists refined the idea of homeostatic regulation of stress in our bodies and now refer to the concept of allostasis. Homeostasis implies some optimal set point for each subsystem in the body (e.g., blood pressure, weight, hormone levels), a balance that the body is constantly trying to maintain. Allostasis recognizes that the balance of systems is dynamic and always occurs in relation to other body systems. The most important idea in understanding persistent stress responses is that homeostasis is always a reactionary process, whereas allostasis recognizes that our bodies anticipate and prepare for stressors. In allostatic approaches to stress, our bodies regulate body systems to new levels and set points, not just after we experience a stressor, but sometimes well in advance of a stressor to prepare us for whatever challenge we might face. These anticipatory stressors, usually of the psychological and social variety, can become chronic and interfere with our well-being.

> **Anticipatory stressors, usually of the psychological and social variety, can become chronic and interfere with our well-being.**

Stressors that provoke the stress response are not limited to negative life experiences. A stressor is anything that causes us to adapt. Positive events including a wedding, birth of child, job promotion, and even neutral events like moving can have the same toll as negative events like the death of a loved one. In fact, in the 1960s, researchers found that simply counting the number of positive and negative events you had in the past year indicates your level of risk for illness (Holmes & Rahe, 1967). Therefore it is important to consider the number of stressors we experience in a given time and how chronic the stressors are.

The bottom line is that excessive and/or enduring stress makes us vulnerable to illness. Stress has been implicated in a variety of conditions, from the common cold to cardiovascular disease (see Seligman, 2011, for a discussion). The question is how? In order to understand the answer to this question, we provide a short primer on the physiology of stress. There is no need to memorize new terms that appear in the section below. Aim to understand the big idea, which is how a prolonged stress response interferes with immune function.

> **A prolonged stress response interferes with immune function.**

Physiology of Stress

To understand the physical basis of stress, we begin with an explanation of our nervous system. Our nervous system is divided into two subsystems, the central and peripheral nervous systems. The central nervous system (CNS) is composed of our brain and our spinal cord. All sensory experiences and the interpretation of those experiences are processed in our CNS. The peripheral nervous system (PNS) includes all the sensory and receptive nerves that allow the rest of the body to communicate with the CNS and the body's interaction with the external world. The PNS collects information from our primary senses and delivers it to the CNS. The PNS is further divided into the sympathetic and parasympathetic nervous systems. These subsystems are intimately involved in the human stress response.

The PNS is primitive by design. All mammals share the same basic structure of their PNS. A key point in understanding the modern human stress response is that the PNS has a rudimentary on/off aspect to it. The sympathetic system turns us on. When we face a stressor, the sympathetic system turns on systems that give us energy and devotes resources to our muscles, therefore moving us to action. The sympathetic system increases our heart rate, respirations, and blood pressure while it reduces blood flow to our digestive system and redirects it to our muscles. In contrast, the parasympathetic system slows us down and turns us off, so to speak. It is active during times of calmness. So it reduces our heart rate, respiration, and blood pressure, and, consequently, increases blood flow to our digestive system.

The activation of the stress response is also associated with a variety of chemical changes in the body. Of course, the brain is the master planner of all our stress reactions; its interpretation of events sets our stress responses in motion. When we perceive a threat, the brain coordinates a sequence of steps throughout the body including activating the sympathetic nervous system, which directs the release of activating hormones, like epinephrine and norepinephrine. In turn, the adrenal gland releases glucocorticoids, which set in motion other actions, for example, the uptick of glucose in the bloodstream for energy. At the same time, these chemicals downregulate the release of other hormones like estrogen and testosterone, growth hormones, and insulin.

Many of these physical and chemical changes that occur as part of a persistent stress response also affect immunity. Mild and brief stress may boost immunity (see below), but when the stress response endures it takes a toll on the immune response system. The most convincing evidence in this regard demonstrates the role of glucocorticoids in inhibiting the function and release of immune fighter cells (e.g., lymphocytes, interleukins, and interferons). Consequently, the longer our stress response is activated, the lower our immune functioning, and the more vulnerable we become to disease.

THE PURPOSE OF STRESS

The Good

Before you start to think that you have mistakenly bought a biology textbook, let's switch back to the topic at hand: your stress and the role it has in your life. Take a moment to reflect on why we experience stress in the first place. All aspects of our being serve some functional purpose, given that they have endured throughout millennia. So what function did stress serve in the past, and what function does it serve today?

Let us start with today. When people reflect on how stress is helpful in their lives they sometimes refer to its motivational qualities. Stress is a trigger to try harder or be better prepared. It provides us with the energy we need to accomplish tasks and face challenges. Others refer to stress as a signal, an indicator for the individual to relax or better manage their circumstances. In short-term doses, mild to moderate levels may actually boost aspects of our immune system and even increase the effectiveness of vaccines. Under acute stress, our bodies release some protective chemicals and increase the activity of immune cells, which some studies suggest may even offer defense against certain types of cancer (Dabhar, Malarkey, Neri, & McEwen, 2012; Dabhar et al., 2010). There are also mental benefits to stress. Research has found that short-term stress can improve memory (Yuen et al., 2009). Stress can give us a laser-like focus to address an immediate problem or challenge.

From a historical perspective, and a physiological one, the purpose of stress is much more mundane. Our nervous system is designed the way it is to serve a basic need for survival. It mimics the design of other mammals. Our prehistoric ancestors needed the basic mechanisms to keep themselves alive, like a gazelle needs to stay alive on the African plains. Fundamentally, we all need a nervous system that can be activated in an instant and immediately devote all of our energy and resources to the escape of a physical threat or to stay and fight it off. In the case of a gazelle, it is essential that it has a nervous system that allows it to quickly energize itself to devote all of its resources to escape its predators. Likewise, for humans, when we are in a life-or-death situation, it is imperative to have a system that allows us to quickly energize ourselves to flee, gives us super strength to lift objects, or to fight off an attacker.

> **Our nervous system is designed the way it is to serve a basic need for survival.**

These are the good parts about stress. You may have noticed that nearly all the benefits of stress come with a qualifier such as "short-term" or "acute." This turns out to be a key distinction for understanding the benefits and the risks of stress. In the short term, stress serves as a signal of awareness and allows us to consider our options. The stress response can be very functional. The brain's orchestration of the stress response to activate chemical and body systems for immediate action is critical to survival. However, herein lies the fundamental problem with stress we encounter in modern life.

The Bad

The positive aspects of stress are directly linked to its downfall. In the modern world, threats to our existence rarely occur. Most of us go years without encountering a true life-or-death experience, yet the relic of our system is still primarily designed for this purpose. The end result is that our nervous system is poorly designed for the daily stressors we are much more likely to encounter—a stressful phone call from a parent, a disruptive and annoying student, an argument with a colleague, a deadline, performance evaluations, and high-stakes testing, to name a few. While these events are stressful, they are very different from events that carry potential for death, yet our nervous system responds to these stressful events with the same basic urgency. Thus, to the extent we experience these daily events as enduring stressors, our sympathetic nervous system constantly prepares our bodies for action and operates as if these daily events threaten our existence. The end result of a perpetually

> **The end result is that our nervous system is poorly designed for the daily, non-life threatening stressors we are much more likely to encounter.**

activated sympathetic nervous system is physiological wear and tear on the very body it was designed to protect and preserve.

Back to our prehistoric ancestors and our animal cousins. This system works perfectly fine for them because they do not experience the same sort of daily hassles we encounter in our lives. Their sympathetic nervous systems turn off when they are not in immediate danger. Their parasympathetic nervous system slows down their heart rate, reduces stress hormones, and allows the body to recover from these stressful events. While they rest or graze, gazelles do not stew over an offensive comment made by a friend, or worry about whether they will have time to complete all their paperwork by end of the week. Instead, they relax until they sense danger and their sympathetic nervous kicks on again.

Sapolsky (2004) highlights a telling example of this in the title of his popular book, *Why Zebras Don't Get Ulcers*. As he reviews in the book, zebras and other mammals of the African plains do not get ulcers because their nervous systems turn off and on. For many humans, however, our sympathetic nervous systems stay active, even in the face of mundane stressors. This allows stress hormones to continue circulating, which takes a toll on all the organs required to keep the sympathetic nervous system active.

As we repeat throughout the book, both the amount of stress you experience and also your perception of it determines its effect on your life, happiness, and functioning. A recent study found that both stress and perceptions predicted longevity. In a large national sample, researchers found that people who reported high amounts of stress *and* who believed that stress affected their health had a 43% greater risk of premature death than those who did not (Keller et al., 2012). Conversely, those who reported high stress but believed it did not affect their health had lower rates of mortality. Thus focusing on reinterpreting stress, in addition to reducing it, will go a long way toward improving your health and happiness.

Take-Home Message

In order to learn how to manage your stress response, you must learn to turn on your parasympathetic nervous system and inactivate your sympathetic nervous system more frequently. Another lesson we have learned about stress is that our brains are intimately involved in the stress response. If you learn new ways to interpret life circumstances, your brain is more likely to use its resources wisely and reduce the likelihood of chronic stress responses.

> **If you learn new ways to interpret life circumstances, your brain is more likely to use its resources wisely and reduce the likelihood of chronic stress responses.**

SOURCES OF TEACHER STRESS

If not lions, then what are the typical stressors of teachers? Life-threatening stressors in teachers' everyday work experiences rarely occur. Instead, teachers experience a variety of daily hassles in their work lives that can accumulate and contribute to persistent stress reactions.

Work-Related Stressors

We recently interviewed dozens of teachers from PreK to secondary settings and asked them about the most challenging parts of their job. The themes of their answers were very consistent and sorted into seven categories: lack of administrative support and unrealistic expectations, colleagues, time demands and resources, diverse student needs and differentiated instruction, student behavior and attitudes, parents, and training and preparation.

Administrative Support and Expectations

Many teachers commented on the lack of support and recognition they receive for doing their jobs. Some summarized this sense as a lack of respect for their professionalism.

> "Not having supportive leadership is a huge challenge. I don't feel supported or validated as being competent." —THIRD-GRADE TEACHER

> "We're not in it to be recognized, but we are asking to be treated with respect as experts in our area and that's never the message that's given out." —SIXTH-GRADE TEACHER

Many expressed the belief that they were expected to perform miracles, to do more with less than in years past. To them, it seemed administrators were spending too much time focusing on what was not working and not enough time acknowledging progress or accomplishments.

Many expressed the belief that they were expected to perform miracles, to do more with less than in years past.

> "The expectations are not always realistic. For the most part we have a wonderful staff who put in an incredible amount of time to support children, and I think that instead of that being recognized or celebrated, we spend a lot of time focusing on our flaws. I know we need to improve, but when we don't get any validation or support it makes it really difficult. It makes us wonder why are we working so hard, why are we trying so hard." —FIFTH-GRADE TEACHER

Perhaps most problematic were teachers' experiences of feeling constantly evaluated and criticized. These teachers experienced lack of administrator support as a sense of negative social judgment.

> "I feel like I'm constantly being watched." —ELEMENTARY SPECIAL EDUCATION TEACHER

> "The culture of the school is stunted. My first opinion was it was sad. People were nervous, like of being judged. It's not comfortable. It's not warm. The teachers are phenomenal. It's not like they don't have it. They have it. It's just not fostered. And it trickles down to the children." —THIRD-GRADE TEACHER

Colleagues

A second category of stressors concerns relationships with colleagues. Several teachers commented on ongoing conflicts with other teachers and school staff members. They experienced this as a divisive work environment. Many even commented on these experiences as a form of interpersonal bullying, not unlike the types of interactions that occur between teens.

> "Staff are rude to each other. For all the good things that are happening they get buried under all that other stuff." —Ninth-Grade Teacher

Teachers also expressed feelings about the culture of the school. In some schools, teachers experienced a strong sense of isolation.

> "This school is very much a do it on your own place: 'Close your door,' 'Teach by yourself,' 'Only give each other information that's necessary to do the job but not to enhance the job.' And so I'm struggling the most with getting the help and the . . . even just the enrichment from working with other really quality teachers that is really lacking."
> —Fourth-Grade Teacher

Time Demands and Limited Resources

Nearly all teachers commented on the increase in paperwork and the limited time they have for social interactions with students. They view this as a burden, and usually an unexpected part of teaching. More experienced teachers commented on how the paperwork expectations have grown over time.

> "Managing the stuff, the paperwork, the meetings, the grading, you know, all the stuff you do instead of teaching." —Tenth-Grade Teacher

> "Paperwork is challenging. It is a full-time job here and a full-time job outside of here."
> —Second-Grade Teacher

> "There's too many things for us to do in the amount of time we have to do them. I think the most important work is with the children. But there is all the paperwork on top of the challenges in the classroom. So we end up doing a lot of our work at home."
> —Fifth-Grade Teacher

Many teachers also noted having limited resources and materials to do their jobs effectively.

> "As the new teacher at this grade level, I got hired late and all the materials were taken out of my room. For instance, every time I come across a new math lesson, it says I need tiles. I don't have those tiles, so I have to go find all the materials. A material shortage is a huge issue." —Second-Grade Teacher

Diverse Student Needs and Differentiating Instruction

Teachers often mentioned two aspects of teacher–student interactions as problematic. First, students have enormous needs that are difficult for a single teacher to meet in a school setting. These include learning needs, especially the challenge of matching instruction to students' skill levels when a vast variety of skill levels exist in a given classroom.

"The most challenging would be the variation of learners in the classroom, that really big broad spectrum. I haven't quite figured it out here with this curriculum, but when I teach a lesson, and I have a third of kids who get it, a third who sort of get it but need help, and a solid third of my class is going, 'I need help. I don't get this. I don't know what to do.' So I end up having seven kids around my conference table during math that I'm re-teaching a lesson to, while my independent kids, yes, can work independently but also need some support and I don't know where to be and where to go. I've worked on it, but that, the differentiation, has been a huge challenge for me, especially in math." —Third-Grade Teacher

"Everyone's different. Everyone learns differently and has different needs. And what happens outside of the classroom to these students greatly impacts what happens inside the classroom. I have to build relationships with every one of them. That's just really hard to do when there are 30 in a class, and some of them are very needy." —Fifth-Grade Teacher

In secondary schools and elementary schools the rotation of students creates challenges for planning and preparation because each class is different.

"I mean, every class is different, which makes it even more difficult, because you have to change your mind-set every time a different group comes in. So that's been really difficult too, the fact that just because something works for this class, does not mean it's going to work for the next." —Seventh-Grade Teacher

In addition to academic skill challenges, teachers frequently commented on the social and emotional needs that kids bring to the classroom and the life experiences that undermine their school success.

"Now it's the mental needs of kids, especially the emotional needs. Teaching is just a small part of our jobs. We spend so much time with social skills and basic skills. So many kids don't get their basic needs met, and that's just draining." —First-Grade Teacher

"These kids have just seen so much that we never saw as kids that they should have never seen. I just feel such a burden to teach these kids to be connected." —Fifth-Grade Teacher

An especially challenging stressor for teachers is when they witness a child's difficult life circumstance firsthand, such as when they observe troubling parent–child interactions or when a child experiences the death of a loved one. Teachers often report feeling helpless in these situations and troubled by the suffering of children in their classrooms.

Student Behaviors and Attitudes

Second, a related set of concerns dealt with student actions and motivation. Teachers felt frustrated with students whom they perceived as disrespectful and unmotivated. A subset of teachers mentioned student misbehavior, open defiance and disruptions, and how such behaviors have become more intense in recent years.

> "In this environment, the multitude of behaviors all going on at the same time, that are difficult behaviors. They're not typical third-grade child behaviors. The children are very upset many times and aren't able to manage their emotions and so they manifest in so many ways: lashing out at others, being stubborn and unwilling to cooperate, running out of the room. There's so much going on at one time." —THIRD-GRADE TEACHER

> "The most challenging students are the ones who are just outright defiant. The attention-seeking ones, I can just give attention to, but the power/control ones, that's harder." —SECOND-GRADE TEACHER

> "How ugly they are to each other and handling it in the right way without flipping out because that makes them flip out." —EIGHTH-GRADE TEACHER

> "Unmanageable behaviors that go way beyond my training. Like throwing books and chairs at me, yelling, screaming." —SECOND-GRADE TEACHER

> "The discipline. The constant talking. In a perfect world they would all be quiet and ready to learn, but they're not, and managing that is a challenge." —KINDERGARTEN TEACHER

What teachers found more bothersome, however, was what they perceived as apathy in many students.

> "They say they don't care. I don't know how to make them care. You have to care more than I care. I can't make them want to do it. Half of me feels like I'm failing as a teacher, and half of me is mad at them." —SEVENTH-GRADE TEACHER

> "Kids who don't want to learn and trying to figure out how to motivate them. They won't open up and share with you, they just push back and withdraw." —EIGHTH-GRADE TEACHER

> "When it seems students don't care, it's hard to care yourself." —FOURTH-GRADE TEACHER

Finally, many teachers reported that the most stressful experiences were not student behaviors and attitudes but rather their own perceived failure to help such students. Many teachers carry very high expectations of themselves to help all children, and those who were disrespectful or unmotivated led teachers to feel ineffective, like they were letting the children down.

> "When you know they have ability and they just aren't using it, that is the most frustrating part for me. I like to be able to reach every child, and I beat myself up when I'm unable to." —Eleventh-Grade Teacher

> "When they are not learning. When it is not happening or flowing as well as I want it to. I get frustrated really quickly. I think I take it personally. I feel personally responsible for everything." —Ninth-Grade Teacher

> "When I feel like I haven't gotten through to them or I haven't helped them so they can proceed with their learning or social development." —Sixth-Grade Teacher

Training and Preparation

While commenting on the behavior and academic challenges of students, teachers also distinguished between student behaviors and their own preparation to deal with such behaviors. These obviously go hand in hand, but many teachers expressed a lack of training and preparation in classroom management as a distinct type of stressor. They thought if they were better prepared, the problems would have been more manageable.

> "Not feeling equipped to deal with the discipline issues, not having the training to know how to help them. Because it's almost every day, with the discipline. The things that are in place right now don't really seem to work for the extreme behaviors. For the children who like being in school, like to learn, what we have in place usually works, but for the extreme behaviors, it doesn't work." —Sixth-Grade Teacher

> "The classroom management, the behavior management. That is the number-one most difficult thing. I feel like I wasn't prepared well enough when I came, which I hear from everyone. My background didn't prepare me for being here at all, on top of not being prepared through college, so I think that has been the biggest struggle." —Fourth-Grade Teacher

> "Classroom management. You think you have it down, it's good for a couple weeks, and then it just stops working. You are constantly changing it. And as teachers we are constantly losing more and more power. You have to be very creative to be able to enforce anything." —First-Grade Teacher

> "For some reason my classroom management is not working. With this group of students it keeps falling apart. I was talking to another teacher and she was saying she noticed around her fourth or fifth year hers fell apart." —Eighth-Grade Teacher

Parents

Teachers expressed frustration with parents they regarded as uninterested and unsupportive.

> "These parents don't care. They expect us to babysit their children and get them to learn. When we ask for their help, they're not there." —SECOND-GRADE TEACHER

> "They get upset at me when I call them to tell them what their child did. It's like these kids have no consequences at home, so why should they care here?" —FIFTH-GRADE TEACHER

Life Stress

These work-related stressors add to the types of stress that teachers and all humans are exposed to outside of work, such as relationship stressors at home, conflicts with spouse or partner and children, conflicts with other adults, financial stressors, health stressors, and all of these persist. Teachers carry these stressors into the school building, before their work day even begins.

INEFFECTIVE COPING STRATEGIES

The rest of this book focuses on helpful coping responses, but it is useful to consider common responses that are not helpful. One common way that people under stress cope is through escape. This includes avoiding conflict, using substances, watching TV, or daydreaming. These escape responses are usually ineffective because they are temporary, that is, they have no lasting benefit for inducing relaxation. In addition, these methods do not serve any functional purpose in solving the problems that induced stress in the first place. Active coping responses (e.g., assertive communication, adaptive thinking, relaxation strategies, exercise) fix barriers or conflicts that created the stress. Furthermore, escape coping strategies often cause new problems. For example, excessive substance use or TV watching may create conflict in family relationships. These habits can also reduce our physical well-being.

Another common way that people cope with frustration is to have some sort of cathartic release. For example, some people scream into a pillow or hit something. Do these strate-

---

GROUP ACTIVITY: Your Daily Stressors

Have a group discussion where each person tells about the two most stressful parts of his or her job. Take turns listening to each other and summarizing what you hear each of you saying. Next, have everyone say what one thing they would most like to be different about the way they are coping with their work.

gies work? Unfortunately, this is a myth, probably traceable to Freudian popular psychology. Research shows these cathartic methods, more often than not, increase our stress in the short and long run, and serve no benefit in promoting well-being (Bushman, 2002).

REFLECTING ON YOUR OWN STRESS AND COPING RESPONSE

Self-Assessments

Now take a moment to reflect on your own experiences with stress and coping. In the first chapter, we asked you two global questions about your stress and coping experiences. Here we ask you to reflect on a more detailed survey about stress.

Life Events Questionnaire

First, answer the questions about recent life events developed by John Lochman (2004) in Handout 2.1.* As noted above, the experience of good and bad life events elevates our risk for illness (Holmes & Rahe, 1967), presumably because they increase our chronic stress load (Evans, 2003). If you answered all 12 questions "no," then congratulations! Currently you are at low risk for life event–related illness. If you answered one or two questions "yes," then you are in the yellow, or warning, zone for potential life event–related illness. You should be mindful of the types of life stressors you can control in order to minimize your risk. If you answered three or more questions "yes," then you are at a higher risk for life event–related illness. It is especially important for you to minimize the life stressors you can control and maximize your coping abilities during the coming months.

Perceived Stress Scale

In addition to life events, another good barometer of our stress level is our own perceptions about how we are feeling and coping with daily life circumstances. Answer the questions from the Perceived Stress Scale in Handout 2.2 (Cohen, Kamarck, & Mermelstein, 1983). As with all surveys we ask you to complete, it is best to go with your first gut response and not spend any time fretting over the precise answer.

Cohen and colleagues (1983) developed and tested this measure in a variety of community samples over the past several decades as a tool for monitoring stress in the general population (see Cohen & Janicki-Deverts, 2012). They have found that higher scores on this measure are related to depression, anxiety, physical symptoms, and increased use of health services.

Notice that this scale has some positively worded items (#8, "felt on top of things") and some negatively worded items (#3, "felt nervous and stressed"). For this reason, you will need to reverse the scoring on some of the items before summing them. To derive your total score, reverse the scores on the four positive items (#4, 5, 7, and 8). That is, on these four items 0 = 4, 1 = 3, 2 = 2, 3 = 1, and 4 = 0. So if you marked #4 as in the (1) *almost never*

---
*All handouts are at the ends of the chapters.

TABLE 2.1. Average Scores on the Perceived Stress Scale

Group (age)	Average score	Group (gender)	Average score
18–29	14.2	Males	12.1
30–44	13.0	Females	13.7
45–54	12.6		
55–64	11.9		
65 years and older	12.0		

box, you would convert this score to a 3 on this item. Once you have converted the four positive items, simply add your responses to all 10 items to get your total score.

Compare your total score to the average scores observed based on your age and gender given in Table 2.1. If your total score is more than six points higher than the average score for your comparison group, then you are likely experiencing a moderate to high level of stress. If your score exceeds the average by 12 or more points, you probably perceive a very high level of stress in your life right now.

The Perceived Stress Scale provides you with a better sense of your experience with stressors during the recent months. Notice that this scale focuses on your perception of your own stress, how in control you feel, and how well you believe things are going for you. This aspect of stress, your interpretation of it, will continue to play an important role in our approach to understanding and managing it. If you scored in the moderate range or higher, this book is especially helpful to you because it will help minimize your stress experience. You may want to retake the Perceived Stress Scale midway through the book, after completing several exercises, and again at the end of the book, to see whether your total score decreases.

Your Stress and Coping

The Good

Take a moment to reflect on your experiences with stress and coping. What function does stress serve for you? Are there benefits of stress that you wouldn't want to lose? What about your coping response? What do you do well in terms of coping with stress?

- ☐ I'm aware of my stress and emotions.
- ☐ I'm aware of my thoughts.
- ☐ I know how to change my negative thinking into positive thinking.
- ☐ I have enough pleasant events.
- ☐ I communicate my feelings to others.
- ☐ I have a strong social support network.
- ☐ I know how to activate the relaxation response.
- ☐ I use deep breathing and other relaxation skills.

- ☐ I am happy with my diet and nutrition.
- ☐ I have a good exercise regimen.
- ☐ I have effective problem-solving skills.
- ☐ I practice mindfulness.
- ☐ I am competent in my job.

The Bad

What are things you would like to be different about stress and your coping skills?

- ☐ I would like to be more aware of my stress and emotions.
- ☐ I would like to be more aware of my thoughts.
- ☐ I would like to change my negative thinking into positive thinking.
- ☐ I would like to increase the pleasant events in my life.
- ☐ I would like to better communicate my feelings to others.
- ☐ I would like to expand my social support network.
- ☐ I would like to know how to activate the relaxation response.
- ☐ I want to improve my use of deep breathing and other relaxation skills.
- ☐ I could have a better diet and nutrition.
- ☐ I want to exercise more.
- ☐ I would like to be a better problem solver.
- ☐ I want to learn to practice mindfulness.
- ☐ I need to improve my teaching competence.

BUILDING COMMITMENT TO CHANGE

You have made a commitment to reading the first two chapters of this book. The question now is, what are you going to do next? At this stage of learning the teacher coaching model (TCM), you may find it helpful to reflect on and commit to whatever you want to accomplish next. Take a moment to complete Handout 2.3. Answer as many questions as you can. As always, it works best to actually write things down.

GROUP ACTIVITY: Building Commitment

Assign one or two questions from each category on Handout 2.3 to every participant. Give them a few minutes to write their answers to each question. Then pair off and take turns discussing responses with a partner. As the listener, repeat or paraphrase back the statements that the speaker makes. Comment on how committed the speaker appears to be to making the change. You might also ask if anything could make them even more committed. Report back to the group after both partners have played the role of speaker and listener.

> **IF YOU DO ONLY ONE THING:**
> **Building Positive Emotions—What Went Well**
>
> For the next several nights before you go to bed, take a moment to reflect back on the day. Keep a tablet, piece of paper, journal, or an electronic device you are comfortable writing on next to your bed. Write down three things that went well during the day and why: why it went well, why you enjoyed it, and why you experienced it in a positive way. You do not have to write for long, but it is important that you spend time thinking deeply about what happened, why, and what caused it to happen. Within in a few days, you will notice a difference in your ability to adjust your feelings to be more positive. Give it a try!

SUMMARY

Chapter 2 provided an overview of how our body operates under stress. Teachers encounter a multitude of daily hassles in their work environment that can lead to persistent stress. Chronic stress is dangerous to our health and interferes with our ability to perform our jobs well. Therefore, teachers' use of effective strategies to cope with stressors can result in improved health and work performance as well as overall life satisfaction. You have already completed assessments that evaluated your perceived levels of stress and asked yourself questions to determine your awareness of your stress level. You have also become more in tune with your stress. The next step is to learn to use new ways to cope.

HANDOUT 2.1

Life Events Questionnaire

During the past 12 months, have any of the following events occurred in your family? Please circle one.

1. Did either caretaker lose their job?		Yes	No
2. Did the caretaker become separated or divorced?		Yes	No
3. Was there a death in the immediate family?		Yes	No
4. Was a close family member a victim of a violent crime?		Yes	No
5. Was the family evicted from their house or apartment?		Yes	No
6. Did a close family member become hospitalized or have a serious physical or mental illness?		Yes	No
7. Did any member of the immediate family have a legal problem that resulted in being jailed?		Yes	No
8. Did any member of the immediate family have a debt that they could not afford to pay?		Yes	No
9. Did any member of the immediate family suffer an accidental injury that required hospitalization?		Yes	No
10. Did the family move to a new neighborhood (defined as a new school zone)?		Yes	No
11. Did a new child or another family member come into your family?		Yes	No
12. Did any member of the immediate family have a legal suit?		Yes	No

From Lochman (2004). Reprinted with permission from the author.

From *Stress Management for Teachers: A Proactive Guide* by Keith C. Herman and Wendy M. Reinke. Copyright 2015 by The Guilford Press. Permission to photocopy this handout is granted to purchasers of this book for personal use only (see copyright page for details). Purchasers can download and print additional copies of this handout from *www.guilford.com/herman-forms*.

HANDOUT 2.2

Perceived Stress Scale

The questions in this scale ask you about your feelings and thoughts during the last month. In each case, please indicate your response by placing an "X" over the square representing how often you felt or thought a certain way.

	Never 0	Almost Never 1	Sometimes 2	Fairly Often 3	Very Often 4
1. In the last month, how often have you been upset because of something that happened unexpectedly?	☐	☐	☐	☐	☐
2. In the last month, how often have you felt that you were unable to control the important things in your life?	☐	☐	☐	☐	☐
3. In the last month, how often have you felt nervous and "stressed"?	☐	☐	☐	☐	☐
4. In the last month, how often have you felt confident about your ability to handle your personal problems?	☐	☐	☐	☐	☐
5. In the last month, how often have you felt that things were going your way?	☐	☐	☐	☐	☐
6. In the last month, how often have you found that you could not cope with all the things that you had to do?	☐	☐	☐	☐	☐
7. In the last month, how often have you been able to control irritations in your life?	☐	☐	☐	☐	☐
8. In the last month, how often have you felt you were on top of things?	☐	☐	☐	☐	☐
9. In the last month, how often have you been angered because of things that were outside your control?	☐	☐	☐	☐	☐
10. In the last month, how often have you felt difficulties were piling up so high that you could not overcome them?	☐	☐	☐	☐	☐

From Cohen, Kamarch, and Mermelstein (1983). Reprinted with permission from the authors and the American Sociological Association.

From *Stress Management for Teachers: A Proactive Guide* by Keith C. Herman and Wendy M. Reinke. Copyright 2015 by The Guilford Press. Permission to photocopy this handout is granted to purchasers of this book for personal use only (see copyright page for details). Purchasers can download and print additional copies of this handout from *www.guilford.com/herman-forms*.

HANDOUT 2.3

Building Commitment

Is It a Problem?
- What makes you think that you need to make a change?
- What makes you think that stress or coping is a problem for you?
- What difficulties have you had in relation to your stress or coping?
- In what ways do you think you or other people have been harmed by this problem?
- What makes you feel like you should do something different?

Are You or Others Concerned?
- What about your stress or coping do you, or other people, see as reason for concern?
- What worries you about your stress or coping response?
- Does that concern you? How much? In what ways?
- What do you think will happen if you don't make a change?

Advantages of Making Changes
- How would you like your stress or coping to different?
- How would you benefit from improving your stress or coping?
- In 5 years, what do you think your stress and coping responses will look like?
- If you could make this change immediately, as if by magic, how would your life be different?
- What are the advantages of making this change?

Reasons for Optimism
- If you decide to make a change, why do you think you could do it?
- What encourages you to feel that you can change?
- What would work for you, if you decide to change?
- What would make you feel even more confident that you could make a change?
- When else in your life have you made a big change like this? How did you do it?
- What personal strengths do you have that will help you succeed?

What Are You Going to Do?
- Never mind the "how" for now; what do you want to happen?
- How important is this to you? How much do you want to do this?
- What are you willing to try?
- What do you intend to do?

From *Stress Management for Teachers: A Proactive Guide* by Keith C. Herman and Wendy M. Reinke. Copyright 2015 by The Guilford Press. Permission to photocopy this handout is granted to purchasers of this book for personal use only (see copyright page for details). Purchasers can download and print additional copies of this handout from *www.guilford.com/herman-forms*.

CHAPTER 3

The Teacher Coping Model

Armed with an understanding of the physiology of stress and an awareness of your own stress, you are now ready to learn the teacher coping model (TCM). The TCM identifies the precursors to stress and to relaxation that you can directly control. The model is based on decades of psychological research and is adapted from models that have proven helpful in a variety of contexts. In this chapter, we review the key principles of the TCM. As you will see, this model serves as a road map for the remainder of the book. In subsequent chapters, we focus on strategies to use for influencing the domains of the TCM in positive ways.

A GOOD THEORY ABOUT STRESS

Rather than give you a bag of tricks to cope with stress, we believe it is important to provide you with the big picture, a good theory that you can use independently for years to come. If you only have a bag of tricks when encountering a new situation or novel stressor you will be lost. If instead you have a good theory that tells you why you get stressed and the easiest ways to manage it, you will be in a position to solve your own stress problems that are inevitable over time. In other words, we don't just want to give you some quick and easy strategies that reduce your stress today. We want to give you a framework for addressing any stressors you might experience in the future.

Bandura's social cognitive theory is the foundation of the TCM (Bandura, 1986, 2004). This theory emphasizes the role of thoughts, behaviors, and feelings in understanding human adaptation. Figure 3.1 depicts the basic social cognitive theory. Think about your experiences as being composed of three elements: your thoughts, feelings, and behaviors. When you view the world in this way, thoughts, behaviors, and feelings are intimately connected to one another.

> **Think about your experiences as being composed of three interconnected elements: your thoughts, feelings, and behaviors.**

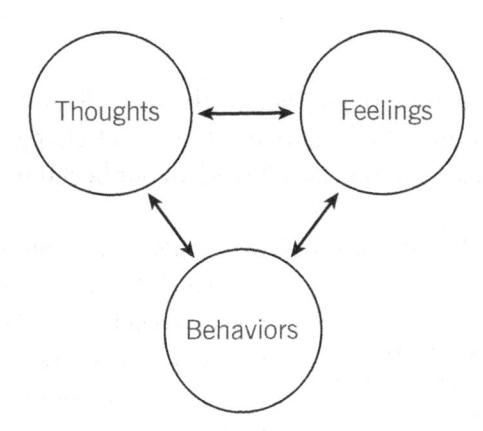

FIGURE 3.1. The social learning model.

It is important to have a common definition of these terms as we move forward. Behaviors refer to our actions, what we do. Behaviors are distinguished from thoughts and feelings in that they are public events. That is, our behaviors can be observed by others, and so they can easily be confirmed and measured. Some examples of adaptive behaviors include exercising, visiting a friend's house, completing paperwork on time, and assertively expressing yourself. These behaviors are observable, and someone else could confirm whether they happened.

Unlike behaviors, thoughts and feelings are private and internal events. We can make them observable when we tell others about our feelings and thoughts or when we write them down. In others words, writing or speaking about our thoughts or feelings is a behavior, but by themselves, when we experience thoughts and feelings, they are private.

Thoughts refer to that stream of consciousness that goes on inside our brains, including words, images, and memories. Thoughts are like a message board with a continuous stream of words and information. A functional way to think of thoughts is as complete sentences. As you read this chapter you may have complete sentences in your mind like, "This makes sense to me. I can do this. This is important to me." Although others cannot see these thoughts that are in your head, you can tell others about your thoughts. As you will see, it can be very helpful to step into this stream of thoughts and pay attention to it.

Like thoughts, feelings are internal events. Feelings refer to emotions that we experience. When you ask people to point to where their thoughts occur, they usually point to their head, whereas for feelings they would often point to their heart. This is a metaphorical way to think of the distinction between thoughts and feelings given that, in reality, our brain is involved in all of our internal experiences. A better way to distinguish feelings from thoughts is to consider feelings as single words of emotional states such as happy, sad, and frustrated. Another point of clarification is that just because you put the word *feel* or *feeling* in front of a thought does not make it a feeling. For instance you might say, "I feel that you are not being helpful." This is an expression of a thought (you are not helpful), rather than a feeling, because there is no emotion expressed.

Interrelations

A key principle of social learning theory is that thoughts, feelings, and behaviors are intertwined. When you change one, the others can't help but change as well. The TCM takes advantage of this simple reality and makes it work in our best interest. Figure 3.2 highlights this relationship.

When you change a thought or a behavior, this will create changes in the other two domains of your experience. Because of this principle, we can easily get into positive or negative cycles with our thoughts, feelings, and behaviors. Perhaps you've experienced these cycles. As an example, read about Amanda, a first-year teacher at Park Elementary School.

> **A key principle of social learning theory is that thoughts, feelings, and behaviors are intertwined.**

Amanda found herself in a runaway, downward spiral that started with a simple mistake. She overslept. From the moment she realized this, her subsequent thoughts, feelings,

---

Downward Spiral

Amanda had a big day. She was struggling in her first year of teaching and was prepping for a new lesson that she hoped would turn her class around. Having worked so late preparing for it the night before, she overslept the morning of her lesson (behavior). When she realized what time it was, she immediately felt tense (feeling) and thought, "This is never going to work. I'm such a screw-up." This thought made her feel even more tense and worried. She scrambled out of bed and got dressed (behavior). She skipped breakfast and drove quickly to work (behaviors). By the time, she got to work, she was exhausted (feeling) and told herself, "This is hopeless" (thought). She felt sad (feeling) and decided not to try her new lesson. What she had hoped would be an exciting day quickly turned into a major disappointment for her that dragged down her spirit for several days after.

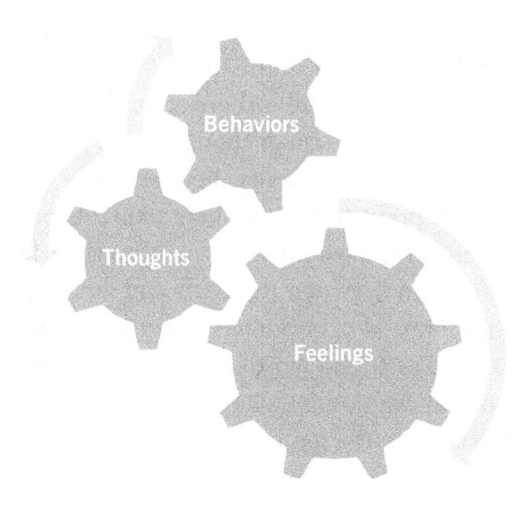

FIGURE 3.2. The links between thoughts, feelings, and behaviors.

and behaviors all turned negative and seemed to conspire against her. Was this downward spiral inevitable? Was there any way for Amanda to turn her morning around? In other words, what if you wanted to stop a negative cycle and turn it around into a positive cycle? That would be pretty handy indeed. The answer, of course, is yes, you can turn cycles around. To alter any cycle, you have two choices: change the way you are thinking or change your actions.

A Negative Cycle

Here is one negative sequence of events that might occur after receiving a negative performance evaluation. You might be very upset about the evaluation, so much so that it continues to affect you the next morning. When you wake up, the following sequence may occur (Figure 3.3):

- Wake up with the thought "I'm stupid. I don't belong as a teacher" (T).
- Decide not to exercise before work and sleep in instead (B).
- Feel tired and sad (F).
- Wake up late and jump out of bed (B).
- Feel tense (F) and think, "Urgh. I'm such a loser" (T).
- Eat breakfast and overeat (B).
- Tell yourself, "I'm so fat and lazy" (T).
- Get to school later, tense and out of breath (B, F).
- Make eye contact with the principal and think, "She thinks I'm a loser" (B, T).
- Skip lunch and miss spending time with coworkers because you are catching up (B).
- Give high rates of reprimands to students and think, "These are awful kids" (B, T).
- End the day feeling exhausted and defeated (F).
- Think, "My evaluation was right. I'm just not cut out for this" (T).

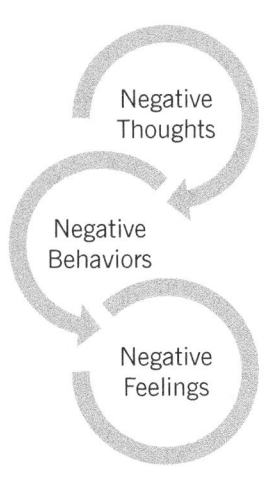

FIGURE 3.3. Negative cycle.

Creating a Positive Cycle

It can be easy to fall into a negative cycle following a negative event like this, but as we have established, events do not cause these cycles by themselves. Rather, it is the thoughts and behaviors we have in reaction to events that can hijack our emotions. In truth, you could intervene and interrupt the negative cycle at any step along the way. Let's say you caught the negative cycle early, right after your first negative thought of the day. Here's how a positive cycle could emerge (Figure 3.4):

> It can be easy to fall into a negative cycle following a negative event like this, but as we have established, events do not cause these cycles by themselves.

- Wake up with the thought "I'm stupid. I don't belong as a teacher" (T).
- Catch yourself: "Wait. I'm not gonna let this get me down. I'll stick with it and get better. This is just one evaluation. I can do this" (T).
- Decide to go exercise before work as planned (B).
- Feel more energized and optimistic (F).
- Tell yourself, "I'm proud of myself for exercising even though I *didn't* feel like it" (T).
- Eat lunch with colleagues and have a good conversation (B).
- Think, "I'm lucky to have such good coworkers" (T).
- Feel grateful (F).
- Arrive at afternoon class early and talk with your students (B).
- You are smiling and laughing with them (B).
- Think, "I'm really getting the hang of this" (T).
- Go home relaxed (F).

Notice that a positive cycle doesn't always quickly click your mood back to happy after feeling extremely disappointed. Positive cycles are the accumulation of many positive

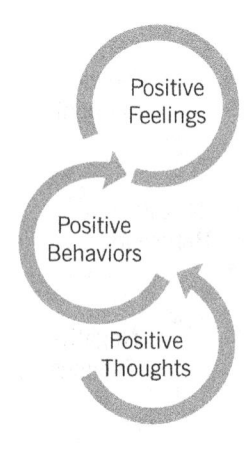

FIGURE 3.4. Positive Cycle

thoughts and behaviors. But it does take a first step, an awareness of an emerging negative cycle and a willingness to change a thought or behavior. In the example, you caught your first negative thought of the day and didn't let it lead to more negatives. Instead, you challenged the negative thought and found a new more adaptive way of thinking. Thinking "I'll get better at this" may not have completely shifted your mood to being happy. Rather, it shifted your mood away from being devastated to a more manageable level of disappointment. By lessening how horrible you felt, you were then able to make more adaptive decisions, like exercising, which made it more likely that more positive thoughts and feelings would follow. This minimization of negative and accumulation of positives shifts us to more positive cycles with our thoughts, feelings, and behaviors.

Which One Is Most Difficult to Control?

Now think for a moment about which of these aspects of your experience would be most difficult to control directly: your thoughts, feelings, or behaviors. Take a moment, choose one, and think about why.

Most people would agree that we have direct control over our behaviors, so let's take that one off the table. It is true that habits can be difficult to change, but at the end of the day, we do make decisions about our actions. I can choose to go for a walk after work or to watch TV. I can choose to prepare dinner or to go to a restaurant. I can choose to read this book or not.

Some people will guess that thoughts are the most difficult to control. The reason people believe this is that thoughts are internal, and they sometimes seem so automatic. Many of us seldom take time to reflect on our thoughts, so they may just seem like they happen to us. The truth is, we do have a fair amount of control over what and how we think. It can take practice first to even become aware of our thoughts and second to alter them, but it can be done. Several chapters in this book teach you how to master your thoughts and use them to manage stress.

That leaves feelings. We have the least direct control over our feelings. We do not have a ready switch to suddenly be happy or irritated or proud and excited. The key word, though, is "direct" because we do have a fair amount of indirect control over our emotional life. We influence our emotions through our thoughts and behaviors. Thus we can also learn to monitor our emotions, to become more aware of them, and to use these skills to our advantage. By paying attention to our emotions, we become more in tune with them and then use them as a barometer for gauging changes in our thoughts and behaviors.

> **We influence our emotions through our thoughts and behaviors.**

When thinking about controlling stress and anxiety, we can also think about emotions or feelings, more broadly, to include physiological reactions. Physical reactions that accompany feelings—the physical indicators of sympathetic nervous system arousal such as rapid heart rate, sweating, fidgeting, and rapid breathing—can provide clues to what we are thinking about and how we are feeling.

The Big Idea

When it gets down to it, we don't have a lot of control over some of the events in our lives. Things happen; sometimes bad things happen, and we are challenged in some way to respond to them. If we have an emotional overreaction and we want to change it, to feel less overwhelmed about the situation or bothered by it, we really have one of two choices: we can change our behavior or we can change our thoughts. We can change our response to what happened by acting differently; we might choose to confront it by talking with people about it or by exercising. Or we can reinterpret it and think about it differently.

THE TCM

The TCM is based on these really basic principles of psychology. If you learn to manage your thoughts and behaviors, your feelings will follow suit. All other aspects of emotional wellness follow from this idea. Figure 3.5 illustrates these ideas with the specific strategies that we describe in the next chapters.

Basically, the TCM focuses on equipping you with the skills you need to induce calmness and relaxation more frequently and to make it more common for you to experience

Awareness
Self-Monitoring
Goal Setting
Problem Solving
Deep Breathing
The TCM

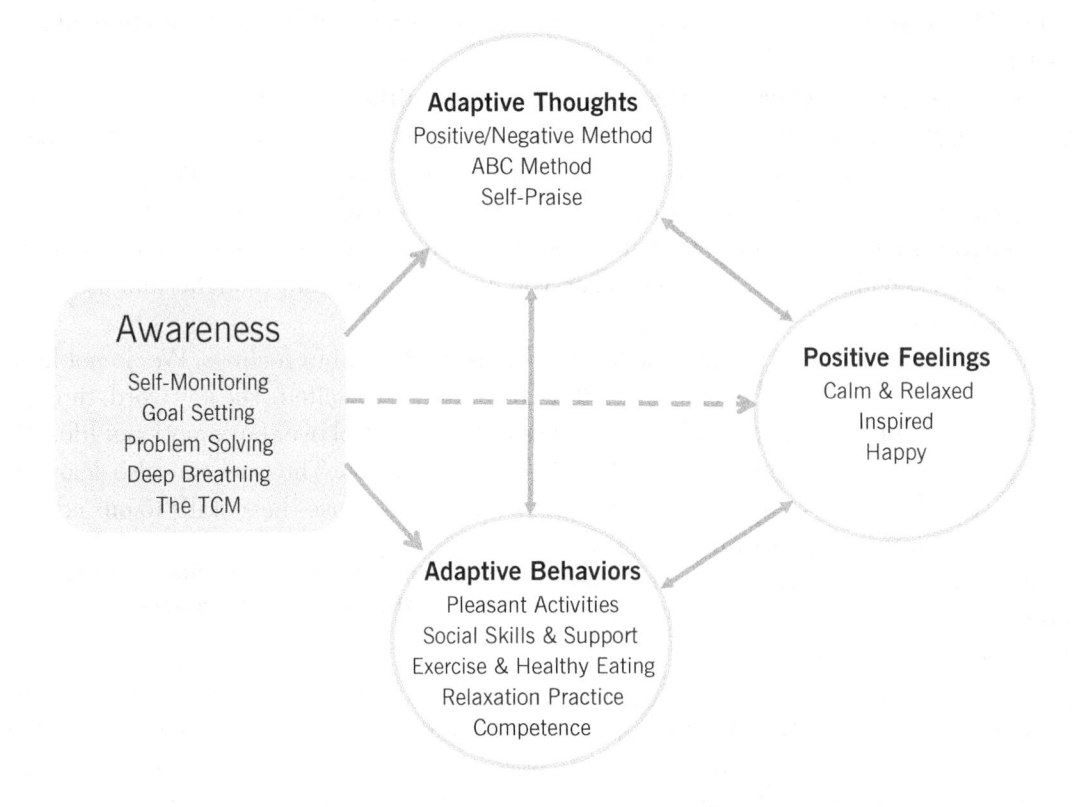

Adaptive Thoughts
Positive/Negative Method
ABC Method
Self-Praise

Positive Feelings
Calm & Relaxed
Inspired
Happy

Adaptive Behaviors
Pleasant Activities
Social Skills & Support
Exercise & Healthy Eating
Relaxation Practice
Competence

FIGURE 3.5. The TCM.

positive feelings like happiness and inspiration. The core skills will focus on developing your awareness of your mood, thoughts, and feelings. Cultivating awareness puts you in the position to choose more adaptive ways of thinking and acting. In the next several chapters we describe the tools you can use to develop new thinking habits and behavior patterns that are aligned with positive emotions.

> **The TCM focuses on equipping you with the skills you need to induce calmness and relaxation more frequently and make it more common for you to experience positive feelings.**

THE TCM BUILDING BLOCKS AND GETTING TO GOOD

A useful metaphor for the TCM is a pyramid of skills not only for coping with stress but also for a broader sense of well-being, what we refer to as *getting to good*. We think of the skills in a hierarchical manner with each building off the ones that are introduced before it. At the top of the building blocks are skills and qualities that go beyond just getting by. Figure 3.6 depicts the TCM building blocks and the corresponding skills.

Awareness

The foundation of the model is developing awareness skills. Building a stable base for your coping building blocks requires that you first have a solid foundation of awareness about your feelings, thoughts, and actions. Central to becoming more aware is to practice self-monitoring. In the next chapter, you will start monitoring your mood on a daily basis. Mood awareness is your barometer for all other skills that follow. It tells you when you need to focus on changing your thoughts and behavior, and it also gives you feedback about what is and is not working for you. Awareness exercises will continue throughout the book as you learn to self-monitor your thoughts and actions in subsequent chapters. Awareness includes goal setting and problem-solving skills. Deep breathing is another awareness tool that sets the foundation for subsequent relaxation skills.

As you attempt to unlearn old patterns and habits and replace them with new ones, you will find doing so requires a fair amount of effort and attention. These are foundational aspects of learning new thoughts and behaviors through daily practices, awareness exercises,

> **Building a stable base for your coping building blocks requires that you first have a solid foundation of awareness about your feelings, thoughts, and actions.**

and skill challenges. As with any new behavior, the more you practice, the easier and sooner it becomes your new habit or automatic process. Think about learning to play the piano or any musical instrument. At first it requires lots of effortful control. The more you practice, the better you get. Eventually, it becomes easier and natural. Then you become more fluent. The same applies to learning any new behavior or thinking pattern. We start with the fundamental skill from which all others will follow: self-monitoring and goal setting.

```
                        ┌──────────┐
                        │ Wellness │
                   ┌────┴──────────┴────┐
                   │ Happiness │  Flow  │
              ┌────┴───────────┴────────┴──────┐
              │           Centering            │
         ┌────┴──────────┬───────────┬─────────┴──┐
         │    Values     │Mindfulness│  Gratitude │
         │  Affirmation  │           │            │
     ┌───┴───────────────┴───────────┴────────────┴───┐
     │              Beyond Survival                   │
┌────┴──────┬──────────┬────────────┬────────────────┴┐
│ Pleasant  │  Social  │Professional│ Exercise and    │
│Activities │Skills and│ Competence │   Healthy       │
│           │ Support  │            │    Eating       │
├───────────┴──────────┴────────────┴─────────────────┤
│                  Adaptive Behaviors                 │
├───────────┬──────────┬────────────┬─────────────────┤
│Positive/  │  ABCs of │ Self-Praise│                 │
│Negative   │ Adaptive │    and     │    Optimism     │
│Thought    │ Thinking │   Reward   │                 │
│Method     │          │            │                 │
├───────────┴──────────┴────────────┴─────────────────┤
│                  Adaptive Thinking                  │
├──────────┬──────────┬────────────┬────────┬─────────┤
│The TCM   │ Problem  │   Self-    │  Goal  │  Deep   │
│Theory    │ Solving  │ Monitoring │Setting │Breathing│
├──────────┴──────────┴────────────┴────────┴─────────┤
│                 Building Awareness                  │
└─────────────────────────────────────────────────────┘
```

Getting to Good ↕

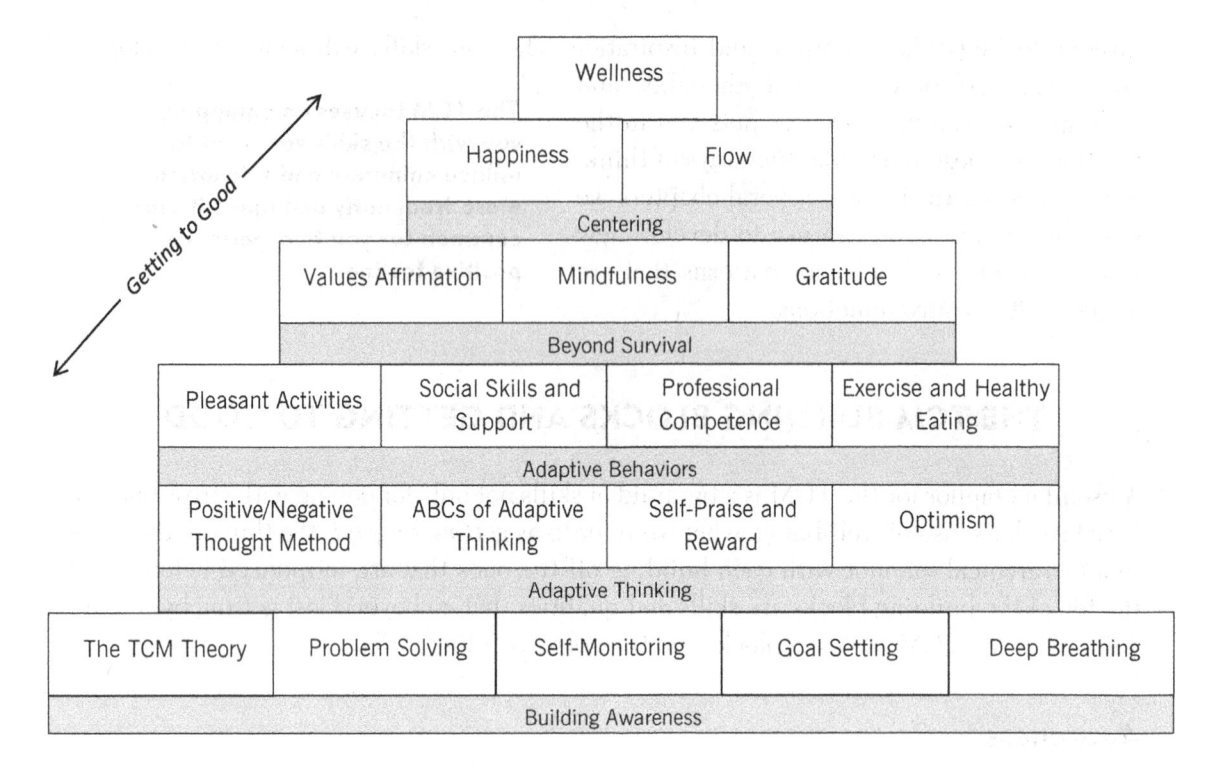

FIGURE 3.6. The TCM building blocks.

As you build awareness, you can think of unpleasant emotions—stress, depression, anxiety—as following from a simple equation. If you simply tallied the number of pleasant activities and thoughts you had in a day and subtracted the number of unpleasant activities and thoughts you would have a pretty good estimate of your overall mood for that day. If you accrued more positives than negatives, you would likely have an overall sense of positive emotion. See Figure 3.7 for a hypothetical calculation. This simple formula provides one path to a better mood. Increasing the number of positive events and thoughts and reducing the number of negatives is the way to go.

Adaptive Thoughts

After a establishing a stable foundation of awareness, you will next focus on adaptive thoughts skills: assessing thoughts and increasing your adaptive, positive thinking skills. We review several strategies that research has shown to help people increase their positive thinking skills. The two primary methods we describe in detail include the positive/negative thought method and the ABC method. Both methods involve learning to monitor your thoughts and intentionally replacing maladaptive thoughts with more functional ways of thinking. Self-praise and reward are additional strategies to support these two methods and encourage you to continue using them.

20 pleasant activities + 100 positive thoughts
− 3 unpleasant events − 7 negative thoughts = **110 positives**

2 pleasant activities + 8 positive thoughts
− 14 unpleasant events − 86 negative thoughts = **90 negatives**

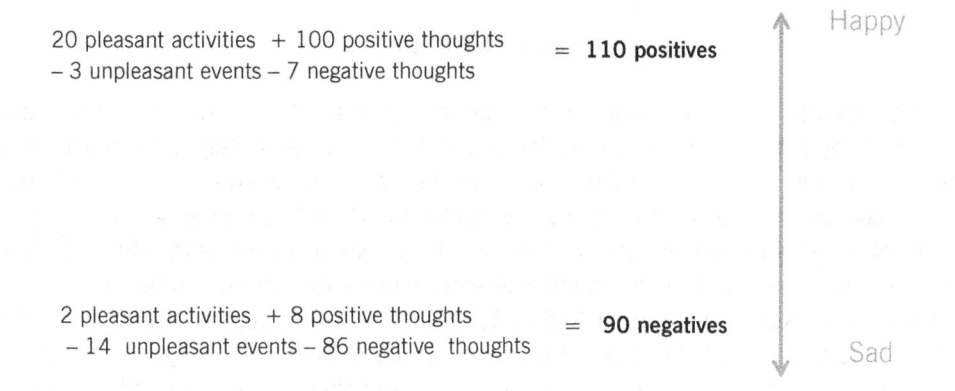

Happy

Sad

FIGURE 3.7. Mood formula.

Adaptive Behaviors

Next, we focus on adaptive behaviors that are associated with positive coping and relaxation. As always, we start with self-reflection and self-monitoring. The key behaviors we focus on include increasing pleasant activities, social support, diet and exercise, and relaxation. You may find you already do well in some of the skills discussed in the adaptive behavior section. That's great! If so, focus your effort and goals on any that you do less well.

In some cases, when people are severely depressed, socially isolated, and spending a lot of time doing nothing much at all, the first step is to get them moving. Depression really is the absence of positive reinforcement in one's life. By gradually withdrawing from the world, emitting fewer behaviors, people who are prone to depression simply give themselves less opportunity for positive interactions with the world. A first step in these cases is simply to activate the person, getting them to emit more behaviors. We do this by first assessing what they are doing now by monitoring how many pleasant activities they engage in on a daily basis, how much movement or exercise they get, and how much social contact they have. Based on these data, we then ask them to set a realistic goal for increasing these behaviors and a monitoring system for tracking it. In turn, we help them come up with a reward system for when they meet their goals. If you find yourself completely worn down and withdrawn, you may want to start with these activating strategies described in Chapter 7.

> **The key behaviors we focus on include increasing pleasant activities, social support, diet and exercise, and relaxation.**

Another key aspect of adaptive behaviors related to teacher stress is professional competence. We devote a full chapter (Chapter 8) to this topic because of its importance to teacher stress. If you are truly struggling with some of the key skill areas of professional competence, telling yourself to relax and engaging in more positive activities can only go so far in reducing your stress as a teacher. The most common struggle we have encountered for teachers involves developing more competence in the area of classroom management, so we devote the most attention to this skill.

Case Example

We were inspired to write this book in part by talking to teachers about their stress and, in many cases, by how few teachers were familiar with the coping strategies we describe in this book. One teacher, Abby, attended one of our workshops on classroom management and was struck by content that was focused on coping. A major part of effective classroom management is for teachers to learn to stay calm and nonemotional when dealing with difficult behaviors. Abby was able to extrapolate these calming strategies in the classroom to other stressors in her life. After our workshop she approached us to discuss a major stressor, her relationship with her boss. She told us that she was not enjoying her job since her school got a new principal. She and her colleagues complained daily about the principal's heavy-handed administrative style, and Abby was going home more and more stressed at the end of the day. We sat with her and asked her to use the ABC method to assess her own thoughts (described in Chapter 6). She quickly became aware of some irrational beliefs that were undermining her happiness. For instance, when she examined her beliefs she realized she was telling herself her that her principal was self-centered and trying to undermine the school and her happiness. These thoughts in turn led Abby to feel angry, suspicious, and helpless. When we discussed with her some alternate ways of thinking about the situation, Abby was able to come up with some new explanations and interpretations that lessened her emotional overreaction (e.g., she considered the possibility that her principal was under her own set of stressors, that she was actually well intentioned and needed support herself). The simplicity of these methods in helping Abby develop more control over her emotional life got her to buy into learning to use these and other coping methods. As she continued to use these cognitive coping strategies she also explored her own behaviors as contributors to her stress levels. Her current most frequent method for coping with stress after work was to go home and drink wine while she watched TV. She experimented with other methods for coping behaviors (described in Chapter 7) and set goals for herself to increase the number of positive activities in her life. She found or rediscovered several hobbies that she had been neglecting. In particular, she increased the amount of time she spent in social settings after work, even deciding to join a running club in her community. As she experimented with these methods, she monitored her mood and retained the activities that made a difference in how she felt and coped. At our last check-in, Abby was trying some of the methods for attaining higher levels of happiness and functioning described in Chapter 9. She attended a local workshop on Zen meditation and did not find that it suited her style. But she later attended a separate mindfulness group at a nearby church and found the style of this presenter fit her perfectly. She tells us the Gratitude Note exercise described in Chapter 6 was a personal favorite of hers.

Beyond Survival

Life is about more than simply surviving and tolerating stress. Thus at the top of the TCM building blocks are skills and activities that encourage you to reach your full potential of wellness and happiness. In later chapters of this book, we describe approaches to mindfulness and well-being that not only allow you to feel less stressed but also to achieve a global sense of satisfaction and well-being that goes well beyond just getting by. In Chapter 9, we review the growing science focused on happiness, and the strategies that have been developed for fostering it. Most of the modern ideas about optimal human function can be traced to Eastern approaches to mindfulness. These approaches have now entered the mainstream of Western medicine and psychological science as innovative methods for promoting health and addressing human maladies; though, it certainly is ironic to describe practices that have existed for millennia as innovative! Innovation here refers to the novel application of these methods in Western cultures, previously underexposed to them. As you will see, these methods both build upon what is described in earlier chapters and also are completely unique and independent. More on that in Chapter 9!

SELF-ASSESSMENTS

Now let's complete a few more self-assessments to help you pinpoint areas that you may want to especially focus on as you learn more about the TCM. For all of these questions, and for every survey in the book, it is important that you answer each item as honestly as you can. This is for your own information only, so be truthful to yourself. Also, we find it is best to not put much thought into your answers, just go with your first gut reaction.

Thinking Habits

Because a large part of the TCM focuses on how thoughts influence feelings and behaviors, it will be important to take time to reflect on your thinking habits. Not everyone thinks alike of course, and there is more than one type of maladaptive thinking pattern. So take a moment to reflect on Handout 3.1 and respond to each item as accurately as you can.

As you have probably surmised to this point in the book, much of the model that we present is based on the assumption that maladaptive thinking contributes to stress responses. The items in Handout 3.1 are devised to tap these tendencies. If you answered yes to any of the first four items (1–4) or no to any of the next four items (5–8), it is likely that the chapter on adaptive thinking will be helpful to you.

Behavior Patterns

Of course, behaviors are also prominent in the TCM. Answer the screening items in Handout 3.2 to assess your behaviors related to stress and coping.

The items in Handout 3.2 ask about adaptive behaviors and optimal functioning. Answering yes to any of these items suggests you could benefit from some of the content of this book. If you answered yes to one or more of the first four items, then Chapter 7 on adaptive behaviors is for you. If you answered yes to either item 5 or 6, then later chapters on mindfulness and self-actualization will be useful to you in moving toward higher-level goals for yourself. If you answered yes to item 7 or 8, answer Handout 3.3 about your classroom and your teaching.

We know that competence (perceived and actual) is related to stress. If you have underdeveloped skills, improving your competence can go a long way toward relieving your stress. The items in Handout 3.3 ask about your perceptions of your teaching and classroom management skills. Answering yes to any of these items points you in the direction of being likely to benefit from Chapter 8. As you know, one aspect of how stressful teaching can be is how competent you feel to do the job. Improving your competence is one way to manage the stress of teaching.

> We know that competence (perceived and actual) is related to stress. If you have underdeveloped skills, improving your competence can go a long way to relieving your stress.

Other Symptoms and Problem Areas

Answer the following four questions to give you a sense about other areas to focus on.

During the past month . . .	Yes	No
1. *Have you been bothered by feeling down, depressed, or hopeless?*	☐	☐
2. *Have you often been bothered by little interest or pleasure in doing things?*	☐	☐
3. *Have you been bothered by feelings of anxiety or apprehension?*	☐	☐
4. *Have you often been bothered by persistent worries or concerns?*	☐	☐

From *http://www.phqscreeners.com*.

These questions are from the Patient Health Questionnaire (PHQ), a family of very brief assessments developed by Robert Spitzer, Janet Williams, Kurt Kroenke, and colleagues that are freely available at *www.phqscreeners.com*. They have been found to be useful for screening people at risk for internalizing problems like depression and anxiety (Kroenke, Spitzer, Williams, & Lowe, 2009; Spitzer, Kroenke, & Williams, 1999). If you answered yes to either of the first two questions, you may want to skip ahead to Chapter 11 and take a more complete depression screening inventory. Answering yes to either of the final two questions may suggest it is worthwhile for you to complete a longer anxiety screening inventory in Chapter 11. Depending on your score on these longer rating scales, you may also want to read that chapter first. Although all of the content of this book is relevant for anyone experiencing internalizing symptoms, more serious depressive episodes or anxiety disorders may suggest the need for more intensive support or treatment. Suggestions for seeking additional support and treatment are provided in Chapter 11.

The next question asks about your use of alcohol:

For men, When was the last time you had more than five drinks in one day?

☐ *Never*   ☐ *In the past 3 months*   ☐ *More than 3 months ago*

IF YOU DO ONLY ONE THING: Three for One

There is pretty consistent evidence of the power of creating more positives than negatives in your life. For this activity, focus on doing three positives for every negative interaction you have with your students. So every time you notice you give a reprimand (any correction including "shhh" counts as a reprimand) focus on doing three positive actions before delivering another reprimand. Simple ways to do this are to give three specific statements any time you catch yourself giving a reprimand. The key will be whether you can accurately monitor your use of reprimands or negative interactions. So you start with paying attention to those, just monitoring them. It may be helpful to get a colleague to observe your classroom and count the number of reprimands (see Chapter 10 for definitions that you can each use) and then compare your results after 10-minute observations. If you are close to the number, then you are probably fairly accurately monitoring your reprimands. When you are using three for one and you reach that goal, also take time to assess your mood (just on a simple 1–10 scale). See if your mood changes in the expected way as your ratio changes.

> **Consistent evidence shows the power of creating more positive than negatives in your life. Here, focus on doing three positives for every negative interaction you have with your students.**

Bonus: Next, try it with your family! For every negative interaction you have with your partner or child be sure to have three or more positive interactions (with praise or affection) before another negative. See if you notice a difference in your mood or a difference in their behavior.

For women, When was the last time you had more than four drinks in one day?

☐ Never   ☐ In the past 3 months   ☐ More than 3 months ago

The National Institute on Alcohol Abuse and Alcoholism devised this question to screen for problematic alcohol use. If you answered, "in the past 3 months," research suggests you may have a problem with your alcohol use. In a large study, that question had a sensitivity and specificity for detecting true alcohol problems above 80%. That's a pretty impressive level of accuracy for a single question. Given that stress can be a trigger for excessive alcohol consumption, we have included information about alcohol abuse in Chapter 11. You may want to skip ahead to that chapter and complete additional screening to see if it would be wise to seek support for your alcohol use in addition to the skills you will develop by reading this book.

SUMMARY

In this opening part of the book, we have set the stage for the coping skills that we describe in the next section. With this knowledge of stress and the TCM as your foundation, you will have a framework to hold together each of the skills we discuss in the subsequent chapters.

HANDOUT 3.1

Thinking Habits

1. I tend to worry a lot. ☐ Yes ☐ No

2. I tend to get down on myself. ☐ Yes ☐ No

3. I tend to overreact to situations. ☐ Yes ☐ No

4. I wish I could learn to control my feelings better. ☐ Yes ☐ No

5. I am an optimist. ☐ Yes ☐ No

6. I find myself thinking more positive than negative thoughts. ☐ Yes ☐ No

7. I usually focus on the bright side of things. ☐ Yes ☐ No

8. I rarely worry too much. ☐ Yes ☐ No

From *Stress Management for Teachers: A Proactive Guide* by Keith C. Herman and Wendy M. Reinke. Copyright 2015 by The Guilford Press. Permission to photocopy this handout is granted to purchasers of this book for personal use only (see copyright page for details). Purchasers can download and print additional copies of this handout from *www.guilford.com/herman-forms*.

HANDOUT 3.2

Behaviors Related to Stress and Coping Screening

1. I wish I had more fun activities in my life. ☐ Yes ☐ No

2. People say I'm too nice. ☐ Yes ☐ No

3. I wish I had more friends. ☐ Yes ☐ No

4. I could learn to relax better. ☐ Yes ☐ No

5. I'm doing OK, but I would like to do even better. ☐ Yes ☐ No

6. I want to reach a state of contentment more often. ☐ Yes ☐ No

7. I do not feel very effective as a teacher. ☐ Yes ☐ No

8. If I were a better teacher I would feel better about myself. ☐ Yes ☐ No

---

From *Stress Management for Teachers: A Proactive Guide* by Keith C. Herman and Wendy M. Reinke. Copyright 2015 by The Guilford Press. Permission to photocopy this handout is granted to purchasers of this book for personal use only (see copyright page for details). Purchasers can download and print additional copies of this handout from *www.guilford.com/herman-forms*.

HANDOUT 3.3

Classroom and Teaching Screening

1. My classroom is out of control. ☐ Yes ☐ No

2. I could improve my classroom management skills. ☐ Yes ☐ No

3. I could improve my instructional management skills. ☐ Yes ☐ No

4. I was not trained to manage these types of student behaviors. ☐ Yes ☐ No

5. I could improve my time management skills. ☐ Yes ☐ No

6. I need help with organization. ☐ Yes ☐ No

From *Stress Management for Teachers: A Proactive Guide* by Keith C. Herman and Wendy M. Reinke. Copyright 2015 by The Guilford Press. Permission to photocopy this handout is granted to purchasers of this book for personal use only (see copyright page for details). Purchasers can download and print additional copies of this handout from *www.guilford.com/herman-forms*.

PART II

COPING STRATEGIES

CHAPTER 4

Awareness

When we learn new coping strategies, we begin by paying attention. Self-monitoring, as it is called, is in itself a valuable intervention that has been shown to create positive changes in people. Learning to pay attention to our habits allows us to pause, reflect, and make different choices. We will repeat this message with each new skill. Self-monitoring also can help us see patterns and triggers for our behavior and consequences that keep them going.

We begin by paying attention to our mood because our emotions are the barometer to our inner experience. By learning to attend to moment-to-moment fluctuations in our feelings, we start to notice thoughts and behaviors that go along with both positive and negative emotions. We become more mindful of ways to bring about adaptive thoughts and behaviors, making it more likely positive emotions will follow.

In this chapter, we provide a set of tools to get you in tune with your feelings. Although the emphasis here is on stress, you will find that these strategies apply equally well to your entire emotional life.

> **By learning to attend to moment-to-moment fluctuations in our feelings, we start to notice thoughts and behaviors that go along with both positive and negative emotions.**

MOOD MONITORING

We recommend that you use a mood monitoring form to help with the process of learning to pay attention to your feelings. We provide two types of mood monitoring forms in our handouts section at the end of this chapter. Each of these forms asks you to rate one or more moods on a scale from 1 to 10. The basic form simply asks you to rate your mood on a single dimension from positive to negative.

Take a look at Handout 4.1. The form includes one rating scale for each day of the week ranging from 1 (negative) to 10 (positive). It also includes space at the bottom to write down any positive or negative thoughts or actions that occurred to you. The purpose of this is to get you to start noticing any connections between your overall mood ratings and what you are thinking or doing.

> ### Mood Monitoring Practice
>
> Take a moment to reflect on how you are feeling right now. Close your eyes and focus inward for a moment. How relaxed versus tense do you feel? Mark a point on the line below. Marks further to the right would indicate high levels of tension. All the way to the right would indicate that you are feeling the most tense you have ever felt. Likewise, marks to the left would indicate increasing levels of relaxation.
>
> ●────────────────|────────────────●
> Relaxed   Tense
>
> How easy was this for you to do? Is it easier for you to rate your mood on a line like this or do you prefer to use a number scale like 1–10? Choose and use the method that makes most sense to you. If it comes naturally for you, then you are well on your way. If this is difficult, continue practicing using the rating form. Also, if you find this challenging, take time to create anchors of your experience as described in the text.
>
> ### GROUP EXERCISE
>
> If you are reading this book as part of a study group, try doing this exercise as a group using physical space. Make one end of the room the relaxed end and the other the tense end. Ask everyone in the group to stand up and find their space on an imaginary mood line. People who line up closer to the relaxed end will be indicating that they are feeling more relaxed, and those at the tense end more tense. Those who line up in the middle will be indicating that they are feeling more neutral, not particularly tense or relaxed. Finally, ask each person to say a few words about why they chose the spot on the line where they are standing. Ask them to identify a thought and/or behavior that goes along with their mood.

Complete the form once a day. We recommend that you keep the form by your bed and use it to reflect back on the day and rate your average mood for the whole day. The first few times you try this you might feel uncomfortable placing a single number on your entire day; however, with practice, this gets very easy to do. The key is to establish an anchor, and your first day or two does this. On subsequent days, reflect back on whether today felt better than yesterday.

If you still find this challenging, take time to establish more concrete anchors. For instance, reflect back on a day or period when you felt as happy (or relaxed) as you have ever felt and use this day as an anchor for 10. Next, reflect back on a day or a period when you felt as unhappy (or tense/stressed) as you ever felt. This day becomes your anchor for negative feelings. Now think of a neutral day, without many highs and lows. This becomes your anchor for a 5. Each day you can use these anchors as comparison points to rate your current mood by asking, "Was my overall feeling today closer to the day I rated as a 10 or the day I rated a 1?" You can establish as many anchors as you need to make this useful for you. You might

> **Key Points: Mood Monitoring**
>
> - Use a Mood Monitoring Form.
> - Complete the worksheet at least once per day at the same time every day.
>   - It becomes easier each day.
> - Jot down any thoughts or behaviors that seem related to mood changes.
>   - Whenever you notice your mood change, ask yourself, "What just went through my mind?"
>   - Get in the habit of writing thoughts, feelings, and behaviors on paper or typing them into an electronic journal.

even create a separate mood rating form where you write down a memorable day to serve as an example of each step in the scale, but try not to get too carried away with precision. The main point of this activity is simply to pay attention to your mood and times that it shifts.

At the bottom of the form, write any thoughts or behaviors that occurred during the day that were related to positive or negative feelings. The goal is to get in the habit of paying attention to these aspects of your inner world, and gradually build on this basic skill.

If mood monitoring comes relatively easy to you, try using Handout 4.2. This handout breaks your mood into three domains. Use it in the same way as the basic mood form. Just rate all three dimensions of your mood rather than just one.

FEELINGS JOURNAL

Another strategy many people find helpful to become more aware of their mood is to keep a feelings journal. Not everyone enjoys journaling, so this is an optional activity. If you are open to it, take 10–15 minutes at the end of the day to write about any positive and negative emotional experiences you had during the day. Write about the circumstances that occurred before and during your emotional experience and try to label your specific emotions. Write down the thoughts and behaviors that occurred along with those emotions. You can simply free-write about these events and let whatever thoughts you have emerge from your writing, or if you prefer, you can add structure to the journal activity by intentionally asking the following questions:

"What happened?"
"What was I feeling?"
"What was I doing?"
"What was I thinking?"
For positive emotions: "What can I do or think to make this happen again?"
For negative emotions: "What can I do or think to make this less likely to happen again?"

DEEP BREATHING

Becoming more mindful of how you breathe is another important aspect of awareness. Your breath is your gateway to the parasympathetic nervous system and the relaxation response. In subsequent chapters, we describe ways to directly control your breathing through various practices like relaxation training and meditation. Here, we want you simply to focus on how you breathe and become more aware of the relationship between your breathing and your feelings.

Take a moment to take several deep breaths. As you do this, pay attention to how you breathe deeply. Which parts of your body move when you take a deep breath? Your shoulders, your chest, your stomach? How long do you take to inhale and exhale when you breathe in deeply? Do you breathe in through your mouth or your nose? The answers to these questions tell you about the mechanics of your breath.

Many of us have learned some misrules about breathing and relaxation. Some of us exaggerate the chest movement when we inhale deeply, mistakenly thinking that the lungs expand outward when they fill with air. If you find that your chest and shoulders rise dramatically when you breathe, you are not maximizing the benefits of deep breathing. Instead, the lungs optimally expand downward with the diaphragm pushing down to make space and in turn pushing the stomach outward. If you are a chest breather it will be helpful to take some time to unlearn this habit. A simple way to do this is to place one hand on your stomach and the other on your chest as you take in several more deep breaths. This time, intentionally push out your stomach as you breathe in and keep your chest relatively flat. Exaggerate the stomach movement the first few breaths. It can be helpful to close your eyes and picture the diaphragm extending downward to make room for your expanding lungs. With a little practice, you can master this new movement and dramatically expand the amount of air your body brings in with each breath.

How long should your exhale and inhale be for a deep breath? You might be surprised how long you can learn to extend each of these movements. The average resting respiration rate is about 15 breaths per minute, which translates to an average inhalation/exhalation rate of 2 seconds. For deep breathing, try to slow this rate to five seconds. Slowly count to five in your head as you breathe in and then again to five as you exhale. With time and practice, you can learn to expand this to a count of 10, 20, and even 30 for each movement. The slower your breathing rate and the longer you keep it at a slow rate, the more you activate your parasympathetic system and all of its other processes (lower heart rate and blood pressure, etc.).

In the coming week, tune in to your breath. Notice it during times of stress and tension. Alter it by slowing it down and notice what effect this has on your body and your mood. At night, take time to practice breathing at a different, slower pace. Pay attention to making your diaphragm expand rather than your chest. As you master effective deep breathing, you will find that you become more aware of tension in your body when it does it exist and ways to

> **As you master effective deep breathing, you will find that you become more aware of tension in your body when it does it exist and ways to slowly release it.**

slowly release it. To gain the optimal benefit from deep breathing, try doing it every day for 10 minutes or longer. You can schedule time to do it at a time that is convenient for you each day (e.g., just before bed), or you can do it mindfully as you experience stress during the day.

GOAL SETTING

Awareness involves being aware of your current behaviors and thoughts, including picturing where you want to be. The ability to set realistic and measureable goals is an important life skill. Throughout this book we ask you to observe and monitor yourself, collect baseline information about your current status, and set goals for yourself based on this information.

With the emphasis on accountability and measureable outcomes in schools, you may have developed a negative association to goal setting. Surely, goal setting can be misused or done poorly. Effective goal setting is meaningful, specific, observable, measureable, and realistic. We begin with "meaningful" because ultimately your goals are about you, and it only makes sense to set goals for yourself that are important to you in some way. The goal's meaning may come from the action itself or a link with a higher ideal. For instance, you may set a goal to increase your exercise behavior. The importance you attach to exercising may be more connected to a larger meaning about your health and emotional well-being than to the action of going to the gym. For instance, you may find the meaningfulness of exercise in staying healthy for your children or grandchildren. Connecting our goals to deeper values and being mindful of them helps us set good goals and usually inspires us to achieve them.

> We begin with "meaningful" because ultimately your goals are about you, and it only makes sense to set goals for yourself that are important to you in some way.

After we establish meaningful goals, we make them specific, concrete, measureable, and observable. These aspects of goal setting help us to know exactly what we are striving for and to determine whether or not we met our goals. "I want to exercise more," would be a nonexample of a specific and measureable goal. Instead, "I will jog for 30 minutes or more three times this week," would be a much more tangible and useful goal. Finally, goals need to be realistic and staggered. We begin to determine how realistic goals are by figuring what our current behavior looks like. We may set a goal to increase our exercise behavior to 7 days a week, but that is probably not a realistic first step if we currently do not exercise at all. We can picture what our ultimate goal might be (exercise every day), but rather than shooting for that all at once, we set goals in a staggered sequence (called *shaping*) with small steps that gradually increase until we reach the ultimate goal.

> Connecting our goals to deeper values and being mindful of them helps us set good goals and usually inspires us to achieve them.

Take a moment now to set a goal for yourself for reading this book using Handout 4.3. Start by setting a specific and measureable goal that you would like to accomplish by the end of the book. For instance, "I would like to lower my daily stress rating on a scale of 1 to

10 from its current level of 8 to a 5 or lower" would be both specific and measureable. Or you might simply set goals around using the strategies such as, "I will try one or more stress management strategies per week and find at least three that I will continue to use after completing the book." After setting a goal, be sure to write down why it is important to you to ensure it is a meaningful goal. Make a commitment to one or more steps required for you to meet your goal. Finally, complete the scales on the handout that ask about importance and confidence. Reflecting on questions like these help affirm your commitment to following through on your goals.

PROBLEM SOLVING

Awareness also involves considering how we define and attempt to solve problems. Problem solving follows naturally from goal setting. We use problem solving multiple times every day. If you try to reduce and manage your stress level, you are by definition engaged in a problem-solving process. It is useful to reflect on how we solve problems. In fact, much research has focused on defining how to solve problems most efficiently, and there has been remarkable consistency in the steps that researchers have identified that are used by effective problem solvers (D'Zurilla & Nezu, 2007). These include some variation of the following: (1) defining the problem, (2) brainstorming solutions, (3) choosing and implementing a solution, and (4) evaluating whether the solution worked.

Defining the problem involves many of the elements of good goal setting. Problems are more likely to be solved when we define them in observable and concrete ways. Good problem definitions also involve focusing on things that we personally control. In this way we are more likely to define problems in ways that make them more solvable. For instance, if you have a conflict with a coworker, an example of a poor problem definition would be "Jerry is a jerk." This violates every key aspect of a good definition. First, it is not observable. "Jerk" is a vague term that is open to interpretation. Second, it defines the problem in a way you cannot directly control. A more effective definition would be, "When Jerry says negative things about me to other teachers, I feel very frustrated and hurt." This definition is explicit about Jerry's behavior and its impact on you.

After you create a clear definition, take time to brainstorm potential solutions. You can do this on your own or with a friend, to help come up with ideas. Sometimes we get in ruts with our solutions and fail to think of original ideas; having someone else enter with new ideas can get us out of such ruts. If you do it on your own, write down any and all possible solutions that come to mind. At this stage, the goal is not to judge whether ideas are feasible or helpful. That comes next. In the brainstorming phase, we just want to stretch our thinking and come up with as many possible ideas as we can. In the "conflict with a coworker" example, you might brainstorm the following ideas:

☐ Tell Jerry how his actions are making me feel and ask him to stop.
☐ Ignore him.

- ☐ Throw a snowball at him.
- ☐ Tell myself it doesn't matter; my friends are my friends and won't be affected by his comments.
- ☐ Talk to the principal about it.
- ☐ Talk to my coworkers about it and get their advice.
- ☐ Play a practical joke on Jerry.
- ☐ Call in sick for a week.
- ☐ Go on a vacation.
- ☐ Take a deep breath whenever it happens.

Notice a couple things about this list. First, not all of these are good ideas. Throwing a snowball at Jerry or calling in sick for a week are probably not effective solutions. At this step, however, it doesn't matter. You might write these ideas down to make yourself laugh and also to help yourself start thinking outside of your normal solutions. Although these ideas might not be helpful, writing them down may open your thinking to new ideas that actually might be beneficial. Second, notice that some of the solutions involve actions you might take, while others involve thinking in new ways. When you brainstorm, focus on your own behaviors and thoughts that you can change in relation to the problem.

After generating ten or more solutions, evaluate which one has the best chance of achieving desirable results. Also decide which ones you are willing and able to do. In this step, you are judging the feasibility of your ideas. You might decide to combine two or more of the ideas. For instance, in the previous example, you might choose to take a deep breath whenever the problem happens and also to change the way you think about it. After making your choice, implement it.

Finally, it is important to monitor whether your solution worked. As you work through the problem-solving steps, think about the outcome that would indicate that you solved the problem. In the previous example, you might define the problem in relation to your mood. For instance, at the start of the problem-solving process you could rate your frustration about the situation as an 8 and set the goal to get it to be less than 5 as an indicator of success. You might also define success in relation to you taking an action. If you have tended to avoid conflict in the past, you might define a successful solution as taking the risk to talk to Jerry directly about the problem and to express yourself in an assertive manner.

Group Exercise

Ask for a volunteer to work through a current life problem using the problem-solving steps. Encourage members of the group to provide input and feedback about each step using the guidelines in the text for effective problem solving. Come up with a clear and specific definition of the problem, brainstorm as a group a list of potential solutions, ask the volunteer to choose one of them, and then develop an evaluation plan.

Set a timeline for when you will enact the plan and assess your progress. When you reflect on whether it is working, decide whether it was successful. If not, you will need to revisit an earlier step. You may find that you need to define the problem in a different way, or you may decide you defined the problem accurately, but you want to try a different solution. In either case, when you implement a new solution, be sure to monitor progress and evaluate its success. The hallmark of effective problem solvers is not that they get the right solution the first time; rather, they persist longer and try more solutions than less effective problem solvers.

> **The hallmark of effective problem solvers is not that they get the right solution the first time; rather, they persist longer and try more solutions than less effective problem solvers.**

This week, reflect on a problem in your life that you would like to solve. Use Handout 4.4 to work through the problem-solving steps. Write down the problem and solutions, then

---

If You Do Only One (Two) Things

Monitor Your Mood

Truly, if you only do one thing in this chapter, take time to monitor your mood using one of the forms. Becoming more aware of your mood is the foundation for all that follows in this book, so take time to do this one thing during the coming week. Commit to doing it every night before bed for the entire week, and you will be better prepared for the next set of activities. You may be surprised that simply paying attention to how you feel in a more intentional way can itself make a difference in how you cope.

> **You may be surprised that simply paying attention to how you feel in a more intentional way can itself make a difference in how you cope.**

Strengths Self-Assessment

We hope you have already taken to mood monitoring. If you have, we included a bonus must-do self-awareness activity. This one will not take long, and it comes with immediate proven benefits for you. For this activity, you need to have access to the Internet. Go to *www.viame.org/survey/Account/Register* and complete the VIA Inventory of Strengths (developed by Christopher Peterson and Martin Seligman). You will need to register your name and create a password, but the survey and results are free. The survey will ask you a series of questions about qualities and whether these qualities describe you. At the end of the survey, you will receive a strengths profile. These will be the qualities that most define your virtues. Simply completing this exercise and reading the results has been shown to promote a sense of well-being and happiness. Awareness of your strengths and virtues and knowing how to use them as a resource helps people cope with adversity. This a good place to start on your self-improvement journey; becoming aware of what you already do well.

enact and evaluate one or more of the solutions. Use this method whenever you encounter new problems.

SUMMARY

Awareness is the foundation for effective coping. Take time this week to use these methods to your advantage. In particular, be sure to develop your mood monitoring muscle! The strategies described in subsequent chapters will only work if they are built on a solid foundation of awareness.

Awareness is the foundation for effective coping.

HANDOUT 4.1

Basic Mood Monitoring Form

Positive		Positive		Positive		Positive		Positive		Positive		Positive
10		10		10		10		10		10		10
9		9		9		9		9		9		9
8		8		8		8		8		8		8
7		7		7		7		7		7		7
6		6		6		6		6		6		6
5		5		5		5		5		5		5
4		4		4		4		4		4		4
3		3		3		3		3		3		3
2		2		2		2		2		2		2
1		1		1		1		1		1		1
Negative		Negative		Negative		Negative		Negative		Negative		Negative
Sunday		**Monday**		**Tuesday**		**Wednesday**		**Thursday**		**Friday**		**Saturday**

Positive thoughts or activities that made me happy: _____

_____

Negative thoughts or activities that made me unhappy: _____

_____

From *Stress Management for Teachers: A Proactive Guide* by Keith C. Herman and Wendy M. Reinke. Copyright 2015 by The Guilford Press. Permission to photocopy this handout is granted to purchasers of this book for personal use only (see copyright page for details). Purchasers can download and print additional copies of this handout from *www.guilford.com/herman-forms*.

HANDOUT 4.2

Mood Monitoring Form with Three Feelings

	Happy	Calm	Relaxed			Happy	Calm	Relaxed
	10	10	10			10	10	10
	9	9	9			9	9	9
	8	8	8			8	8	8
	7	7	7			7	7	7
	6	6	6			6	6	6
	5	5	5			5	5	5
	4	4	4			4	4	4
	3	3	3			3	3	3
	2	2	2			2	2	2
	1	1	1			1	1	1
	Sad	Mad	Anxious			Sad	Mad	Anxious

Sunday — Monday — Tuesday — Wednesday — Thursday — Friday — Saturday

Positive thoughts or activities that made me happy, calm, or relaxed: _____

Negative thoughts or activities that made me sad, mad, or anxious: _____

From *Stress Management for Teachers: A Proactive Guide* by Keith C. Herman and Wendy M. Reinke. Copyright 2015 by The Guilford Press. Permission to photocopy this handout is granted to purchasers of this book for personal use only (see copyright page for details). Purchasers can download and print additional copies of this handout from www.guilford.com/herman-forms.

59

HANDOUT 4.3

Goal-Setting Sheet

My overall goal in reading this book is to: _____

_____

_____

This goal is important to me because: _____

_____

_____

To achieve this goal I commit to doing the following:
- ☐ Read the entire book.
- ☐ Do at least one exercise or activity in every chapter.
- ☐ Do every exercise or activity in every chapter.
- ☐ Read the following chapters and do at least one exercise in each:

    Chapters _____ _____ _____ _____ _____ _____
- ☐ Create a plan for positive coping based on this book.

How important is it for me to meet my goal? Circle a number and write it in the blank below:

    0   1   2   3   4   5   6   7   8   9   10

Not Important   Very Important

I rated the importance _____. Why did I choose this number and not one number lower?

_____

How confident am I that I can meet this goal? Circle a number and write it in the blank below:

    0   1   2   3   4   5   6   7   8   9   10

Not Confident   Very Confident

I rated my confidence _____. Why did I choose this number and not one number lower?

_____

What could I do to help myself become more confident: _____

_____

_____

_____

From *Stress Management for Teachers: A Proactive Guide* by Keith C. Herman and Wendy M. Reinke. Copyright 2015 by The Guilford Press. Permission to photocopy this handout is granted to purchasers of this book for personal use only (see copyright page for details). Purchasers can download and print additional copies of this handout from *www.guilford.com/herman-forms*.

HANDOUT 4.4

Problem-Solving Sheet

What is the problem? *Define it in a way that makes it specific, observable, and solvable.*

_____
_____
_____
_____
_____

What are some possible solutions? *Brainstorm as many as you can, including ideas for changing what you are doing and how you are thinking.*

_____
_____
_____
_____
_____

Which solution has the best chance for success? *Choose one that you are willing and able to do and believe will work.*

_____
_____
_____
_____
_____

Did it work? *Decide how you will monitor and measure progress and a reasonable timeline for determining success.*

_____
_____
_____
_____
_____

If yes, *congratulations! Reward yourself.*

If no, *keep trying. Return to a prior step and repeat the process.*

From *Stress Management for Teachers: A Proactive Guide* by Keith C. Herman and Wendy M. Reinke. Copyright 2015 by The Guilford Press. Permission to photocopy this handout is granted to purchasers of this book for personal use only (see copyright page for details). Purchasers can download and print additional copies of this handout from *www.guilford.com/herman-forms*.

CHAPTER 5

Adaptive Thinking I
The Positive/Negative Thoughts Method

Now that you have been paying attention to your mood, you are in a good position to start monitoring and changing your thinking patterns. Recall the TCM suggests that one primary method for influencing your emotional life is through your thinking habits (see Figure 5.1). This chapter focuses on the tools and strategies to create new, more adaptive thoughts that bring about calming and positive emotions.

There are two different broad approaches for learning new thinking habits (Lewinsohn, Muñoz, Youngren, & Zeiss, 1992). You can choose which you want to use based on a brief description of each. If you don't have a strong preference, you can try both and see which method works better for you. Many people find that they enjoy using aspects of both methods from time to time.

The first method, called the positive/negative thoughts method, involves tracking your thinking and doing activities that increase your positive thoughts and decrease your negative thoughts. This involves creating lists of positive thoughts or doing activities that elicit them, and calling them forth intentionally throughout the day. The second method, called the ABC method, targets emotional overreactions. It involves systematically noticing your negative thoughts that go along with negative emotions and replacing them with more adaptive thoughts. This method works especially well for people who are comfortable debating ideas or using logical arguments to reach new conclusions.

If you prefer to start with the ABC method, first read the sections "Becoming an Expert on Your Thoughts," and "Disclaimer," and complete the self-assessments. Then skip ahead to the next chapter. Otherwise, continue with "Positive/Negative Thoughts Method."

BECOMING AN EXPERT ON YOUR THOUGHTS

Thoughts come at us so quickly and they feel so automatic that learning to become an expert on your thoughts requires concentrated effort and practice. We strongly recommend that

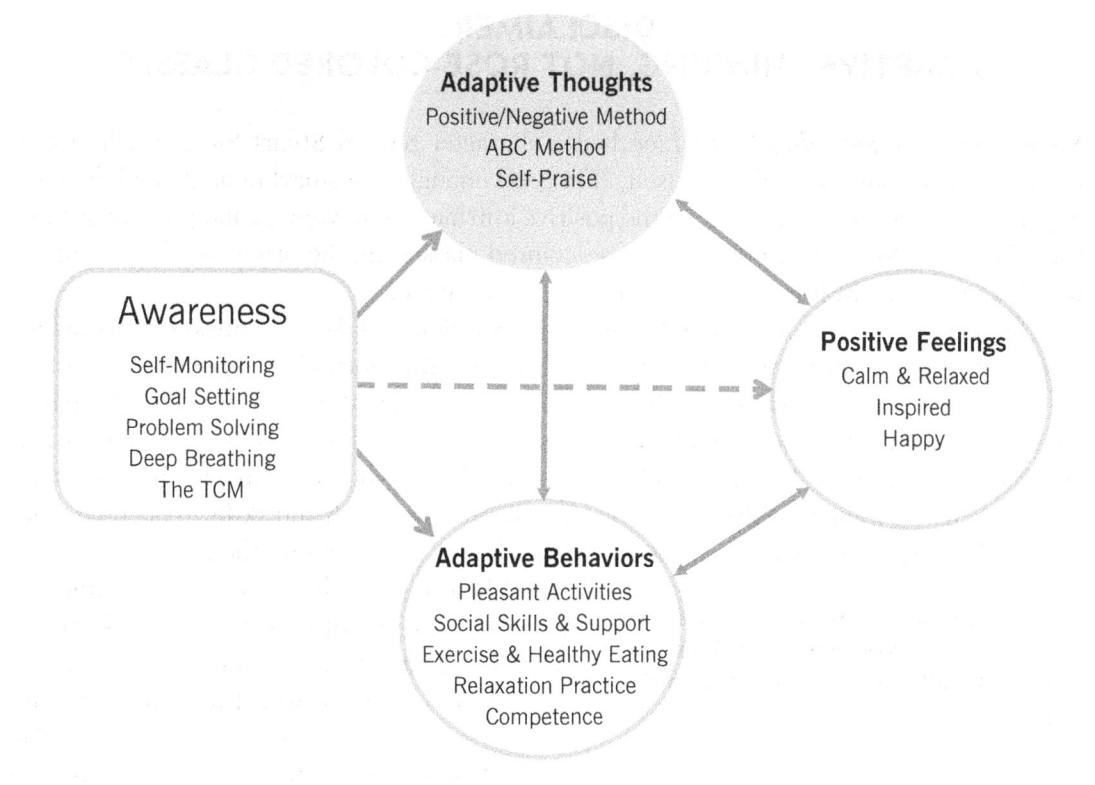

```
                    Adaptive Thoughts
                   Positive/Negative Method
                        ABC Method
                        Self-Praise

   Awareness
  Self-Monitoring                              Positive Feelings
  Goal Setting                                  Calm & Relaxed
  Problem Solving                                  Inspired
  Deep Breathing                                    Happy
     The TCM

                    Adaptive Behaviors
                    Pleasant Activities
                   Social Skills & Support
                  Exercise & Healthy Eating
                    Relaxation Practice
                        Competence
```

FIGURE 5.1. Adaptive thoughts in the TCM.

you do some or all of the exercises in this chapter to become accustomed to new ways of thinking. One key trick we have learned over the years is that it is important to do the actual work of writing your thoughts on paper. It does not work as well when we leave our thoughts floating as abstract concepts in our heads. We are more likely to notice our thoughts when we write them down, and we are better able to judge their accuracy and usefulness when we see them outside our heads.

Another good idea is to write your thoughts down on paper (or electronically) as soon as possible after they occur. It is much harder to recall what we were thinking about an upsetting morning event when we wait until the end of the day to record it. So try to get in the habit of carrying a notebook with you or an electronic device you are comfortable using so you can document your thoughts during the day. It does get easier, and you will need to use the tools less over time, but to start, get in the habit of writing your thoughts down.

> **Thoughts come at us so quickly and they feel so automatic that learning to become an expert on your thoughts requires concentrated effort and practice.**

> **We are more likely to notice our thoughts when we write them down, and we are better able to judge their accuracy and usefulness when we see them outside our heads.**

DISCLAIMER:
ADAPTIVE THINKING, NOT ROSE-COLORED GLASSES

Many years ago, *Saturday Night Live* had a character named Stuart Smalley who sat in front of a mirror and recited to himself, "I'm good enough, I'm smart enough, and doggone it, people like me." It was a spoof on the positive affirmation movement and popular suggestions for trying to cope by putting on rose-colored glasses and ignoring the realities of the world. Unfortunately, it gave positive thinking a bad name.

To be clear, it is *not* our goal to teach you to experience "fake" happiness or to convince yourself that things are great when they are difficult. It is normal to experience upsetting feelings when we face adversities. It only becomes problematic when we do not recover, when upsetting feelings become overreactions, or when they linger for days or months longer than is useful to us. It is ultimately up to you to judge whether your thoughts are functional and if you want to replace them. In this chapter, we teach you skills to become more aware of your thoughts and to handle adversities better, *not* to ignore them.

> **In this chapter, we teach you skills to become more aware of your thoughts and to handle adversities better, *not* ignore them.**

When we talk about adaptive thinking, we are not talking about pretending that the world is perfect. Instead, we are proposing that many of us think about the world in unhelpful ways that actually makes our problems worse. The methods we describe here are not intended to create robotic adherence to things you do not actually believe. Rather, these strategies will help you better evaluate which thoughts you want to keep and which ones you want to discard. It is ultimately your choice.

As we rush through life, we often take our thoughts for granted. Some thoughts are repetitive and have been part of our daily thinking habits from childhood. If these repetitive thoughts that you have developed are adaptive in that they help you cope and move forward, then by all means, continue to think them. If, instead, as you become aware of some of your habitual thoughts, you find some that are no longer useful for you and even some that are simply not accurate, you may want to replace them with ones that can be more functional. These methods will only work if you choose new thoughts that you actually believe.

> **As we rush through life, we often take our thoughts for granted.**

SELF-ASSESSMENT

Take a moment to assess you own beliefs and attitudes using Handout 5.1. This questionnaire lists different attitudes or beliefs people sometimes hold. Read each statement carefully and decide how much you agree or disagree with the statement. For each of the attitudes, indicate to the right of the item the number that best describes how you think. Be sure to choose only one answer for each attitude. Because people are different, there are no right or wrong answers to these statements. To decide whether a given attitude is typical of your way of thinking, simply keep in mind what you are like *most of the time*.

This scale is the Dysfunctional Attitude Scale (DAS; Weissman, 1979), which is a widely used measure of maladaptive thinking associated with stress and depression. Derive your total score by adding all of your responses. Scores range from 40 to 280, with higher scores indicating higher levels of dysfunctional thinking. Calculate your total score by reverse scoring the adaptive items and then summing all items. Although there is no cutoff score, in general higher scores are significantly associated with depressive symptoms and stress.

The total score gives you some sense of your thinking habits. It is most important to look back over the items that you rated above a 4 to see which types of maladaptive attitudes you are more likely to possess. Each of these items represents a common type of dysfunctional belief. If you think in these ways, you are likely making yourself more upset about events than is useful to you. Being more mindful of these attitudes gives you a head start in learning to pay attention to your thinking errors. You may have also noticed that the items on this scale revolved around several themes. These include beliefs about approval, love, achievement, perfectionism, entitlement, power/omnipotence, and autonomy. See if the beliefs that you endorsed were more likely to fall within one or more of these areas. If so, this gives you another clue as to the types of thinking errors you are inclined to make.

POSITIVE/NEGATIVE THOUGHTS METHOD: PLANTING POSITIVE THOUGHTS AND REDUCING NEGATIVE THOUGHTS

Much like nurturing a garden, we have to attend to both removing the weeds (negative thoughts) and planting new seeds (positive thoughts). Just because you pull the weeds of your garden doesn't mean flowers will grow in their place. In the positive/negative thoughts method, you will use one or more strategies for planting new thoughts and one or more for removing negative ones. Peter Lewinsohn developed many of the strategies used in this method and described them in his popular book, *Control Your Depression* (Lewinsohn, Muñoz, Youngren, & Zeiss, 1992).

Big Ideas of the Positive/Negative Thoughts Method

- Your mood is determined by the ratio of positive to negative thoughts you are having.
- You must work on both ends of the equation.
- There are many strategies for increasing positive thoughts and decreasing negative thoughts.
- As a general rule, try to limit your number of negative thoughts and actions (including gossiping; more on that in Chapter 7).

Tracking Your Positive and Negative Thoughts

The first step in this approach is simply to keep track of your positive and negative thoughts throughout the day. Do this for several days so that you generate a fairly lengthy list of examples. You can use Handout 5.2 for this purpose, or simply keep track of them in a notebook or on an electronic device that is accessible to you throughout the day. Write these thoughts down as they occur; if you wait to do this just at the end of the day, you will miss a lot. Forcing yourself to pause and notice your thoughts several times during the day also helps cultivate a habit of self-awareness.

Common Negative Thoughts for Teachers

Handout 5.3 includes a list of negative thoughts that teachers tell us they commonly experience. Take a look at this list and mark the ones that you recognize in yourself. Then for each negative thought, write a positive replacement thought. For instance, if you checked "I'm a terrible teacher," a possible positive replacement thought would be, "I'm not terrible. I do a lot of things well and I will keep improving if I keep trying."

Strategies for Generating Positive Thoughts

Inspiration and Recalling Your Passions

Take a moment to reflect on why you became a teacher in the first place. See if you can tap into that passion that excited you and called you to action. Write these thoughts down and/or talk about them with a colleague or a friend. Use Handout 5.4 to document these thoughts and reread them from time to time.

Here are some examples from teachers we have talked with.

"Knowing that I can be someone for [students], be there for them, and through that I can teach them."

"I had really bad first- and second-grade teachers. I hated it. And then my third-grade teacher was young and she made learning fun, so I thought 'I want to be a teacher so I can help kids learn to like school.'"

"It was just comfortable like it was what I was supposed to do. I babysat and have always been involved with kids."

"I think I've always been a teacher. It was something I always felt like I was good at. I always was someone who took care of others, and that's the part I gravitate to, so in some ways I'm a caretaker."

"I have dyslexia and I have sat in that seat, and I want to help children. Unlock that struggle for them."

"I've always liked being in school. I've always loved being in this environment."

The Best Thing about Being a Teacher

Likewise, documenting what you most enjoy about being a teacher and rereading the list on a regular basis can help generate positive thoughts. In our interviews with teachers, it was remarkable how consistent the responses were. Nearly every answer had some version of "the kids" in it. The specific ways that students made teaching enjoyable varied by teacher, though. Here are some of the responses:

"The best thing about being a teacher would be the bond you form with kids. I really love to make that relationship. Like at the end of the day now, you tell the kids that you love them and they hear that. Then when a kid walks out the door and says, 'Love you Ms. T. . . .' and I don't say it first that really shows me they know I'm not just saying I care about them, that I really mean it, so that they feel comfortable saying it to me."

"We all just are a community in here, and I would say seeing that community grow is the best thing. You start at the beginning of the year with everyone really shy, strangers, and everybody's kind of like, 'Who are you?' Then you reach a point where you're just a community. I love watching my kids socialize and building. I see them as little citizens, and how I can help them go out into the world and be successful."

"The relationships with kids. I enjoy talking with them. I like listening to them and all the interesting things they think—the things they find interesting, I enjoy hearing. I like helping them work through problems, whether it's social things or personal things. I like to see them grow, not just physically but in all areas of their lives."

"I just love the kids. I love teaching them. I love getting to know them and supporting them. And when they go on to other grades and they still come back to check in, that just is so gratifying."

"It's about the whole child. It's not just about the academics, it's about making them successful."

"I just get so much in return from the kids for what I do for them."

"The kids crack me up. It's the comic relief!"

"The kids. Interacting with the kids. Seeing how much they grow and change in a year."

"Seeing the kids get excited."

"When you see that lightbulb turn on for the children. Unlocking that unknown so they can succeed in other areas."

"Being around the kids. I love kids and their ideas and how creative they can be. I learn so much from them, probably just as much as they learn from me. Figuring out how their minds work, it's fun."

> **GROUP ACTIVITY**
>
> Take time to share these stories about how you became a teacher and the best part of being a teacher in your groups. It can be empowering and inspiring to share your stories and hear the stories of others. Be sure to document your story and any that inspire you so you can return to read them in the future.

Within each of these statements is a set of adaptive thoughts that you can write down and recall during times of stress. When you find thoughts that tap into your positive emotions (i.e., simply by thinking them they bring about a positive feeling in you), write these down. You can use these to your advantage in the future. Take a moment to write down the best part of being a teacher using Handout 5.5.

Coping Thoughts

One thing we hear over and over again from effective teachers is that they have developed coping thoughts for dealing with the most stressful situations. Coping thoughts are simple mantras that you can repeat to yourself when you feel yourself getting upset. A common scenario in which teachers need to use coping thoughts occurs when they are managing difficult student behaviors in the classroom. Effective discipline requires that adults remain calm and deliver consequences in a matter-of-fact manner. Obviously, this can be challenging when managing behaviors that upset us. Positive coping thoughts include the following:

"I can get through this. This won't last forever."
"It's okay to be upset. It will pass."
"I've handled this before."
"Just remember to breathe."
"One step at a time."
"Keep focused on what I need to do."
"Remember to stay calm."
"Take your time. There's no rush. Time is on my side."
"I will learn from this. It will get easier each time."
"Remember to praise students who are meeting expectations."
"I can do this."
"Staying calm shows that I am in control."
"If I get upset now, he may learn that his misbehavior works to get my attention and the problem could get worse."
Single words repeated over and over: *relax, peace, calm, breathe.*

The most effective coping thoughts for you may be very personalized. Try some of these generic mantras given above, but also see if you can find a thought that works especially well to calm you down. Here are some specific coping thoughts teachers have used to manage difficult times.

> "My attitude sets the tone."
> "I don't fight with 8-year-olds."
> "Remember to notice the ones being "good" when I feel stressed."
> "I should be as forgiving as my students."
> "This situation will not matter in 5 years."
> "Ask myself, 'Is this situation affecting the entire class or just me?'"
> "I am a model for these children for how to manage my anger by staying calm. For some children, I may be their only positive coping model."
> "People don't care what you know until they know that you care."

Coping thoughts can also come from inspiring quotes that you have heard over the years. Check out *www.my-inspirational-quotes.com/category/special-quotes/teacher-quotes* for some quotes that other teachers have found inspiring and use them in your daily practice, like a mantra that you repeat to yourself during times of stress.

Coping thoughts can include images or ideas. We discuss guided imagery as a coping strategy in Chapter 7. For now, know that any image or idea that you find relaxing—a nature scene like a beach, mountain, or meadow; a camp fire; a memory of a time you felt at peace—can be used as a coping tool during times of duress. Think of these, write them down using Handout 5.6, and use times of stress as a signal to think about them.

Using Priming and Cues

Priming involves intentionally thinking positive thoughts throughout the day. A great way to do this is to write down a set of positive thoughts that you would like to think more. It could be things like any of the inspiring thoughts you generated earlier or any positive thought that gives you positive emotions:

> I am grateful for _____ [fill in the blank].

Once you have a list, set a goal to read it three or more times a day. Think about when you have a few minutes during the day. Before you get out of bed in the morning and just before you fall asleep at night are two times that work well. Also, choose one or more times during the day when you will read the list, perhaps at lunch or during a planning time. When you read the list, it is important to read it actively, thinking about each positive thought and why it is important to you (rather than passively reading words).

You can use cues in this method to prompt the positive thoughts as well. Think of any habit or routine that occurs throughout your day. A common one is looking at the clock or a watch. Whenever you do this habit or routine, tell yourself that you will think one positive thought on your list. It can be the same thought throughout an entire day or you can have several thoughts. For instance, every time you catch yourself glancing at the clock, you might think, "I am grateful for the chance to be a positive influence in these students' lives." Or, "I am proud of myself for committing to becoming a better teacher." Or even simply, "I am calm. I am relaxed."

You can add cues to your environment by placing dots or sticky notes in random places around your desk or the room. When you see these cues, use them as a prompt to remind yourself to think the positive thoughts you want to generate more in your mind. With practice, these thoughts will start emerging on their own.

Giving Yourself Credit

Few of us take time to pause during the day to give ourselves credit for our accomplishments, and doing so would yield a shift in our thinking. With this technique, you simply schedule one or more times during the day to take time to acknowledge your accomplishments. As always, this is most effective if you take time to put it in writing. So first choose at least one time during the day when you can spend 5 minutes reflecting on what you have done to that point in the day. It could be during lunch and/or at the end of your work day. Sit down and write several examples of anything that could be construed as an accomplishment. Think beyond just big successes—accomplishments come in all shapes and sizes, and we too often make the mistake of only celebrating or even acknowledging huge accomplishments. Instead, take time to notice all the details of successes, no matter how small, that you have during each day. Some days that might include very simple things like getting out of bed, taking time to eat breakfast, driving slowly to work, remembering to take a deep breath when you noticed yourself getting frustrated, and so on. We are much more inclined to notice even the smallest mistakes we make, and we rarely give as much attention to the smallest achievement. It takes effort, but it is worthwhile, because when you do this, you start generating positive thoughts that weren't there before. You will find that, with time, it comes naturally to notice every small positive step you make.

You can write these down on a blank sheet of paper. Try to write at least five at first, and then increase it to at least 10 per day. Become an expert at noticing the small things that contribute to a successful day.

Self-Rewarding Thoughts

Self-praise is an important skill that we reference often in this book for several reasons. First, many of us forget to routinely praise ourselves. Second, self-praise is a type of reward in itself that encourages whatever behavior you praise. As a strategy for increasing positive thoughts, write down 10 or more self-praise statements that you would like to add to your thought routine. As always, these should be ideas or thoughts that you truly believe or want to believe. These thoughts can be general, global qualities that you want to remind yourself about (e.g., "I am good at _____," "I always try my best." "I am a team player," "I am brave and strong," "I like that I take risks," "I am a hard worker"), or they can be in-the-moment acknowledgements of something you have done (e.g., "I did an excellent job of leading the class discussion," "I like how I stayed calm when that student was being disruptive," "I'm pleased that I stood up for myself in that meeting," "I liked how I just expressed my ideas," "I feel really good that I am going to the gym right now, even though I was tired when I got home").

Strategies for Reducing Negative Thoughts

Worry Time

One reason that worry persists is because it is unstructured and we allow it to occur at any time. Worry time involves scheduling a time during the day where you allow yourself to worry, setting a timer for no more than 20 minutes, and then ending your worry session at that time. If you find yourself worrying outside of your worry time, simply say to yourself, "Not right now. I will allow myself to worry during my worry time." If it is something you want to be sure to worry about during worry time, write it down; get it out of your head and onto paper. Although it may sound silly and unrealistic, we find that this new habit makes it more likely that you will better confine your worrying to this scheduled time. If you give yourself permission to worry, it takes away some of its angst and gives you more control over it. Interestingly enough, we also find that over time people tend to use less and less of their worry time, sometimes ending it after only a few minutes. These people found that once they thought about a particular concern, they no longer felt a need to dwell on it.

> **If you give yourself permission to worry, it takes away some of its angst and gives you more control over it.**

Time Projection

Looking forward in time can be a useful strategy to reduce negative thoughts. The strategy here is to imagine the future and ask yourself whether the events of today will have any bearing on the future. You might ask yourself any of the following questions:

"What will people remember about today a year [5 years, 100 years] from now?"
"What's the worst thing that could happen? How will I deal with it if it does?"
"What's the best thing that could happen?"

Projecting forward in time helps us to think more realistically about events and reduce our sense of catastrophe in the moment. Looking forward, we generally realize that our strong reactions are temporary and will dissipate in time.

Exaggeration/Blowing Things Out of Proportion

One creative way to diminish negative thinking is to imagine the worst-case scenario. This works especially well if you can be as ridiculous as possible and exaggerate possible negative outcomes. The goal is to get yourself to realize how your real problems are usually on a much smaller scale than how catastrophic we make them seem. For instance, if you were embarrassed about a public mistake you made, blowing it out of proportion might involve sitting down and picturing how the entire world might respond to your mistake. You might envision T-shirts being made with your picture and a caption that reads, "Can you believe how stupid that was?" Newspaper headlines proclaim you as a village idiot. In comparison, the actual consequences of your public mistake are minor.

USING THE METHOD

Choose one of the positive methods and one of the negative methods to use this week. Before you introduce a new strategy, be sure to spend at least several days collecting baseline data about your thinking habits by writing down your thoughts as they occur without trying to change them. This baseline will give you a sense of your positive to negative thought ratio. Based on this ratio, you can set new goals, but keep them realistic. For instance, if you notice during your baseline that you seem to think four negative thoughts for every positive thought, you might set a goal to reduce that to two negatives for every positive. In order to reach your goal, you can select one positive and negative strategy to practice during the coming week. When you achieve that goal the following week, you can use the same strategies or choose new ones and set a goal of one positive to one negative. Ultimately, you may want to set the goal of having two or three positive thoughts for every negative.

Goal Setting

Using Handout 5.7, take time to set your goals for the week related to the positive/negative thoughts method. Be sure to complete all parts of the form, as it will make it more likely your efforts will pay off.

SUMMARY

The positive/negative thoughts method is your first tool for turning around maladaptive thinking. By paying attention to our thoughts and then intentionally changing them, we make it more likely that we will elicit positive thoughts in the future. In turn, by thinking in more adaptive ways, we become more optimistic and, consequently, the positive emotions and health associated with optimism become accessible to us.

> **By thinking in more adaptive ways, we become more optimistic and the positive emotions and health associated with optimism become accessible to us.**

IF YOU DO ONLY ONE THING

We have included two must-do activities this chapter, one designed to increase positive thoughts (the Gratitude Journal), the other to decrease negative thoughts (Written Self-Disclosure). It is your choice which one to focus on now. You might decide to do both, as they are each very effective strategies for boosting health and happiness.

Gratitude Journal

Keep a gratitude journal this week in which you spend 10 minutes at the end of every day writing down what you are grateful for. Really think about each item that you write and why you are grateful for it. Use some or all of the items as your positive thoughts that you would like to recall during the day. You might even rate your mood before you start writing and again after 10 minutes. Chances are you will notice a positive shift. The more you do it, the more this positivity will permeate your day.

Written Self-Disclosure

We describe the health benefits of written self-disclosure in Chapter 7, but the exercise works here as well. It is designed to have you write about an upsetting experience and then discard them so it can function as a method for reducing negative thinking. The benefits of this simple method are astounding and include not only stress reduction but also improved immune functioning and reduced health service visits (Pennebaker, 1997). The directions are below:

> Please write about a deeply emotional and difficult time in your life, preferably one that you have refrained from talking about at length with others. Focus on writing about your deepest thoughts and feelings surrounding the event. It is important that you write continuously for the entire time. If you run out of things to say, just repeat what you have already written. In your writing, don't worry about grammar, spelling, or sentence structure. Just write. Write for 20–30 minutes.

Be forewarned, these writing activities can be exhausting. It is common for people to feel sad or anxious or even angry in the immediate aftermath of the writing activity. These feelings will pass, and you will feel stronger for it. If they persist or if they become overwhelming, then stop the task. In the very unlikely event that you experience overwhelming feelings that persist, or certainly any thoughts of harming yourself or others, you should consult with a mental health professional immediately.

HANDOUT 5.1

Dysfunctional Attitude Scale

	Totally Agree	Agree Very Much	Agree Slightly	Neutral	Disagree Slightly	Disagree Very Much	Totally Disagree
It is difficult to be happy unless one is good looking, intelligent, rich, and creative.	1	2	3	4	5	6	7
Happiness is more a matter of my attitude toward myself than the way other people think about me.	1	2	3	4	5	6	7
People will probably think less of me if I make a mistake.	1	2	3	4	5	6	7
If I do not do well all the time, people will not respect me.	1	2	3	4	5	6	7
Taking even a small risk is foolish because the loss is likely to be a disaster.	1	2	3	4	5	6	7
It is possible to gain another person's respect without being especially talented at anything.	1	2	3	4	5	6	7
I cannot be happy unless most people I know admire me.	1	2	3	4	5	6	7
If a person asks for help, it is a sign of weakness.	1	2	3	4	5	6	7
If I do not do as well as other people, it means I am a weak person.	1	2	3	4	5	6	7
If I fail at my work, then I am a failure as a person.	1	2	3	4	5	6	7
If you cannot do something well, there is little point in doing it at all.	1	2	3	4	5	6	7

(continued)

From Weissman (1979). Reprinted with permission from the author.

From *Stress Management for Teachers: A Proactive Guide* by Keith C. Herman and Wendy M. Reinke. Copyright 2015 by The Guilford Press. Permission to photocopy this handout is granted to purchasers of this book for personal use only (see copyright page for details). Purchasers can download and print additional copies of this handout from *www.guilford.com/herman-forms*.

Dysfunctional Attitude Scale *(page 2 of 3)*

	Totally Agree	Agree Very Much	Agree Slightly	Neutral	Disagree Slightly	Disagree Very Much	Totally Disagree
Making mistakes is fine because I can learn from them.	1	2	3	4	5	6	7
If someone disagrees with me, it probably indicates he/she does not like me.	1	2	3	4	5	6	7
If I fail partly, it is as bad as being a complete failure.	1	2	3	4	5	6	7
If other people know what you are really like, they will think less of you.	1	2	3	4	5	6	7
I am nothing if a person I love doesn't love me.	1	2	3	4	5	6	7
One can get pleasure from an activity regardless of the end result.	1	2	3	4	5	6	7
People should have a chance to succeed before doing anything.	1	2	3	4	5	6	7
My value as a person depends greatly on what others think of me.	1	2	3	4	5	6	7
If I don't set the highest standards for myself, I am likely to end up a second-rate person.	1	2	3	4	5	6	7
If I am to be a worthwhile person, I must be the best in at least one way.	1	2	3	4	5	6	7
People who have good ideas are better than those who do not.	1	2	3	4	5	6	7
I should be upset if I make a mistake.	1	2	3	4	5	6	7
My opinions of myself are more important than others' opinions of me.	1	2	3	4	5	6	7
To be a good, moral, worthwhile person I must help everyone who needs it.	1	2	3	4	5	6	7
If I ask a question, it makes me look stupid.	1	2	3	4	5	6	7

(continued)

Dysfunctional Attitude Scale *(page 3 of 3)*

	Totally Agree	Agree Very Much	Agree Slightly	Neutral	Disagree Slightly	Disagree Very Much	Totally Disagree
It is awful to be put down by people important to you.	1	2	3	4	5	6	7
If you don't have other people to lean on, you are going to be sad.	1	2	3	4	5	6	7
I can reach important goals without pushing myself.	1	2	3	4	5	6	7
It is possible for a person to be scolded and not get upset.	1	2	3	4	5	6	7
I cannot trust other people because they might be cruel to me.	1	2	3	4	5	6	7
If others dislike you, you cannot be happy.	1	2	3	4	5	6	7
It is best to give up your own interests in order to please other people.	1	2	3	4	5	6	7
My happiness depends more on other people than it does on me.	1	2	3	4	5	6	7
I do not need the approval of other people in order to be happy.	1	2	3	4	5	6	7
If a person avoids problems, the problems tend to go away.	1	2	3	4	5	6	7
I can be happy even if I miss out on many of the good things in life.	1	2	3	4	5	6	7
What other people think about me is very important.	1	2	3	4	5	6	7
Being alone leads to unhappiness.	1	2	3	4	5	6	7
I can find happiness without being loved by another person.	1	2	3	4	5	6	7

Scoring: Reverse score the shaded items by taking 8 minus the number you circled (if you circled 3, your reverse score would be 8 − 3 = 5). Then sum all items to obtain your total score.

HANDOUT 5.2

Common Negative Thoughts and Their Positive Replacements

Negative Thoughts	I have this thought sometimes	Positive Replacement Thought
I'm a terrible teacher.		
It's awful to be disrespected.		
This will never work.		
I can't stand this.		
This is too hard.		
This is not fair.		
I have too many students.		
I can't do this.		
I am losing control.		
I hate being disrespected.		
His parents just don't care.		
She's doing this on purpose.		
I can't let him get away with that. It will make me look weak.		
No one ever supports me.		
This paperwork is such a waste of time.		
I don't know what I'm doing.		
This is hopeless.		
He doesn't care, so why should I?		
I must get control of this classroom.		
These students should listen to me.		
He always acts this way.		

From *Stress Management for Teachers: A Proactive Guide* by Keith C. Herman and Wendy M. Reinke. Copyright 2015 by The Guilford Press. Permission to photocopy this handout is granted to purchasers of this book for personal use only (see copyright page for details). Purchasers can download and print additional copies of this handout from *www.guilford.com/herman-forms*.

HANDOUT 5.3

Tracking Positive and Negative Thoughts

Positive Thoughts	Negative Thoughts
Total:	**Total:**

From *Stress Management for Teachers: A Proactive Guide* by Keith C. Herman and Wendy M. Reinke. Copyright 2015 by The Guilford Press. Permission to photocopy this handout is granted to purchasers of this book for personal use only (see copyright page for details). Purchasers can download and print additional copies of this handout from *www.guilford.com/herman-forms*.

HANDOUT 5.4

Why I Became a Teacher

I became a teacher because . . .

_____
_____
_____
_____
_____
_____
_____
_____
_____
_____
_____
_____
_____
_____
_____
_____
_____
_____
_____
_____
_____
_____
_____
_____

From *Stress Management for Teachers: A Proactive Guide* by Keith C. Herman and Wendy M. Reinke. Copyright 2015 by The Guilford Press. Permission to photocopy this handout is granted to purchasers of this book for personal use only (see copyright page for details). Purchasers can download and print additional copies of this handout from *www.guilford.com/herman-forms*.

HANDOUT 5.5

What I Like Most about Being a Teacher

What I like most about being a teacher is . . .

___

From *Stress Management for Teachers: A Proactive Guide* by Keith C. Herman and Wendy M. Reinke. Copyright 2015 by The Guilford Press. Permission to photocopy this handout is granted to purchasers of this book for personal use only (see copyright page for details). Purchasers can download and print additional copies of this handout from *www.guilford.com/herman-forms*.

HANDOUT 5.6

My Coping Thoughts

My coping thoughts for dealing with stress:

_____

_____

_____

_____

_____

_____

_____

_____

_____

_____

_____

_____

_____

_____

_____

_____

_____

_____

_____

_____

From *Stress Management for Teachers: A Proactive Guide* by Keith C. Herman and Wendy M. Reinke. Copyright 2015 by The Guilford Press. Permission to photocopy this handout is granted to purchasers of this book for personal use only (see copyright page for details). Purchasers can download and print additional copies of this handout from *www.guilford.com/herman-forms*.

HANDOUT 5.7

Positive and Negative Method Goal Setting

This week I am going to use the following strategies for increasing positive thoughts and decreasing negative thoughts:	
Positive Strategy	**Negative Strategy**
☐ Inspiration and recalling passion ☐ Priming ☐ Using cues ☐ Acknowledging accomplishments ☐ Self-rewarding thoughts	☐ Worry time ☐ Time projection ☐ Exaggeration
My current rate is _____ positive thoughts for every _____ negative thought. By the end of the week my goal is to have _____ positive thoughts for every _____ negative thought. Each day, I reach my goal I will reward myself with the following self-rewarding thoughts: _____ _____ _____. When I reach my goal for 3 or more days in a row, I will reward myself with _____ _____ _____ [bigger reward].	

From *Stress Management for Teachers: A Proactive Guide* by Keith C. Herman and Wendy M. Reinke. Copyright 2015 by The Guilford Press. Permission to photocopy this handout is granted to purchasers of this book for personal use only (see copyright page for details). Purchasers can download and print additional copies of this handout from *www.guilford.com/herman-forms*.

CHAPTER 6

Adaptive Thinking II
The ABC Method

An alternate, or supplemental, way to increase your adaptive thinking comes from the work of psychologist Albert Ellis. Ellis was deeply influenced by the Greek philosopher Epictetus, who suggested that humans are not troubled by events but by the way they think about them. He went on to develop a popular and effective method of psychotherapy for reducing stress, anxiety, and depression called rational emotive behavior therapy (REBT) (Ellis, 1997, 2003). In therapy, Ellis played the role of a lawyer arguing against the maladaptive thinking patterns his clients had developed. What has evolved from REBT over the years was the use of methods for self-improvement to teach individuals how to be their own guides and emotional self-defense lawyers.

The ABC Method is the foundation for REBT. ABC is an acronym that stands for the basic elements of effective self-monitoring. A stands for *activating event*. This includes any event or happening that evokes an emotional response. B stands for your *beliefs* about the event, including your thoughts, attitudes, and images. C stands for *consequence*, or the emotional consequences that follow from the event and your beliefs. Quite often we mistakenly assume that events in our life lead to our emotional consequence. As the Greek philosopher so aptly stated and Ellis later articulated, it is more accurate and helpful to realize that beliefs or thoughts about events make us feel particular ways. The reason this is such an adaptive approach to the problem is that we often have little control over many of the events that occur in our life. If we allowed our emotional lives to be controlled by events, we might feel helpless, like a boat adrift in the sea or butterfly fluttering on a windy day. Instead, we become empowered when we recognize that we have control over our beliefs.

> **ABC is an acronym that stands for the basic elements of effective self-monitoring.**

The idea behind the ABC method is that our reactions to events are due to our beliefs about the events, as opposed to the event itself. If we slow down and look at our reason for

> **Goals of the ABC Method**
>
> - To handle the negative thoughts that you *do* have in a more adaptive way.
> - To be more resilient in the face of adversity by challenging your beliefs and evaluating how accurate they are.

reacting the way we do, we may be able to see where we are using faulty logic and dispute it. We can apply scientific thinking, hypothesis testing, and critical thinking skills to our self-dialogues. By disputing the faulty, nonresilient thoughts, we can replace them with more reasonable ones.

The ABC method is useful when you find yourself overreacting to situations. An overreaction occurs when you react so strongly that it hinders your functioning. A good rule of thumb to follow is if you continue to ruminate about something for more than a day, you need to do something different. At this point, you have two choices: you can either change your behavior or change your thinking. Changing your behavior could possibly mean expressing the feeling you have to someone; alternately, you might change your perspective.

> **A good rule of thumb to follow is if you continue to ruminate about something for more than a day, you need to do something different.**

SELF-ASSESSMENT

Because we are talking about overreactions, take a moment to think about what things are most likely to push your buttons. What things really annoy you when they happen? Handout 6.1 is a list of common areas that you might find more or less challenging. Look over the list and check the areas that are most likely to push your buttons, either because you feel less effective in handling them or because something about them activates your emotional responses.

It helps to be mindful of the areas or topics that most commonly get you riled up. Staying aware of these "push-button adversaries," as they are called, will help you become more mindful of when you may need to use the skills described below.

SELF-MONITORING: ABC

The ABC Worksheet

In this method the first step, as usual, is self-monitoring. Begin by monitoring and documenting your emotions and thoughts as they occur throughout the day for later review. In subsequent steps, after you master self-monitoring, you then use skills to alter your maladaptive thoughts by arguing against or using Socratic questions to challenge them and find more adaptive ways of thinking.

This week, use the ABC Worksheet to document your emotional reactions. Whenever you have an emotional reaction, write it down. Start with your emotional consequences. This is usually our first clue that we need to pay attention to our thoughts—we are often aware of when we have having strong emotions, and so this is our signal for doing the work. You may feel more than one emotional in response to any given event, so write them all down. Next, reflect on what happened just prior to your emotional reactions and write this in the activating event section; be sure to stick with the facts (who, what, where, when). Finally, reflect on your interpretation of the event, your thoughts and beliefs, that are connected to each emotional consequence you listed in C.

Rating Your Beliefs

Use Handouts 6.2 and 6.3 for this activity. Handout 6.2 is an ABC Worksheet with instructions, and Handout 6.3 is an ABC Worksheet that you will use when you are fluent in the method and no longer need instructions. Note also that Handout 6.2 includes two extra columns for rating how strongly you believe each belief you write in the B section from 1 (not at all) to 100 (completely). Try practicing rating your beliefs in the "Before" section. This tool will come in handy for a later step in this method, where you assess whether you were successful in changing your emotional overreaction.

Examples

Let's return to the example from Chapter 1 to illustrate the use of the ABC Worksheet. Recall that three teachers had different emotional reactions to hearing that they would be having weekly performance evaluations. Ms. Phipps felt angry. Figure 6.1 is what her ABC Worksheet looked like. Mr. Gonzalez on the other hand felt anxious. Figure 6.2 is what his ABC Worksheet looked like. Notice a few important details. First, note that the activating event for Mr. Gonzalez and Ms. Phipps are identical, but their beliefs about the event

Activating Event	**B**eliefs	**C**onsequences (Emotions)
My principal announced at our faculty meeting that she would start doing weekly classroom observations starting next week.	1. She is wasting my time. 2. She's just trying to show she's in charge. 3. She is incompetent and has no business telling me how to teach.	1. Frustrated 2. Annoyed 3. Angry

FIGURE 6.1. Ms. Phipps's ABC Worksheet.

86   COPING STRATEGIES

Activating Event	**B**eliefs	**C**onsequences (Emotions)
My principal announced at our faculty meeting that she would start doing weekly classroom observations starting next week.	1. My principal is going to discover that I am an impostor. 2. I am not a good teacher. 3. I'm going to lose my job.	1. Anxious 2. Sad 3. Anxious and depressed

FIGURE 6.2. Mr. Gonzalez's ABC Worksheet.

and the consequences are very different. Next, notice that when he completed the form, Mr. Gonzalez noticed that he was actually feeling several different emotions. He was most aware of his anxiety, but upon reflection, he also sensed some sadness and depression, so he wrote these in the C section. Finally, notice that each belief was distinctly related to each of the feelings that he identified.

Finally, recall that Ms. Malcolm actually experienced positive feelings after hearing that her principal would be doing observations in her class. Do the ABCs apply here? Yes, we have already clearly established that positive feelings arise from positive thoughts. It can be helpful to be aware of the types of beliefs that lead us to feel in positive ways. Figure 6.3 is what Ms. Malcolm's Worksheet looked like. Again notice the activating event is the same. Instead of feeling worried or angry, Ms. Malcolm was feeling excited and inspired because she believed the observations represented an opportunity for her to improve as a teacher.

Activating Event	**B**eliefs	**C**onsequences (Emotions)
My principal announced at our faculty meeting that she would start doing weekly classroom observations starting next week.	1. I'm going to learn a lot from this experience. 2. This is going to give me a chance to become a great teacher. 3. It will be great to get to know my principal better.	1. Excited 2. Inspired 3. Enthused

FIGURE 6.3. Ms. Malcolm's ABC Worksheet.

Identifying Your Beliefs

Pinpointing your beliefs and thoughts that are connected to your specific emotions is a very important skill in this process. It takes practice. To identify the thoughts tied to your emotional reaction, ask yourself, "What about this event led me to feel this way?" Do this for each of the emotions that you are feeling, because there is likely a specific thought, belief, or image connected to each feeling. For instance, if you discover that you are feeling angry and sad after a negative performance evaluation, you may find yourself thinking a series of thoughts connected to this evaluation. Pinpointing what beliefs are tied to your anger enables you to ask, "What is it about getting negative feedback that makes me angry?" You may find a string of thoughts connected to this feeling like any or all of the following:

> **To identify the thoughts tied to your emotional reaction, ask yourself, "What about this event led me to feel this way?"**

Thoughts That May Bring About Anger

"It's not fair."
"My principal is out to get me."
"No one notices how hard I'm trying."
"This was a setup. No one could be effective with this class."

Next, think about any beliefs that are connected to other feelings. For instance, if you were also feeling sad, you would ask, "What about my negative review makes me so sad?"

Thoughts That Might Bring About Sadness

"I'm not good at this."
"This is hopeless."
"I'm going to lose my job."
"Nobody likes me."

Notice how these are different than the thoughts above related to anger and how they might bring about a very different emotional response. This level of precision is really important as you attempt to uncover the most damaging beliefs. Often the most upsetting thoughts are not the ones closest to the surface or the ones we are first aware of. Sometimes they are layered in a series or string of ideas that we really have to take time to unravel.

Perhaps you were also feeling embarrassed. Note the thoughts related to embarrassment are also likely different than those that elicit anger and sadness.

> **Often the most upsetting thoughts are not close to the surface. Sometimes they are layered in a string of ideas that we have to take time to unravel.**

Thoughts Related to Embarrassment

"My colleagues are going to think I can't teach."
"I don't want to show anyone these evaluations."
"That was a stupid thing to do."

It is important to come up with beliefs as statements rather than questions. For instance, you might first come up with the thought like, "What will people think about me?" This question is connected to the upsetting thought, but it is the answer you have formulated in your mind that is affecting you most. For instance, you might figure out that you are really thinking the statement, "People will think I'm incompetent when they find out."

When you think you have found the key belief tied to your feeling, a way to test this is to ask, "Is just thinking this thought right now enough to make me feel as upset as I feel about the event?" For instance, if you believe the thought that makes you most angry is that your principal is out to get you, you would consider whether just thinking that gets you riled up. If so, then you probably have tapped into the key belief. If not, you may need to dig a little deeper.

Practice

Try the following examples to see whether you can guess what might be some thoughts behind the emotional overreaction.

> Mr. Caldera is nearing the end of his third-period math instruction when he notices three students in the back texting and not paying attention. Mr. Caldera stops his instruction, charges to the back of the room, waves his finger at the students, and shouts, "I am not going to tell you again! Put those away and start paying attention!" He hovers over them for several more seconds before quickly turning and walking to the front of the room. The class notices Mr. Caldera is flushed and visibly shaking as he begins instruction again.

The first question for you to consider is whether this was an emotional overreaction. Some teachers might respond no, that Mr. Caldera was perfectly justified to be as angry as he was and to let the students know about it. When we provide similar scenarios to teachers, they frequently tell us they have been in his shoes and it likely was the buildup of repeated interactions that led to this level of frustration. These are all important points. Mr. Caldera feels the way he feels; clearly this was a frustrating situation for him. It is not up to us to judge him. Rather, it would be up to him to decide for himself whether this was an overreaction or whether it was functional for him in some ways. If we asked Mr. Caldera if he thought this was an effective interaction, what would he say? We're guessing that he would have preferred not to get so upset, and that he may have actually been more effective if he had remained calmer. If so, and he was willing to reflect on his own thinking after the fact, let's try to guess what his ABC Worksheet would look like. Take a moment to complete

Handout 6.4. Remember to start with C first. Write down two or three emotions that you think Mr. Caldera was feeling. Next, write down A, just the facts of the activating event. Finally, write down any beliefs that Mr. Caldera may have been thinking about A that led him to experience the feelings you wrote for C.

What did you write? Was this easy or hard? Take a look at one possible response in Figure 6.4. Don't worry if the beliefs you wrote weren't identical to the ones in Figure 6.4. There are many potentially right answers here. Ultimately, it would be up to Mr. Caldera to tell us what he was thinking. Your A and C should have been similar to the example in Figure 6.4. The key test of whether you are on track with uncovering maladaptive beliefs is to see whether the types of thoughts you generated match the feelings and intensity you wrote in Step C.

Ms. Simone prides herself on sticking with even the most challenging students. This year, there is one boy in her class, Jacob, whom she has been unable to connect with. Today, she has planned an activity that she thinks will bring him around. She introduces the activity to the class. All the children seem to be having fun, but suddenly Jacob says, "This is stupid," and storms out of the class. Ms. Simone's heart sinks, and she has trouble finding the energy to make it through the rest of the day.

Was this an emotional overreaction? It depends, and as always it would be up to Ms. Simone to decide. If she had strong feelings that persisted through the day and she had difficulty doing her job, she might decide this was an overreaction. Let's look at her ABC Worksheet. Take a moment to complete Handout 6.5. Start with C, and be careful. Try to guess what she was feeling and not focus on what your own reaction might have been. Then write the facts of the event at A. Last, write a few beliefs that may have been driving the emotions you wrote for C.

Activating Event	**B**eliefs	**C**onsequences (Emotions)
I was teaching third-period math and was delivering instruction when I saw three students texting.	1. These are the most disrespectful students I have ever met. They don't care about anything but themselves. 2. This happens every single day. 3. I'm never gonna get through to them.	1. Furious 2. Frustrated 3. Defeated/hopeless

FIGURE 6.4. Sample completed ABC Worksheet for Mr. Caldera.

Activating Event	**B**eliefs	**C**onsequences (Emotions)
I was leading a class activity that I had planned as a way to involve Jacob when he shouted that it was stupid and left the room.	1. It's my fault that I can't reach Jacob. I'm letting him down. I'm not a very good teacher. 2. I tried so hard to make this work. Nobody ever appreciates me. 3. I should just give up.	1. Sad 2. Hurt 3. Defeated/hopeless

FIGURE 6.5. Sample completed ABC Worksheet for Ms. Simone.

Take a look below at what we wrote for this example in Figure 6.5. Compare your responses to ours. We noted that the C in this case might be tricky, because another reasonable emotion response to this event would be to experience some version of anger or frustration. It is possible that Ms. Simone was feeling these things in addition to what we wrote, but we focused on sad and hurt because the scenario focused on her low energy and heartbreak. These implied to us internalizing moods. Regardless, if you wrote down anger, the key is that your beliefs matched these feelings. Here, we wrote that one thought or belief that could lead someone to feel sad is the idea that the person is a bad teacher or was somehow failing in responsibilities. Hurt feelings are often tied to feeling unappreciated, unnoticed, or unsupported. Finally, hopeless feelings are usually connected to beliefs about things never getting better and the decision to give up.

Group Activity

Ask one person in the group to share a recent overreaction. As a group, walk through each step of the ABC method, writing the responses for each category on the board. Start with C, the person's emotional reaction, and ask the person to specify all the feelings he or she had in response to the event. Next, for A, write who, what, where, when aspects of the event (just facts, like a police report, without interpretations). Finally, fill in B, by asking the person, "What thoughts or beliefs about A led you to feel the emotions of C?" Try to get the person to indentify specific thoughts and interpretations that were connected uniquely to each feeling.

Digging Deeper: The Funnel Technique

Another strategy to get at core upsetting beliefs is called the funnel technique, or funneling. Funneling involves asking a series of questions repeatedly until you get to the root belief or thought that is most upsetting. The key question is, "Why does that belief bother me so much?" For instance, imagine you wrote down, "My principal thinks I'm incompetent." You realize this thought makes you upset but not as distraught as you were feeling. You ask yourself, "What about thinking that the principal thinks I'm incompetent upsets me the most?" You might answer that your principal may always view you this way. Again, ask, "What about my principal always viewing me as incompetent is so upsetting?" You might conclude you are worried that your principal may decide not to support renewing your contract. At the bottom of the funnel is this belief that you are going to lose your job, and it is this belief that matches the intensity of your anxiety. Use Handout 6.6 as a tool for facilitating your use of the funnel method.

> **Funneling involves asking a series of questions repeatedly until you get to the root belief or thought that is most upsetting. The key question is, "Why does that belief bother me so much?"**

Common Thinking Errors

Another tool for becoming more aware of your own maladaptive thoughts is to learn more about the most common types of thinking errors that humans make. Drs. Ellis and Aaron Beck have documented many common types of thinking errors. As you read about each of these, reflect on which types you are prone to make.

All-or-None Thinking/Overgeneralization

One common mistake is to think about events in extreme terms and label them in ways that make you believe they occur more or less frequently than is true. The words to watch out for as cues that you may be overgeneralizing include *always* or *never*. If you catch yourself thinking in these terms, you are likely thinking in a way that is not helpful to you and that increases the chances of an overreaction. These types of thoughts and labels can be harmful because they are rarely true. They represent exaggerations, and to the extent we believe them or take them for granted, we are likely to get overly upset about the event. Examples of all-or-none thinking and overgeneralization include the following:

> **The words to watch out for as cues that you may be overgeneralizing include *always* or *never*.**

"My husband *never* appreciates me."
"This *always* happens to me."
"These students are *never* respectful."

When you catch yourself thinking in these terms, try asking yourself, "Is it true that it is *always* (or *never*) the case?" or "Can I think of an example that counters this belief?" You might also simply eliminate *always* or *never* and focus on the event right now. "These students are not being respectful right now," conveys a different, less emotional tone than the belief that they are *never* respectful.

Moralization

Another common mistake is to add moral terms to our thinking. Moralization puts added and usually unnecessary weight on interpretations. The key words here are *must* or *should*. If you catch yourself thinking in these terms, you may add a moral burden to your interpretations that increase the chance they will bring about extreme emotional responses. Examples include the following:

> **Moralization puts added and usually unnecessary weight on interpretations. The key catchwords here are *must* or *should*.**

"I *should* get more praise for my effort."
"This behavior *must* stop."
"I *must* get control of my classroom."
"Students *should* listen."

The reason this thinking is a problem is that it exaggerates the problem. Instead, try simple replacement phrases like "I would prefer it if . . ." or "It would be better if . . ." This type of language is accurate, and it lessens the emotional burden to the moral interpretations.

Catastrophizing

Using catastrophizing language also increases the likelihood of overreactions. Words to listen for here include *awful* and *terrible*. These words imply something catastrophic and overwhelming has happened, when in fact, the event being described is usually much more mundane. Some examples include the following:

"This is just *awful* that I don't get any support."
"It's *terrible* that these kids don't know how to behave."
"It's *awful* that these parents are not involved."

Eliminating these words from our beliefs and interpretation is an effective response to them. Replacing them with more neutral language like, "I don't like it when . . ." or "I wish this were different . . ." can also lessen the emotional response. Alternately, you can ask yourself Socratic questions to challenge some of these beliefs. One student we were working with on using these skills came up with a brilliant counter to catastrophic thinking. When he caught himself thinking in those terms, he simply asked himself, "Is this really a catastrophe like 9/11?" The answer to this question is nearly always no, and it prompted him to think about the situation in more realistic ways.

Personalization

When we misinterpret an event as being intentionally directed at us, it automatically heightens our emotional response to it. Humans are prone to believe the world revolves around us, and so we often interpret whatever happens as being connected to us in some way. In reality, most events have nothing to do with us. When we interpret events, especially negative events, in any overly personal way, we make it very likely that we will have a strong emotional reaction to them.

Mind Reading

When we assume the reasons that people act the way they do, we are making the thinking error of mind reading. For example, if your principal fails to say hello in passing and you believe it is because she is angry at you, you are likely making yourself more upset than needed. There are a dozen reasons why a person may not say hello in a particular moment that have nothing to do with you. Perhaps she was deep in thought and did not even notice you, or perhaps she was rushing to another pressing matter. The most important way to avoid mind reading is to become aware of our tendency to do it and then if needed, to check things out with the other person. Ask them whether your perception is correct. Usually you will discover there was some other explanation for their behavior that you had not considered.

Some teachers are prone to the mind reading in relation to student behaviors. If you find yourself thinking, "He is doing this on purpose," or "She's trying to make me mad," check your thoughts. Assigning malicious motives to students will only get a bigger rise out of you. Consider the many benign reasons that students might act out that have nothing to do with you. Alternatively, use an empowering approach to behavior change (such as that described in Chapter 8) that examines the function or purpose of behavior through a lens that focuses on how behaviors develop over time rather than as an affront to you.

Fortunetelling

If you find yourself making negative predictions about the future ("This will never work," "Things don't go my way, so this won't turn out well") you may be committing the fortunetelling error. "I have a headache, so my whole day is shot," becomes a self-fulfilling prophecy. Interrupting and changing such thinking habits puts you in a better position to manage your mood.

Which Thinking Errors Do You Make?

Take a moment to decide which thinking errors you are prone to make. If you are not sure, listen for the key words described above to see which errors you catch as you track your thoughts during the week. Once you become aware of your thinking errors, you will become an expert at detecting them. For instance, if you become aware that you have a habit of thinking in extremes, you will quickly become attuned to times the words *always* or *never* appear in your thoughts, and this will become your cue to stop and come up with more adaptive thoughts.

Identifying Core Beliefs

Dr. Aaron Beck distinguishes between surface beliefs, what he called automatic thoughts, and core beliefs about the self. Automatic thoughts are more accessible to us, and with a little practice, we can become more aware of them. These are important because they trigger our emotional experiences, they are fairly easy to manipulate, and they give us clues about lingering perceptions of ourselves. These automatic thoughts are tied to our core beliefs. It can take a bit more practice and effort to become aware of these beliefs and in turn to change them because they may have persisted unquestioned for much of our lives.

You can have adaptive or maladaptive core beliefs about yourself. Adaptive core beliefs are things like "I'm competent," "I have a good life," "I'm a hard worker," and "Things work out for a reason." On the other hand, there are some common maladaptive core beliefs that you may want to watch for.

If you start tapping in to these types of beliefs, it is useful for you to know. These beliefs can be changed, but it takes persistence and practice. You would first decide what new core belief you would like to replace for the maladaptive thought. Next, the new belief is substituted for the maladaptive thought through systematic rehearsing and practicing, perhaps using some of the methods described in the positive/negative thoughts method in Chapter 5.

Maladaptive Core Beliefs

- "I'm defective."
- "I'm unlovable."
- "I'm incompetent."
- "The world is unsafe."
- "People are out to get me."
- "People owe me."
- "Life is unfair."
- "You can't trust people."

CHALLENGING MALADAPTIVE THINKING: ABCDE

After you monitor your thoughts and start detecting your thinking habits, you are in a position to take the next step. The ABC method expands to the ABCDE method to challenge maladaptive thoughts. *D* stands for *dispute* and *E* stands for *effect*. Dispute refers to taking time to actively argue against and challenge your beliefs. For some of your beliefs, this will be easy. After you become aware of them and write them down, you may be able to decide quickly that that was an unhelpful way of thinking and come up with a new alternative. For instance, a simple trick to change thinking errors consists of changing awful language to preference language.

On the other hand, you may be attached to some beliefs and reluctant to give them up. For others, you may struggle to think of an adaptive alternative. In these circumstances, the best methods involve active questioning through deductive reasoning or Socratic processing. Some excellent questions for challenging your maladaptive thoughts and deriving new adaptive ones are given below:

"What is the evidence for this belief? Are there alternate explanations?"
"What's the worst that could happen? How would I deal with that?"
"To the extent the belief is true, what can I do about it?"
"Is this belief helpful to me? Is there a more helpful way to think about the situation?"
"What would I tell a friend who had a similar type of thought to think instead?"
"What will people be saying about this in 100 years?"

The goals of this process are to start thinking like a scientist, to not accept your beliefs as fact, and to be open to alternate ways of thinking about situations. As you come up with new beliefs, write these down and assess the effect. The effect part of the method is concerned with checking whether your efforts have paid off. To determine effect, ask yourself,

GROUP ACTIVITY: Hot Seat

Ask one person in the group to share a recent overreaction and the types of maladaptive thoughts he or she has been having about the event. Now ask for a volunteer to sit in a chair at the front of the room. The person with the overreaction will then direct the maladaptive thoughts to the person in the hot seat. This person's task is to argue against all of these maladaptive thoughts. For instance, the person with the overreaction might say, "This is hopeless. This will never work." The person in the hot seat could respond, "That is fortunetelling. It won't work if I don't try. But I'm willing to do my best." Go back and forth and then switch roles. The idea is to make these thoughts and coping alternatives explicit. Also, it can be helpful for someone having an overreaction to hear other people generate alternative coping thoughts that he or she might not have considered.

"How do I feel now?" If you have successfully identified and changed the most upsetting thought and a corresponding alternative belief, then you will likely feel better. To be clear, you may not be feeling perfect; it is still reasonable for you to be disappointed or annoyed. The goal is to lessen your emotional response so it no longer disrupts your life.

> **If you have successfully identified and changed the most upsetting thought and a corresponding alternative belief, then you will likely feel better.**

If the answer is no and the effect remains the same as the original consequence, then you have more work to do. Some common culprits of this outcome are that you still have not identified the most upsetting thought, so you may need to do some more work with funneling or simply reflecting on what about the event bothered you. Another possibility is that you have yet to identify a more adaptive alternative thought. Sometimes the problem is that you have found a new thought but do not fully believe it. To be effective you need a new belief that is acceptable and believable to you.

The ABCDE Worksheet

Handouts 6.7 and 6.8 provide ABCDE Worksheets for you to use in the coming weeks. Handout 6.7 includes instructions. As with the ABC Worksheets you can switch to Handout 6.8 without instructions once you become fluent in the method.

Examples

Let's return to our example of the teachers who experienced different emotional consequences after a faculty meeting. Ms. Malcolm did not need to complete Steps D and E, because her feelings and thoughts were already adaptive and positive. However, Ms. Phipps felt angry, so she worked through Steps D and E. She first rated how much she believed each of her thoughts at Step B as being 85–100, meaning she believed them very strongly, which is why she had a strong negative reaction. The more we believe our negative thoughts to be true, the more upset we will be. However, we typically accept our beliefs to be true without much critical thought. This is why disputing is important—it allows us to challenge our beliefs by asking Socratic questions and to arrive at new, adaptive ways of thinking.

In Step D, Ms. Phipps asked herself what evidence she had that her principal was trying to annoy her, was trying to exert her power, or was incompetent. Ms. Phipps then asked if there was evidence against those beliefs. She also asked herself what she would say to a colleague who was thinking similar thoughts. Finally, she asked herself whether it was helpful in any way for her to believe these thoughts. These questions helped her arrive at new ways of thinking, and she wrote her new thoughts down. Her new thoughts included the belief that her principal was actually well intentioned, and that she truly believed the principal had the best interest of the students at heart. She also acknowledged that it was ultimately the principal's decision, and it was within her role to do the observations. Finally, she realized that she had too quickly dismissed the principal as completely incompetent in teaching matters and that she might learn something from the experience if she remained open and respectful.

Ms. Phipps re-rated her beliefs from Step B and found that she no longer believed the original maladaptive thoughts very much. Finally, she evaluated her new feelings and found that her negative mood had been replaced by a more neutral and accepting emotional experience, seen in Figure 6.6.

Mr. Gonzalez felt anxious and sad that the principal would be visiting his classroom. He followed the same steps by rating the strengths of his beliefs, disputing these beliefs, and then evaluating any new effects. He evaluated the evidence for and against his beliefs and questioned what could be the worst thing that realistically might happen. He arrived at new adaptive beliefs and a more positive emotional experience, seen in Figure 6.7.

Activating Event	**B**eliefs	Before	After	**C**onsequences (Emotions)
My principal announced at our faculty meeting that she would start doing weekly classroom observations starting next week.	1. She is wasting my time.	100	10	1. Frustrated
	2. She's just trying to show she's in charge.	90	10	2. Annoyed
	3. She is incompetent and has no business telling me how to teach.	85	5	3. Angry

Disprove/Dispute/Debate	**E**valuate
1. She's just doing her job. She means well.	1. Accepting
2. She IS in charge and it is her decision. I do think she believes this will be helpful to us.	2. Resigned
3. I actually don't know much about her teaching background. Regardless, she may have some good ideas and the only way I will hear them is if I show her some respect.	3. More tolerant

FIGURE 6.6. Ms. Phipps's ABCDE Worksheet.

Activating Event	Beliefs	Before	After	Consequences (Emotions)
My principal announced at our faculty meeting that she would start doing weekly classroom observations starting next week.	1. My principal is going to discover that I am an impostor.	90	10	1. Anxious
	2. I am not a good teacher.	95	15	2. Sad
	3. I'm going to lose my job.	75	0	3. Anxious and depressed

Disprove/Dispute/Debate	Evaluate
1. This is a chance for me to get feedback, and that is one of the best ways to learn and grow as a teacher.	1. Energized
2. I do a lot very well as a teacher, my students like me and are learning, and I am doing everything I can to get better at it.	2. Resolved
3. I'm not that bad! The worst that is likely to happen is that I will get some feedback about areas for improvement, and I will improve, which, is the whole point.	3. Accepting

FIGURE 6.7. Mr. Gonzalez's ABCDE Worksheet.

Practice

Let's return to Mr. Caldera and Ms. Simone and see if we can help them develop more adaptive beliefs. Look back at Figures 6.4 and 6.5, and try to dispute the maladaptive beliefs at Step B. Then look at Figures 6.8 and 6.9 to compare your responses to the ones they developed for themselves.

GROUP ACTIVITY

Return to the ABC example from earlier in the group, and now complete the D and E parts of the method. Take turns disputing each maladaptive belief that was identified earlier and ask the person to choose the ones that best fit his or her situation. Ask the person to re-rate his or her beliefs identified at Step B and see if you can help them reach a new effect (E).

> **IF YOU DO ONLY ONE THING: Gratitude Note**
>
> Building off your gratitude journal from the previous chapter, try this activity that is proven to promote a lasting sense of wellness in a single swoop. Think of someone who has made your life better. It may help to close your eyes and see the first person who pops into your mind when you think of someone who has had a positive influence on you. Now find time to write a thank-you note to the person, a note of gratitude. Make it specific and detailed, not just a generic thank-you. It should be at least a page of writing, about 300 words. Now to make it even more meaningful, deliver the note in person and read it aloud. Arrange a time and place to meet with the person where you can express your gratitude. Read the note to them, or if you're an artist, sing it to them! Seligman's research tells us you will be feeling happier and less depressed one month after doing this. We're guessing the person who receives your message of gratitude will also benefit!

SUMMARY

In this chapter, we focused on a second method for increasing our adaptive thoughts. The ABC method is a structured and systematic tool that you can use to become more aware of your automatic thoughts and restructure the ones that are not helpful to you. As you

Activating Event	**B**eliefs	**C**onsequences (Emotions)
I was teaching third period math and was delivering instruction when I saw three students texting.	1. These are the most disrespectful students I have every met. They don't care about anything but themselves. 2. This happens every single day. 3. I'm never gonna get through to them.	1. Furious 2. Frustrated 3. Defeated/hopeless

Disprove/Dispute/Debate	**E**valuate
1. I can only be effective if I stay calm. I need to find another strategy. 2. This happens a lot, not every day; some days are better than others. 3. They want me to give up. Everyone gives up on them.	1. Disappointed but less angry 2. Annoyed 3. Empowered

FIGURE 6.8. Sample completed ABCDE Worksheet for Mr. Caldera.

Activating Event	**B**eliefs	**C**onsequences (Emotions)
I was leading a class activity that I had planned as a way to involve Jacob when he shouted that it was stupid and left the room.	1. It's my fault that I can't reach Jacob. I'm letting him down. I'm not a very good techer. 2. I tried so hard to make this work. Nobody ever appreciates me. 3. I should just give up.	1. Sad 2. Hurt 3. Defeated/hopeless

Disprove/Dispute/Debate	**E**valuate
1. I'm trying my best. This won't work overnight. Many people have given up on Jacob. I'm not gonna be one of them. 2. I just have to stick with it and know for myself that I'm doing the right thing. 3. If not me, then who will help Jacob. I may not see the difference I'm making yet, but believing in Jacob will last him his lifetime.	1. Patient 2. Committed 3. Encouraged

FIGURE 6.9. Sample completed ABCDE Worksheet for Ms. Simone.

become more fluent in this method, you may find that you are better able to be mindful of your overreactions as they occur and ask the Socratic questions to identify more adaptive thoughts in the moment. Still even Aaron Beck, the famed psychiatrist who developed similar methods in his well-established treatment approach for depression, claims that he occasionally still pulls out his worksheets to write down his feelings and the events and thoughts that preceded them. It is a useful tool and one that works best when we write things down.

HANDOUT 6.1

List of Common Challenging Areas

_____ Conflicts at school

_____ Conflicts with peers

_____ Interactions with authority figures

_____ Interactions with family members

_____ Success

_____ Failure

_____ Being alone

_____ Difficult assignments or projects

_____ Hectic schedule

_____ Change

_____ Social situations

_____ Disrespectful students

_____ Interactions with parents

_____ Grading

_____ State assessments

_____ Performance evaluations

Other (specify):

_____ _____

_____ _____

_____ _____

_____ _____

From *Stress Management for Teachers: A Proactive Guide* by Keith C. Herman and Wendy M. Reinke. Copyright 2015 by The Guilford Press. Permission to photocopy this handout is granted to purchasers of this book for personal use only (see copyright page for details). Purchasers can download and print additional copies of this handout from *www.guilford.com/herman-forms*.

HANDOUT 6.2

ABC Worksheet (with Instructions)

Instructions: Whenever you have an emotional reaction, write it down. Start with your emotional consequences (C). You may feel more than one emotion in response to an event, so write them all down. Next, reflect on what happened just prior to your emotional reactions and write this down in the activating event (A) section; be sure to stick to the facts (who, what, where, when). Finally, reflect on your interpretation of the event, your thoughts and beliefs (B) that are connected to each emotional consequence you listed in (C).

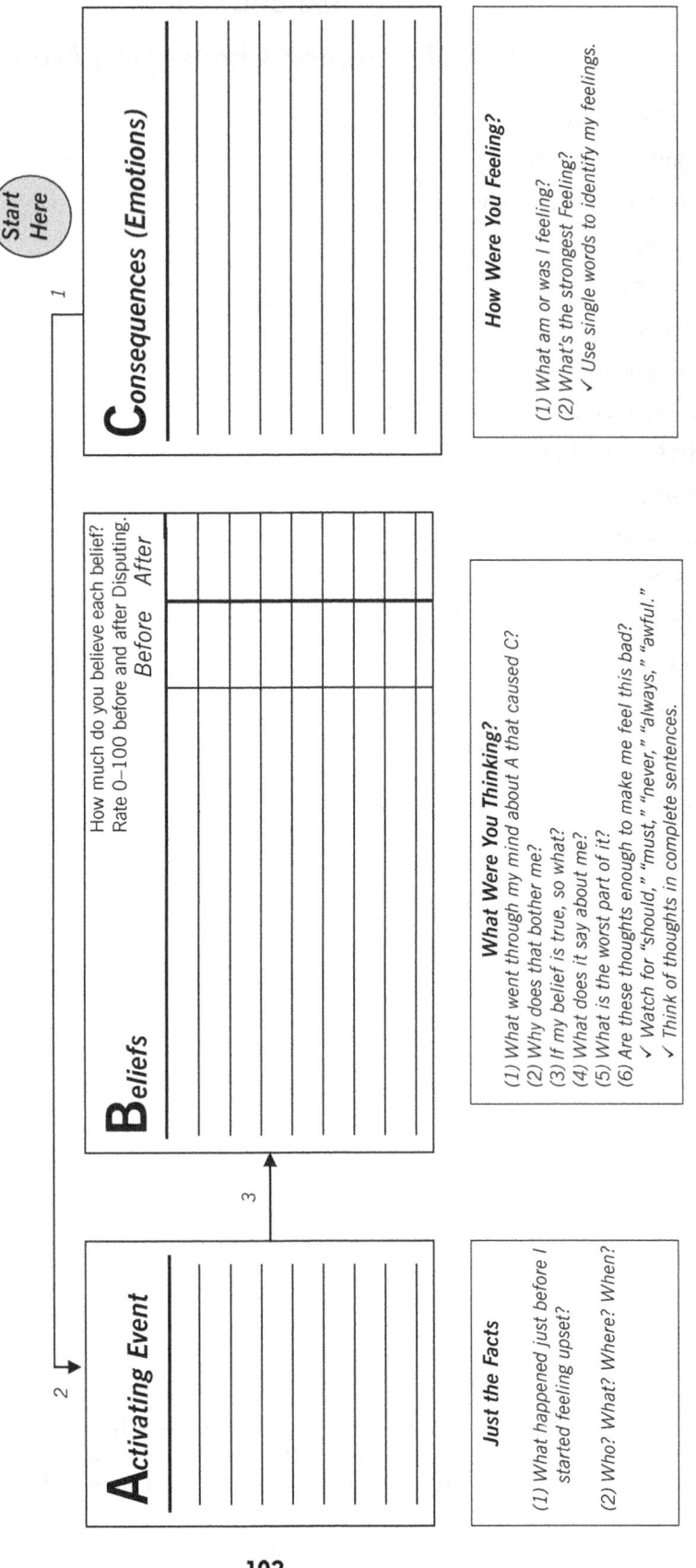

Activating Event

Just the Facts

(1) What happened just before I started feeling upset?
(2) Who? What? Where? When?

Beliefs

How much do you believe each belief?
Rate 0–100 before and after Disputing.
Before   After

What Were You Thinking?

(1) What went through my mind about A that caused C?
(2) Why does that bother me?
(3) If my belief is true, so what?
(4) What does it say about me?
(5) What is the worst part of it?
(6) Are these thoughts enough to make me feel this bad?
   ✓ Watch for "should," "must," "never," "always," "awful."
   ✓ Think of thoughts in complete sentences.

Consequences (Emotions)

Start Here

How Were You Feeling?

(1) What am or was I feeling?
(2) What's the strongest Feeling?
   ✓ Use single words to identify my feelings.

From *Stress Management for Teachers: A Proactive Guide* by Keith C. Herman and Wendy M. Reinke. Copyright 2015 by The Guilford Press. Permission to photocopy this handout is granted to purchasers of this book for personal use only (see copyright page for details). Purchasers can download and print additional copies of this handout from www.guilford.com/herman-forms.

HANDOUT 6.3

ABC Worksheet (without Instructions)

Activating Event	**B**eliefs	**C**onsequences (Emotions)

From *Stress Management for Teachers: A Proactive Guide* by Keith C. Herman and Wendy M. Reinke. Copyright 2015 by The Guilford Press. Permission to photocopy this handout is granted to purchasers of this book for personal use only (see copyright page for details). Purchasers can download and print additional copies of this handout from www.guilford.com/herman-forms.

HANDOUT 6.4

Complete Mr. Caldera's ABC Worksheet

Activating Event

Beliefs

Consequences (*Emotions*)

HANDOUT 6.5

Complete Ms. Simone's ABC Worksheet

Activating Event	**B**eliefs	**C**onsequences (Emotions)

From *Stress Management for Teachers: A Proactive Guide* by Keith C. Herman and Wendy M. Reinke. Copyright 2015 by The Guilford Press. Permission to photocopy this handout is granted to purchasers of this book for personal use only (see copyright page for details). Purchasers can download and print additional copies of this handout from *www.guilford.com/herman-forms*.

HANDOUT 6.6

The Funnel Method

Ask Yourself:

Q1: What about this thought bothers me so?

Q2: What about this thought upsets me most?

Q3: If this were true, what about it would be so upsetting?

Q4: Does just thinking this thought make me as upset about the situation as I ever felt?

If yes, you have found the key belief.

If No, keep asking Qs 1–3 until you hit the belief that leads you to answer Q4 as a yes.

- First Thought
- Answer to Question 1
- Answer to Question 2

From *Stress Management for Teachers: A Proactive Guide* by Keith C. Herman and Wendy M. Reinke. Copyright 2015 by The Guilford Press. Permission to photocopy this handout is granted to purchasers of this book for personal use only (see copyright page for details). Purchasers can download and print additional copies of this handout from *www.guilford.com/herman-forms*.

HANDOUT 6.7

ABCDE Worksheet (with Instructions)

Instructions: Whenever you have an emotional reaction, write it down. Start with your emotional consequences (C). You may feel more than one emotion in response to an event, so write them all down. Next, reflect on what happened just prior to your emotional reactions and write this down in the activating event (A) section; be sure to stick to the facts (who, what, where, when). Next, reflect on your interpretation of the event, your thoughts and beliefs (B) that are connected to each emotional consequence you listed in (C). Actively dispute each maladaptive belief (B) using socratic questions and write down more adaptive beliefs in (D). Finally, ask yourself how you feel now to see if you have a new effect (E).

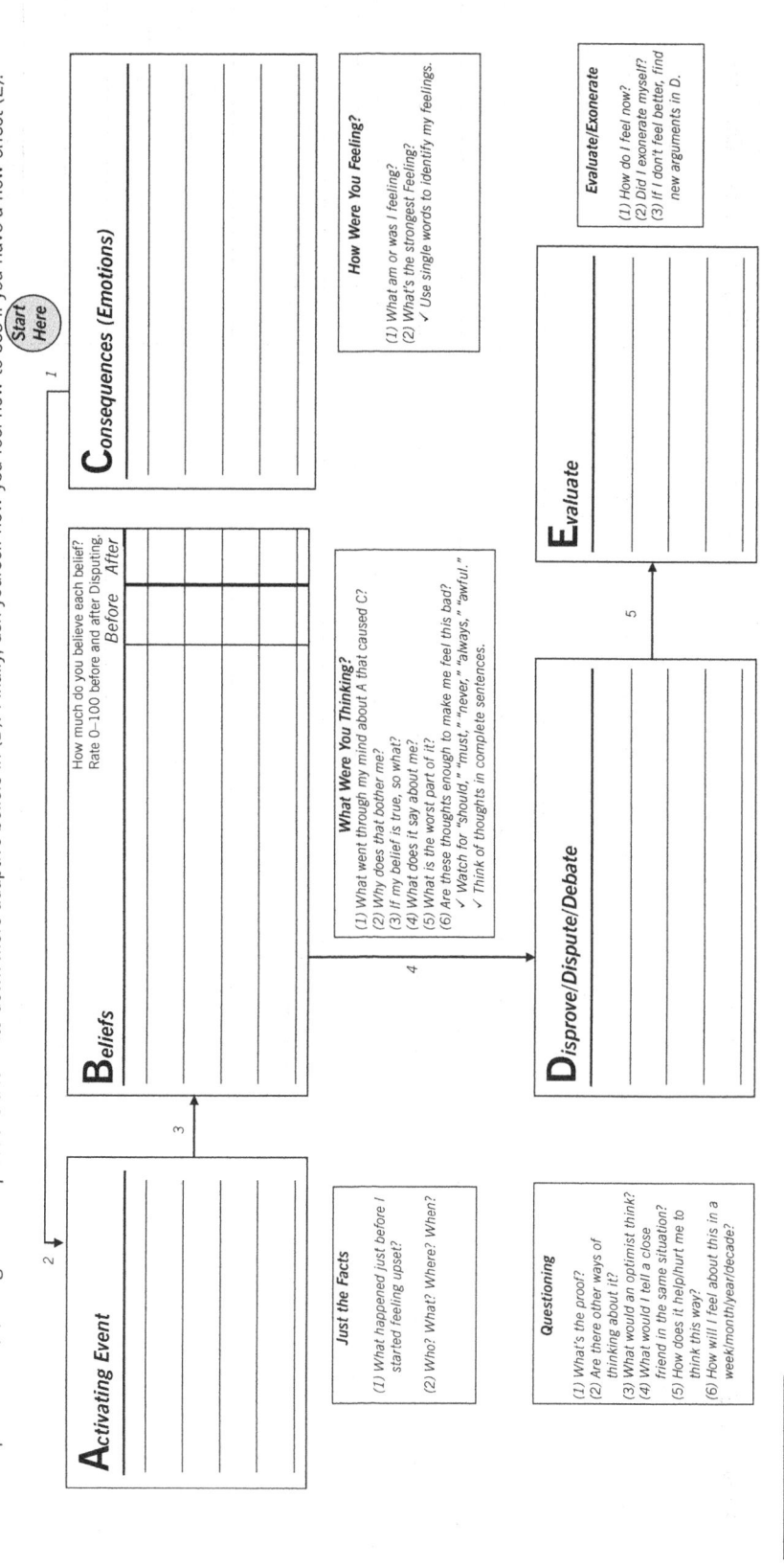

Start Here → 1

Consequences (Emotions)

How Were You Feeling?

(1) What am or was I feeling?
(2) What's the strongest feeling?
✓ Use single words to identify my feelings.

Beliefs

How much do you believe each belief?
Rate 0–100 before and after Disputing.
Before | After

What Were You Thinking?

(1) What went through my mind about A that caused C?
(2) Why does that bother me?
(3) If my belief is true, so what?
(4) What does it say about me?
(5) What is the worst part of it?
(6) Are these thoughts enough to make me feel this bad?
✓ Watch for "should," "must," "never," "always," "awful."
✓ Think of thoughts in complete sentences.

Activating Event

Just the Facts

(1) What happened just before I started feeling upset?
(2) Who? What? Where? When?

Disprove/Dispute/Debate

Questioning

(1) What's the proof?
(2) Are there other ways of thinking about it?
(3) What would an optimist think?
(4) What would I tell a close friend in the same situation?
(5) How does it help/hurt me to think this way?
(6) How will I feel about this in a week/month/year/decade?

Evaluate

Evaluate/Exonerate

(1) How do I feel now?
(2) Did I exonerate myself?
(3) If I don't feel better, find new arguments in D.

From *Stress Management for Teachers: A Proactive Guide* by Keith C. Herman and Wendy M. Reinke. Copyright 2015 by The Guilford Press. Permission to photocopy this handout is granted to purchasers of this book for personal use only (see copyright page for details). Purchasers can download and print additional copies of this handout from *www.guilford.com/herman-forms*.

HANDOUT 6.8

ABCDE Worksheet (without Instructions)

Activating Event

Beliefs

Before   After

Consequences (Emotions)

Disprove/Dispute/Debate

Evaluate

From *Stress Management for Teachers: A Proactive Guide* by Keith C. Herman and Wendy M. Reinke. Copyright 2015 by The Guilford Press. Permission to photocopy this handout is granted to purchasers of this book for personal use only (see copyright page for details). Purchasers can download and print additional copies of this handout from www.guilford.com/herman-forms.

CHAPTER 7

Adaptive Behaviors

By now, you understand the truism that what we do affects our mood. That's good because we can choose what we do. When we make positive choices, better feelings result. In this chapter, we capitalize on this notion by focusing on several behaviors that are especially important in determining our mood: your positive-to-negative ratio, pleasant activities, social supports and communication, relaxation, healthy eating and exercise, and minimal interventions.

A lot of strategies are described in this chapter. To sort through the long list of potential strategies, you can approach this chapter in a couple of ways. First, you might simply read through the chapter once and see which sections most resonate with you, then try the

Selecting Sections to Focus On

- Do you view yourself as a negative person or do others give you feedback about your negativity?
  - Consider starting with the "Increasing Your Positive-to-Negative Ratio" section.
- Are you often bored, apathetic, or depressed? Or do you simply wish you had more time for fun in your life?
  - The "Pleasant Activities" section may be perfect for you.
- Do you experience a lot of stress in your relationships at home or at work?
  - Try the "Effective Communication and Social Problem Solving" section.
- Do you experience a lot tension or mental stress?
  - The "Relaxation Skills" section will be helpful for you. In truth, this section is for everyone!
- Are you bothered by your eating or your exercise habits?
  - The "Healthy Eating and Exercise" section has ideas for you.

methods in that section. Second, you might attempt one method in each section. Third, take a moment now to reflect on which aspects of your behavior are most troubling to you, if any. Answer the questions on the prior page to select sections to read.

INCREASING YOUR POSITIVE-TO-NEGATIVE RATIO

Recall that a basic premise of the TCM is that more positive thoughts and actions will lead to more positive emotions. In prior chapters we focused on increasing positive thoughts. Here the focus is on increasing positive behaviors (see Figure 7.1). Several lines of research and guidelines for optimal positive-to-negative ratios suggest a target rate of at least three positives for every negative (see Seligman, 2011). Strive for this ratio in your daily interactions and notice the effect it has on your mood when you achieve it.

> **Strive for a 3:1 positive-to-negative ratio in your daily interactions and notice the effect it has on your mood when you achieve it.**

Adaptive Thoughts
Positive/Negative Method
ABC Method
Self-Praise

Awareness
Self-Monitoring
Goal Setting
Problem Solving
Deep Breathing
The TCM

Positive Feelings
Calm & Relaxed
Inspired
Happy

Adaptive Behaviors
Pleasant Activities
Social Skills & Support
Exercise & Healthy Eating
Relaxation Practice
Competence

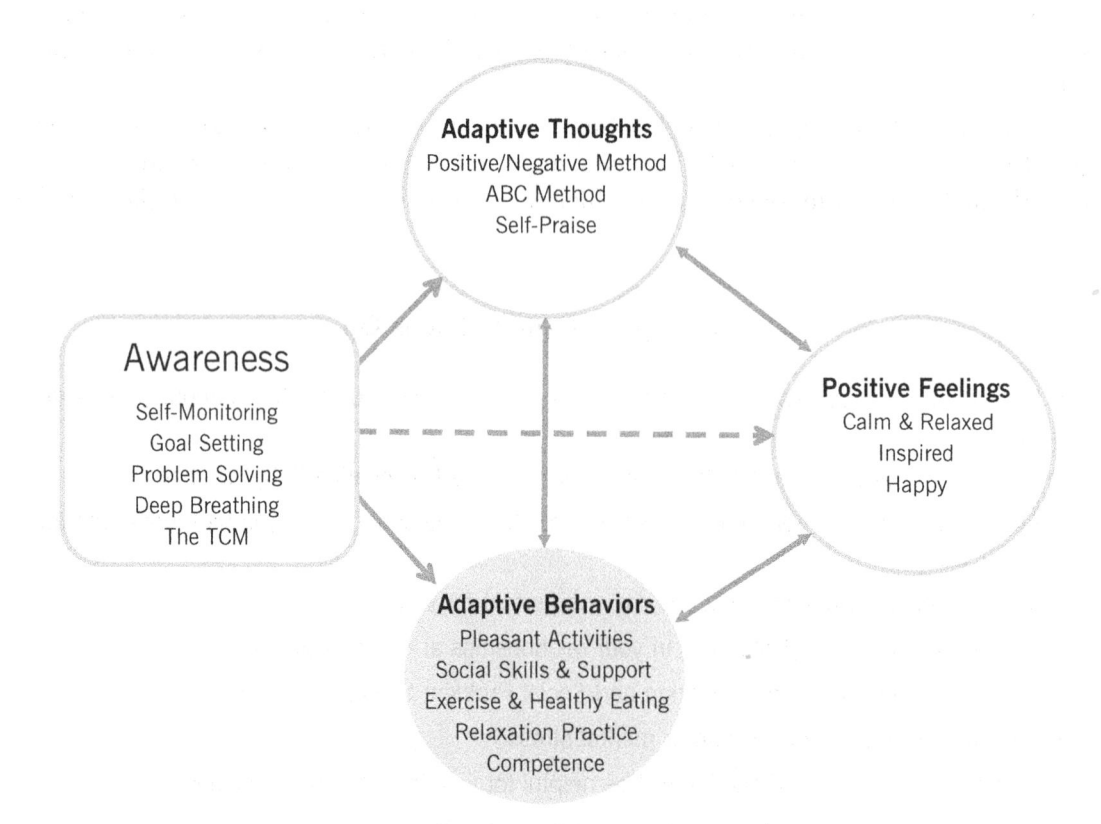

FIGURE 7.1. Adaptive behaviors in the TCM.

In the Classroom

Increasing your positive-to-negative ratio of interactions with students will improve your mood. The best news is that this is also one of the most effective methods for reducing disruptive behaviors in the classroom (see Chapter 8). Thus this method will be part of a positive feedback cycle, whereby you increase your positive behaviors (praise and compliments), which elicits more positive behaviors in students, improves your mood, and makes it more likely you will continue to increase your positive behaviors. Each positive iteration increases the likelihood you will have more positive thoughts and in turn more positive emotions. Chapter 8 describes several strategies for increasing your positive interactions in the classroom.

In Your Friendships

Increasing positive and reducing negative interactions with your friends and coworkers will also have a positive effect on your mood. One of the most important ways to do this is to monitor the positivity in your conversations. Gossip is a major culprit in undermining our mood for this very reason. If you find yourself engaging in gossip, defined as negative conversations about others (criticizing, judging, or ridiculing them), know that it will take a toll on your emotions. Gossip is enticing because it makes us feel aligned with our friends or coworkers who are expressing similar negative thoughts. Unfortunately, any temporary positive alliance that gossip creates comes at a cost to your emotional well-being. It is a form of co-rumination where you and one or more others share negative thoughts about yourself or others, and you inadvertently reinforce each other for this negative expression. Each negative comment counts as a negative thought and action on your positive to negative formula. Recall that as you mount more negative points during your day, your mood gradually follows suit.

To break a gossip cycle, you first need to be mindful of it, notice it, and intend to change it. If you decide you would like to reduce your gossip behavior, set a goal to do so, and develop a plan. Some simple strategies in the moment are to change the topic and if need be walk away from negative conversations. You might also avoid those who are most likely to engage in gossip. You can tackle it head on by telling your friends your concerns or about your goal, "I've been thinking that I would like to be more positive about things, and one thing I would like to change is to try to focus more on the positives of others. So if you catch me saying negative things about others, let me know, so I can switch it around."

At Home

In exactly the same way, the types of interactions you have with family members have a profound effect on your mood. When it comes to parenting, the same behavior management principles you use in the classroom also apply to your children. The strategies described in Chapter 8 for increasing positive interactions work equally well with your child(ren). You can also monitor the number of positive to negative comments you make toward your spouse or partner. Set a goal for yourself to gradually increase your ratio to a final goal of three to four positives for every negative. One trick is to simply take note of any negative comment you make and then tell yourself you will need to deliver three or four positives before you give another negative. You might preplan some compliments. Take time reflecting on all the positive attributes of your child(ren) and your spouse or partner. Write these out and then use them throughout the day as compliments or praise statements.

PLEASANT ACTIVITIES

Pleasant activities refer simply to activities that you find pleasurable or enjoyable. It is specific to you and your interests and preferences. Many of us take pleasant activities for granted and do not spend much time thinking about them or planning them. Perhaps we spend time planning big events, like vacations or trips, which are important. However, daily pleasant activities are the ones that affect our daily mood. We find it is helpful to be just as planful about arranging daily pleasant activities as we are about planning big events.

Daily pleasant activities are the ones that affect our daily mood.

A first step in becoming more proactive about pleasant activities is to spend time thinking about what you enjoy doing. Take a moment now to reflect on activities you find pleasurable and write them down. It can be even more helpful to read over a list of activities and decide which ones you like, or if you haven't tried some, which ones you would like to try. If we only reflect on want we have done, we may limit ourselves. For one, we may forget things that we used to enjoy but no longer do. Second, we may never have experienced some activities, so we would not intuitively include them on a list of things we would like to try.

For this reason, researchers have developed lists of pleasant activities. Most notably, Douglas MacPhillamy and the eminent psychologist Peter Lewinsohn surveyed hundreds of adults and had each generate a list of activities they enjoyed (MacPhillamy & Lewinsohn, 1972). They compiled these lists into a single comprehensive survey called the Pleasant Events Schedule, which includes more than 300 activities. We have included the schedule in Handout 7.1. Read this list and pick 20 activities you enjoy or think you would enjoy and write them on Handout 7.2.

After you generate your list, start tracking how often you engage in pleasant activities. For the next week, use Handout 7.3 to track the number of pleasant events you experience. This will give you a benchmark to use as you set goals for increasing the number of pleasant activities each week. In subsequent weeks, you can use Handout 7.3 to set goals based on how many activities you did in a prior week. If you did only two pleasant activities during the prior week, set a goal of doing three or four during the coming week. Then use Handouts 7.2 and 7.3 to pick which activities you would like to do and schedule them on the calendar. To work, you need to treat these scheduled pleasant activities with a similar level of priority as something you commit to doing (e.g., a doctor's appointment). The bottom of Handout 7.3 asks you to write down how you will reward yourself for meeting your goals.

This is an important aspect of pleasant event scheduling, so take time to think about an appropriate reward. Then be sure to reward yourself when you meet your goals.

Fun in the Classroom

The principle of positive activities applies equally well to your time in the classroom. It is easy to lose sight of this in the era of accountability, but learning should be fun. Students learn more and faster when they are enjoying themselves. Just as important, enjoyable activities translate into positive emotions for you and your students. In addition, fun classrooms make classroom management easier and more effective.

How do you bring fun into your classroom? The first step is to make having fun a priority. If it is important to you, then commit to finding ways to have more fun and do more pleasant activities in the classroom. The specific ways

> **Fun classrooms make classroom management easier and more effective.**

you will have fun may vary somewhat depending on the age of your students. For younger students, short and simple games like Simon Says may be appropriate, but these same games may not be fun for older students.

Here are some ideas we have heard from other teachers:

- Play 1- to 2-minute games (like Simon Says or Guess the Animal for younger students and 20 Questions for older students).
- Have a dance party.
- Take a 1-minute wiggle break.
- Start and/or end the day with a praise circle in which everyone says one positive thing about the day.
- Set a goal to laugh and smile more.
- Use humor (although avoid sarcasm).
- Allow students to earn the privilege to tell the class a joke.
- Bring a water spray bottle on hot days and allow students to earn the privilege of being misted.
- Turn on music and dance in front of the class (We're not good dancers!).

Of course, as with any classroom routine, you will want to establish rules and expectations about how the activity will work and what is allowed.

How do you have fun in the classroom? Are there fun activities you did in the past that you would like to do again? Take time to complete Handout 7.4 to add fun to your current classroom routine.

Reward Yourself

Many teachers are natural caretakers. It can be easy to lose sight of the need to take care of yourself as you spend your career helping others. Several of the exercises in this book ask you to find time to reward yourself. It is helpful to have some smaller, low-cost rewards that you can give yourself on a daily basis, including self-praise. It is also a good idea to have more intricate, valuable rewards that you give yourself on a less frequent basis for larger accomplishments. Here's a sample list of self-rewards generated by another teacher. Create your own list using Handout 7.5.

Good Incentives for Me
- Go to a restaurant.
- Pleasure reading.
- Get a manicure, facial, or massage.
- Take a day trip.
- Have coffee or tea with a coworker.
- Buy a book.
- Allow myself to have a lesson-plan-free weekend.
- Take a bubble bath.
- Buy some new shoes.
- Buy something frivolous.
- Take a walk in the park.

EFFECTIVE COMMUNICATION AND SOCIAL PROBLEM SOLVING

Social relationships, both at work and home, are a major source of stress for many people. Relationships can be complicated, and one foundation for successful relationships is effective communication skills. Entire books have been written about effective communication. Here we focus on just a few fundamental skills that can be most helpful in dealing with daily interpersonal stressors: listening, assertiveness skills, and social problem solving.

Social Support and Expressing Your Feelings

Quite often teachers don't have or take time to express their pent-up emotions. In our conversations with teachers, it is common for them suddenly to become very emotional, sad, or upset. It's as if many teachers are just getting by, enduring their daily stressors, and suppressing their emotions just beneath the surface. If you give them even a brief moment to reflect and have someone listen to them, these emotions can come flooding out in the form of tears or anger. Based on these observations, it is clear to us that many teachers do not have outlets for expressing their feelings or even time to notice them.

To this point, we hope the awareness exercises and the thought methods in this book have you reflecting on your emotional experiences a bit more than before. Sometimes just thinking about things differently as you have read in the prior two chapters is enough to change and manage our emotions. Sometimes we also need social outlets to express our emotions.

Self-Assessment

Take a moment now to reflect on your own social support network by completing Handout 7.6. The Interpersonal Support Evaluation List (ISEL; Cohen, Mermelstein, Kamarck, & Hoberman, 1985) was designed to measure the functional aspects of social support. This scale is made up of a list of statements, each of which may or may not be true about you. For each statement, circle "definitely true" if you are sure it is true about you and "probably true" if you think it is true but are not absolutely certain. Similarly, you should circle "definitely false" if you are sure the statement is false and "probably false" if you think it is false but are not absolutely certain.

This measure asks about three aspects of social support: appraisal, belonging, and tangible. To score, sum each of these aspects and then derive your total score by summing all three domains. First, reverse score items 1, 2, 7, 8, 11, 12 by subtracting your score on each from 4 (e.g., 4 minus your score on #1). For your appraisal scores add items 2, 4, 6, 11; for belonging add 1, 5, 7, 9; and for tangible add 3, 8, 10, 12.

The ISEL gives you some sense about your social network. If you are satisfied with your network, it will serve as a good foundation for your social coping skills. If you would like to expand it or develop more close relationships, set this as a goal for yourself during the coming weeks. Think of people whom you would like to spend more time with, at work or away from work, and set goals to do so, just as you have been doing with other skills in this book. You might even use the problem-solving form from Chapter 4 to define the social network problem you are having, brainstorm solutions, implement one, and evaluate how it works.

Connecting with Other Teachers

Teaching can be an isolating profession. Depending on the environment in your school, it can feel like you are the only adult drifting in a sea of students who need your help. For this reason, reaching out to other teachers for support, conversation, and connection can yield large benefits for you. The groups we regularly conduct for teachers are very skill based, but we are certain a large part of what is helpful about them is simply the social support they give to teachers. Hearing about the experiences of other teachers can be very validating in stressful school environments, and only another teacher truly understands what it is like to teach.

Teaching can be an isolating profession.

One way to connect more regularly with other teachers is to invite one or more to regular social support meetings or to use this book as a guide for a study group. It is important that these meetings are not just complaint sessions but rather productive, supportive gatherings. Therefore, be sure to have some structured aspect to the group.

The Internet also has a wealth of resources for teachers to connect with one another. Here are few you might consider exploring:

- Teacher.net (*http://teachers.net*) has a variety of resources for teachers including a message board to connect with others.
- It's Not All Flowers and Sausages (*http://itsnotallflowersandsausages.blogspot.com*) is a blog that offers inspiring and also silly stories about the daily experiences of teachers.
- ProTeacher (*www.proteacher.net*) offers a variety of resources matched to the grade level of teachers including chat groups. You will need to create a login for this website.
- Teacher Lingo (*http://teacherlingo.com*) includes teacher resources, blogs, and forums.

Finally, an important life skill is learning to ask for help. Others are so busy in their tasks they might not notice when you are struggling and not offer to help. They can only know if you need assistance if you ask. Get in the habit of noticing when you have reached your limit and when you could use an extra hand at home or at work.

Assertive Communication

Most social problems originate through a failure to communicate clearly with one another, and poor listening can explain the breakdown of much communication. Think about the many ways communication can go awry. In our role as a speaker, it is our responsibility to express our ideas, feelings, and perceptions as clearly as possible. Expressive communication can be seen as occurring on a continuum ranging from passive to aggressive. One key way to distinguish between these forms of communication is to think of expressive communication as a way we assert our rights and protect the rights of others. Aggressive communication is characterized by erring toward the rights of the speaker while infringing on the rights of others. Passive communication is when we err toward allowing others to infringe on our rights. Somewhere between these two extremes is assertive communication, which is defined by a balanced communication style of give and take in which both the speaker and listener express their opinions and ideas without infringing or limiting the rights of the other. Two important components of assertive communication include expressing feelings and listening.

Expressing Feelings

One key to managing relationships and handling social conflict is to become adept at recognizing and expressing your feelings. You have already mastered the first part by monitoring your mood. Once you are aware of your mood, you can use it to your advantage to help guide you through difficult conversations. When you experience a relationship challenge, it is usually based in some negative mood that the conflict has induced in you. Often a good place to start a conversation is by expressing that feeling. There are better and worse ways to express feelings. Avoid blaming others or using "you" language, which can put the other on the defensive and make it less likely they will hear what you are trying to communicate. Instead, use "I feel" language where you focus on yourself and the impact you are experiencing as a result of the relationship problem.

> One key to managing relationships and handling social conflict is to become adept at recognizing and expressing your feelings.

The typical format of an "I feel" statement is given below:

I feel (*single feeling word*) when you (*specific behavior that person is doing or has done*).
I would appreciate it if you (*specific behavior change you are requesting*).

Use this exact format as you are learning the skill. As you become more comfortable with it, you can vary it a bit, so as not to sound robotic, as long as you adhere to the basic rules: use "I" language, be specific, and avoid judging or blaming.

Let's look at an example. Ms. Oliver is feeling bothered by a repeated experience with her principal. The principal has come into her room on several occasions, interrupted instruction, and made suggestions for Ms. Oliver in front of the class. She decides to meet with the principal and let him know how the interactions are making her feel and to request a specific change. Here is what she said: "I feel hurt and frustrated when you interrupt my class and correct me in front of my students. In the future I would appreciate it if you shared feedback with me in private." This is a very assertive, direct, and respectful way to express the problem and request a change. What if it doesn't work? The truth is that we do not have direct control over how people respond to our requests for change. It is ultimately up to them how they react. The goal of using direct, assertive expressions is simply to express yourself as clearly as possible and make it more likely that you will be heard. These methods increase the likelihood that relational problems will be solved, but they do not guarantee it. If the principal in this case had a very negative reaction to Ms. Oliver's request, she might choose to repeat it. If the principal's reaction evoked a new feeling in Ms. Oliver, she might choose to express the new feeling by saying, "I'm feeling confused now by your response. I hear you saying that you are only trying to be helpful. What I am saying is that I feel uncomfortable and disrespected, which makes it harder for me to be effective." Ms. Oliver might also decide at some point that it is not worth the battle and that it is best to end the conversation, saying, "I just wanted you to know how your behavior was affecting me," and leave it at that. Sticking with your feelings is effective because no one can argue with you about what you feel. Your feelings are your own.

A good place to start any difficult conversation is with whatever feeling you have about starting the conversation itself. An example of how you could open a conversation that makes you feel apprehensive is, "I'm feeling a little anxious about where to start. I really value our relationship and don't want to jeopardize it. At the same time, I decided to take this risk because I really have something I want you to know about." Other beginnings might be, "I'm not really sure where to start here," or "I'm feeling awkward/uncomfortable." Such segues alert the other person that you want to have a meaningful interaction and that you care about the outcome, which makes it more likely you will be heard and understood.

Listening Skills

Effective communication requires not only assertive expression but also the ability to hear what the other person is trying to communicate in return. Good listening skills involve both hearing and understanding what is being said, as well as letting the other person know that you have heard and understood them. In other words, you might be hearing the words that are being spoken, but if the other person doesn't believe that you are listening, then the communication will not be successful.

Conveying understanding involves body posture, eye contact, and tone of voice. In addition, basic listening skills can be summarized by the acronym OARS (Miller & Rollnick, 2013): Open-ended questions ("Tell me more about it"), Affirmations ("I can really see how much this means to you"), Reflective listening ("That really makes you angry when the principal does that"), and Summarizing ("The three things I'm hearing that you really want to be different about this situation are . . ."). *Open-ended questions* are simply questions that require elaboration and more than a single-word response (like yes or no). One common mistake people make when attempting to listen is to interrupt the other speaker to give advice. One way to avoid this is whenever you have an urge to tell someone what to do, stop and try to reframe your thought as a question that may elicit that answer. In other words, ask yourself questions you can pose to make the person say what you are thinking. So if you find yourself wanting to tell a friend or colleague how to solve a problem in the classroom, stop and rephrase your thought as a question. Instead, ask the teacher, "What are some good things that can come from changing your classroom environment?"

Affirmations are verbal or nonverbal behaviors that convey acceptance, support, and encouragement for the speaker. Simple head nods, saying "yes," or more elaborate praise statements all fall in this realm. Effective affirmations are best when they are sincere, so only affirm what you genuinely believe to be true. It is also helpful to provide specific examples rather than global praise statements ("Good job") because it helps both to prompt and reinforce that specific behavior. Furthermore, specific examples are more likely to be perceived as sincere.

Reflective listening refers to paraphrasing comments made by the speaker while giving special attention to the feelings implied by their statements or behaviors. Reflections can vary in depth from a straight paraphrase of what was said to a guess about underlying feelings. These are best given as statements rather than as questions.

Summaries are two- to three-sentence responses that try to link together a series of ideas that were expressed during earlier parts of a conversation. Summaries can serve multiple functions. They show that you are listening and understanding the speaker's perspective. They allow you to agree on what has been said to be sure that you understand the key points of a topic. You can also use summaries to highlight an ongoing theme that you have heard during a conversation. In this way, effective summaries can help the speaker gain new insights into their own internal dialogue by revealing to them patterns of their thinking that they might not have fully considered before. Summaries can also serve as effective transitions to end one topic (like a discussion about things they like about teaching) and begin a new one (things they find challenging about teaching).

RELAXATION SKILLS

Another effective coping behavior is to develop your ability to induce the relaxation response. The relaxation response is not the same thing as relaxing. Watching TV, lying in the sun, or doing other activities that you find relaxing may or may not induce a relaxation response. Herbert Benson first described the relaxation response in the 1970s. He studied stress and coping and was interested in helping people reduce the arousal of the sympathetic nervous system. He went on to describe several methods for activating the relaxation response. All methods involved some variation of two steps: (1) focusing on a repetitive phrase, breath, or movement; and (2) having a passive attitude about our thoughts. Benson also documented two levels of changes that occur as a result of the relaxation response: immediate and long-term. The immediate changes are the physiological effects we have commented on before as the result of activating your parasympathetic nervous system; lower heart rate and respirations, and so forth. The long-term changes are ones that occur after regular practice of methods that induce the relaxation response for a month or longer. These include creating lasting changes in neurochemicals and hormones and in self-perceptions and mood. Below we describe several relaxation methods that can reliably activate the relaxation response.

Deep Breathing

Deep breathing skills are the foundation for virtually any relaxation method. The reason deep breathing is so effective goes back to what we know about the stress response. Although our systems are fairly primitive, we can capitalize on how integrated they are in turning the stress response on or off. Just like the sympathetic nervous turns on in an all-or-none fashion, the parasympathetic does so as well. If you want to activate the relaxation response, you simply have to mindfully intervene in one of the parasympathetic systems. Breathing is our most accessible entry into the relaxation response. When we intentionally slow down our respirations, taking longer and deeper breaths, we activate the parasympathetic system. Because the various subsystems work in unison, when our breathing rate slows, so does our heart rate, blood pressure, and all the other systems associated with relaxation. This implies that if you want to feel relaxed, a very useful and effective way to do this is to intentionally slow your breathing.

> **If you want to feel relaxed, a very useful and effective way to do this is to intentionally slow your breathing.**

As we described in Chapter 4, some simple strategies for accessing your breathing are to consciously inhale to a count of five and exhale to a count of five. You can gradually try increasing your exhale and inhale to a count of ten or higher. If you slow your breathing rate down to five or six respirations a minute for 10 or 15 minutes, you will find that you have activated the body's relaxation response. Your heart rate will be lower, your blood pressure will drop, and your digestive system will become active.

Try adding basic visualization to your breathing. For instance, as you breathe in, think about inhaling new, clean air and while exhaling, releasing toxic, stressful air. You might picture the air as it goes in and out, or visualize a balloon inside your stomach expanding and collapsing with each breath. Any relaxing, peaceful imagery of the breathing process will help further focus your attention and elicit the relaxation response.

Progressive Muscle Relaxation

Another reason deep breathing is effective is because it gives us a focus for our attention. This is another element of any relaxation method in that it focuses our attention to the moment and away from our worries and concerns.

Progressive muscle relaxation also activates the relaxation response by systematically reducing muscle tension in addition to relying on breathing. In this method, you continuously scan your body for muscle tension, intentionally contracting your muscles one at a time, and then relaxing them. In this way you are teaching yourself to become more aware of muscle tension and developing control over it. When we relax our muscles we activate the relaxation response.

To practice, find a comfortable position, preferably lying down with your eyes closed. Focus your attention on your breathing as before. When you feel settled, scan your body for muscle tension and just try to relax.

1. Starting with your hands, clench your fists one at a time, and hold that tension for a count of 5 and then release it all at once. Notice what it feels like in your hand and arm when your muscles are tense and the difference when you relax.
2. Take a deep breath and then repeat the process in the other hand.
3. Next, move up to other muscles in the arm, one at time.
4. Tighten your forearm and then relax it.
5. To tighten your bicep, curl your first up toward your face and feel the tension in your upper arm.
6. Shrug your shoulders toward your ears for 5 seconds and then release them down. You should feel tension in your shoulder and upper back and then notice it dissipate with the release.
7. Tighten the muscles of your neck by bringing your chin toward your chest and holding it. Release it and take a deep breath.
8. Follow the same process for your chest, stomach, buttocks, and legs.
9. With each step, tighten the muscles one at a time, notice the tension, release it and then breathe deeply.
10. Finally, repeat these steps with the muscles in your face by smiling, raising your eyebrows, and squishing your nose.
11. For one last step, try tensing all the muscles in your body at once, holding, and then releasing.

At the end of the process (which can take 15–20 minutes), you should notice a gradual reduction in muscle tension and a lowering of heart rate. Research has shown that doing these types of exercises several times a week can help you be more mindful of muscle tension throughout the day, have lower levels of stress, anxiety, and depression, and have more positive perceptions of yourself.

Mini-Muscle Relaxations

Once you become accustomed to progressive muscle relaxation, you can use it in brief sessions throughout the day. You might take 2 minutes to take in several deep breaths and tense all the muscles of the body at once, and then release them. Repeating this a few times can induce the relaxation response after you become proficient in this method. If you have even a little more time, you might do groups of muscles (arms, body, legs, and face) one at a time and then finish by tensing the entire body at once.

Autogenic Relaxation

German psychiatrist Johannes Schulz developed autogenic training in the 1930s. It is based on the assumption that repeating statements silently to oneself about feeling heavy and warm can focus attention and induce deep states of relaxation. Studies have shown comparable benefits of autogenic training as other forms of relaxation, so the choice of methods is yours. Give each a try and see which one works best for you or that you most enjoy. The steps of autogenic relaxation are the following:

1. Find a quiet place free from distractions. Lie on the floor or recline in a chair. Loosen any tight clothing and remove glasses or contacts. Rest your hands in your lap or on the arms of the chair.
2. Take a few slow, even breaths. Remember to breathe from the diaphragm.
3. Repeat to yourself, "I am completely calm."
4. Focus on your hands. Quietly and slowly repeat to yourself several times, "My hands are becoming heavy and warm. Warmth is flowing into my hands." Next, repeat, "My right hand is warm and relaxed," then, "My left hand is warm and relaxed." Then quietly say to yourself, "I am completely calm and relaxed."
5. Focus your attention on your arms. Quietly and slowly repeat to yourself, "My arms are becoming warm and relaxed. Warmth is flowing into my arms." Again, repeat, "My right arm is warm and relaxed," and "My left arm is warm and relaxed." Then quietly say to yourself, "I am calm."
6. Continue on by focusing on your shoulders, your neck, and then your back. For each body part, repeat the phrase, "My _____ is becoming heavy and warm. Warm and relaxed."
7. Focus on your legs. Quietly and slowly repeat to yourself several times, "My legs are very heavy." Then say to yourself, "I am completely calm."
8. Focus on your feet and repeat, "My feet are becoming heavy and warm. I can feel

the warm blood flowing to my feet." Then quietly say to yourself, "I am calm and relaxed."
9. Quietly and slowly repeat to yourself several times, "My heartbeat is calm and regular." Then quietly say to yourself, "I am relaxed and calm."
10. Quietly and slowly repeat to yourself, "My breathing is calm and regular." Then quietly say to yourself, "I am completely calm."
11. Quietly and slowly repeat to yourself six times, "My abdomen is warm." Then quietly say to yourself, "I am calm."
12. Quietly and slowly repeat to yourself six times, "My forehead is pleasantly cool." Then quietly say to yourself, "I am completely calm."
13. Enjoy the feeling of relaxation, warmth and heaviness. When you are ready, quietly say to yourself, "Arms firm, breathe deeply, eyes open."

You can vary the phrasing. The key is to use repetitive phrases and focus your attention on the sensations they induce. Note the repetition of words like *calm*, *relaxed*, *heavy*, and *warm*. Simply repeating these terms as you scan your body will activate the relaxation response.

Guided Imagery

Guided imagery involves creating a relaxing scene of your choice and making it as real and vivid in your imagination as possible. By tuning in and focusing on this scene, you slow your body and your breathing. The key of this approach to relaxation and to creating a vivid scene is to focus on every sense that you experience in the scene. You can practice this in the real world when you are experiencing relaxing places by asking yourself, "What do I hear, smell, taste, feel, and see?" Try to notice every sensory detail and then incorporate these memories into your imagery scene.

For instance, one common scene for guided imagery is a beach. Think of all the sensations you have experienced when you were relaxed at a beach. Sounds might include the crashing waves, the sound of the breeze in your ear, the movement of palm leaves, and perhaps even the distant laughter of children playing. Touch sensations might include the warmth of the sun at specific places on your body, the coolness of a breeze, the sand between your toes. Sights include all the colors that you see at a beach, the shades of blue in the ocean and the sky, fluffy white clouds, and the color of the sand and trees. Smells might include the salty smell of the ocean, suntan oils, or tropical drinks. Tastes would include any relaxing food or drinks you have at the beach.

Relaxation Tapes

Many people find it helpful to be guided through these methods with relaxation tapes. Many such tapes exist and can be helpful in activating the relaxation response as long as they follow similar scripts to those described above. Alternately, you might create your own tape by reading one of the scripts above and taping it. You can listen to it and let it guide you through the steps. Finally, if you are using this book in a study group, think about taking turns leading the group in one or more of the relaxation methods described above. The key to being an effective guide is to have a calm voice and a slow, steady pace, pausing 5 seconds or more between each step.

HEALTHY EATING AND EXERCISE

It probably goes without saying, but nutrition and exercise are critical to promoting physical health and emotional well-being. The connection between these healthy habits and your emotional life are manifold. The most obvious is that what you eat and how active you are directly influence the circuitry of your body, your hormones and neurotransmitters, which in turn influence the emotional experiences you have. For instance, exercise activates neurotransmitter patterns associated with a sense of well-being, including the release of endorphins at the active regulation of the emotion centers of the brain (Sarris, Kavanagh, & Newton, 2008). Certain foods also induce healthy metabolism and can even activate certain hormones. A case in point is the literature that has emerged about omega-3 and its benefits in reducing depression (Mischoulon et al., 2009) and suicidality (Huan et al., 2004).

> What you eat and how active you are directly influence the circuitry of your body, your hormones and neurotransmitters, which in turn influence the emotional experiences you have.

A second way eating and exercise affect your mood is their role in influencing your self-perceptions. When we engage in healthy habits, we often feel better about ourselves. When we lose weight and increase muscle tone, we can develop more positive views of ourselves. Research has even shown that these physical changes can lead people to feel more self-confident and empowered in other areas of their lives.

Yet another way healthy habits invite positive changes in our mood is through social mechanisms. When we develop healthy habits and people notice, we start receive more positive feedback from the world. If we lose weight and look healthier, people often respond to us in more favorable ways, which can lead us to think more positive thoughts and continue the healthy behaviors. Of course, weight loss will be most enduring if you focus on internal benefits (e.g., your mood) and goals that you set about behaviors that you have direct control over (what you eat and how much you exercise) rather than outcomes that are more distal and less controllable (like the number on a scale and how people view you). We simply note that often there are positive feedback loops in the environment that we bring about whenever we engage in positive behaviors.

Most of us know these things about the benefits of nutrition and exercise, yet many of us struggle to permanently adopt new healthier routines. There are more than 1,000 commercial diet plans available to choose, but which approach works best for you? How is a consumer able to make wise decisions with such a proliferation of diet alternatives on the market? Available research comparing popular diet approaches (e.g., Atkins, Ornish, Weight Watchers, The Zone) suggests that each approach results in modest weight lost and cardiovascular benefits (Dansinger, Gleason, Griffith, Selker, & Schaefer, 2005). Not surprisingly, the benefits are strongest for those who adhere most closely to the plan for the longest period of time. The two potential lessons that have emerged from this research are (1) all plans may share some factors in common that work, and (2) whatever approach you decide to take, sticking with it is key to how much you will benefit.

What might be some common factors across diet programs? There are two that we know of. One is to use the same methods we have described here for adopting any new behavior. It begins with self-monitoring. Research has documented for decades that simply writing down everything we eat and paying attention to calories can have a profound effect on our behavior. There are now new software programs and websites that make this task easier. Another related strategy is reflection. In this case, a key approach to eating less and differently is to pause more often when we eat. We'll come back to this in the mindfulness chapter, but for now know that eating smaller portions and setting goals about lengthening the time you sit and eat helps with the monitoring and reflection process. If now you currently wolf down your food in 5 minutes or less, simply set the goal of having yourself sit for 30 minutes while you consume your meals. Try scheduling and self-rewards for meeting your goals. The same approaches work for meeting exercise goals. After establishing your baseline habits, as before, set small and realistic goals for changing your habits.

One caveat to note is that not every method works for all people; in fact, some people with extreme behaviors such as severe eating disorders may find that some methods of weight trigger disordered eating. As with all the methods in this book, we describe strategies that research suggests will increase the probability of success for most people. Your task is to use those methods that work for you.

MINIMAL INTERVENTIONS

What are you able and willing to commit to doing at this point? How much time and effort have you put into learning these exercises? The good news is sometimes it doesn't take much. If you are still holding out on committing to working through some of the exercises and activities, try one of these and see what happens.

Literature has emerged in recent years showing the benefits of even minimal interventions. Reading this or other high-quality self-help books and exercising are examples of minimal interventions. Here are a few others.

Written Self-Disclosure

Nearly two decades ago, James Pennebaker (1997) began a series of studies on the benefits of writing about emotional experiences. Since that time, Pennebaker and others have uncovered compelling evidence that writing about emotion experiences for 20–30 minutes a day can yield remarkable health benefits in just a few writing sessions. Compared to people who wrote about more mundane topics (like what they were planning to do for the day), those who wrote about emotional experiences were more likely to report persistent feelings of wellness and relaxation, reduced somatic indicators of stress (lower heart rate, respirations, and blood pressure), reduced health care visits, and even increased immune responsiveness as measured by blood tests.

There are a few variations of the procedure, but most involve some version of the following instructions:

> "Please write about a deeply emotional and difficult time in your life, preferably one that you have refrained from talking about at length with others. Focus on writing about your deepest thoughts and feelings surrounding the event. It is important that you write continuously for the entire time. If you run out of things to say, just repeat what you have already written. In your writing, don't worry about grammar, spelling, or sentence structure. Just write. Write for 20–30 minutes."

There is no need to put your name on the paper or to save it, unless you wish to do so. Benefits appear to begin nearly immediately, but persistent benefits are more likely to appear after three or four consecutive days. You can write about the same event on each day or different ones. Possible topics include upsetting events of your life, major conflicts or problems in the past or present, or important events that you have not revealed to others or discussed in depth.

Set a goal for yourself about how many days you would like to try this. Choose four consecutive days to gain the greatest likelihood of benefit. On subsequent days, remind yourself you only have three or fewer days left and praise yourself for your effort. On the final day, you might focus on wrapping it up or tying together ideas from the prior days, making connections to present day circumstances. It is up to you where you want to take it, as long as your focus remains on expressing your deepest thoughts and emotions.

Be forewarned, these writing activities can be exhausting. It is common for people to feel sad or anxious or even angry in the immediate aftermath of the writing activity. These feelings will pass, and you will feel stronger for it. If they persist or if they become overwhelming, then stop the task. In the very unlikely event that you experience overwhelming feelings that persist, or certainly any thoughts of harming yourself or others, you should consult immediately with a mental health professional.

Plants and Nature

It probably won't surprise you that many people find nature relaxing and that accessing it can have health benefits; however, you might be surprised about the stress relief benefits of incorporating nature into your daily life in the simplest of ways. A line of research has emerged in recent years to test ways to use nature to our benefit in our home and workplaces. Research has revealed that simply adding a plant to a social environment lessens the stress response (lower heart rate and blood pressure) when confronted with a stressor (Frumkin, 2001). Adding pictures of nature, watching nature shows, and visualizing nature all produce the same benefit. Using nature is a very simple strategy for creating an environment conducive to relaxation and positive coping. Of course, if you get plants and they all

> **IF YOU DO ONLY ONE THING: Exercise**
>
> The literature is well established that regular exercise prevents and treats negative moods (Sarris et al., 2008; Teychenne, Ball, & Salmon, 2004). Commit to doing some form of exercise over the next several days, any type of exercise you like to do or wish to do more of. Ideally, it should be an activity that gets your heart pumping a bit that suits your current level of fitness. Schedule your exercise into your calendar and treat it like an appointment you can't miss. Before you begin exercising, take a moment to rate your mood over the past week, on a scale of 1–10. Then each time you prepare to exercise take a moment to rate your mood in that particular moment on a scale of 1–10. Each time you finish your exercise, rate your mood again on the same scale. See if you spot any trends. Does your mood typically improve after you exercise? After several days, take time for an overall mood rating. What's your mood been like on average over the past several days? Chances are you will see an upward trend in your mood and a decrease in your stress with each day you exercise.

die, that may not be relaxing. So if you add plants to the environment, choose ones that match you level of attention to them and willingness to keep them alive. Many tropical indoor plants require minimal care (e.g., watering once a week and nothing else).

Using nature is a very simple strategy for creating an environment conducive to relaxation and positive coping.

SUMMARY

Choosing to engage in more adaptive behavior is yet another way to manage your mood. The more positive actions you do allows you to add to your daily mood formula and shift the balance toward a positive mood. Pleasant activities, effective communication, successful social interactions, relaxation, and healthy habits set the stage for you to maintain a good mood throughout the day and manage any adversities that emerge. In the next chapter, we consider another set of behaviors that are critical for teacher coping: teaching competence.

HANDOUT 7.1
Pleasant Events Schedule

	Activity	Like or Want to Try
1.	Being in the country	
2.	Wearing expensive or formal clothes	
3.	Making contributions to religious, charitable, or other groups	
4.	Talking about sports	
5.	Meeting someone new of the same sex	
6.	Taking tests when well prepared	
7.	Going to a rock concert	
8.	Playing baseball or softball	
9.	Planning trips or vacations	
10.	Buying things for myself	
11.	Being at the beach	
12.	Doing artwork (painting, sculpture, drawing, movie-making, etc.)	
13.	Rock-climbing or mountaineering	
14.	Reading the scriptures or other sacred works	
15.	Playing golf	
16.	Taking part in military activities	
17.	Rearranging or decorating my room or house	
18.	Going naked	
19.	Going to a sports event	
20.	Reading a "how-to" book or article	
21.	Going to the races (horse, car, boat, etc.)	
22.	Reading stories, novels, nonfiction poems, or plays	
23.	Going to a bar, tavern, club, etc.	
24.	Going to lectures or hearing speakers	
25.	Driving skillfully	
26.	Breathing clean air	
27.	Thinking up or arranging a song or music	
28.	Getting drunk	
29.	Saying something clearly	
30.	Boating (canoeing, kayaking, motor-boating, sailing, etc.)	
31.	Pleasing my parents	
32.	Restoring antiques, refinishing furniture, etc.	
33.	Watching TV	
34.	Talking to myself	
35.	Camping	

(continued)

From MacPhillamy and Lewinsohn (1972). Copyright by the authors. Reprinted by permission.

From *Stress Management for Teachers: A Proactive Guide* by Keith C. Herman and Wendy M. Reinke. Copyright 2015 by The Guilford Press. Permission to photocopy this handout is granted to purchasers of this book for personal use only (see copyright page for details). Purchasers can download and print additional copies of this handout from *www.guilford.com/herman-forms*.

Pleasant Events Schedule *(page 2 of 8)*

	Activity	Like or Want to Try
36.	Working in politics	
37.	Working on machines (cars, bikes, motorcycles, tractors, etc.)	
38.	Thinking about something good in the future	
39.	Playing cards	
40.	Completing a difficult task	
41.	Laughing	
42.	Solving a problem, puzzle, crossword, etc.	
43.	Being at weddings, baptisms, confirmations, etc.	
44.	Criticizing someone	
45.	Shaving	
46.	Having lunch with friends or associates	
47.	Taking powerful drugs	
48.	Playing tennis	
49.	Taking a shower	
50.	Driving long distances	
51.	Woodworking or carpentry	
52.	Writing stories, novels, plays, or poetry	
53.	Being with animals	
54.	Riding in an airplane	
55.	Exploring (hiking away from known routes, spelunking, etc.)	
56.	Having a frank and open conversation	
57.	Singing in a group	
58.	Thinking about myself or my problems	
59.	Working on my job	
60.	Going to a party	
61.	Going to church functions (socials, classes, bazaars, etc.)	
62.	Speaking a foreign language	
63.	Going to service, civic, or social club meetings	
64.	Going to a business meeting or a convention	
65.	Being in a sporty or expensive car	
66.	Playing a musical instrument	
67.	Making snacks	
68.	Snow-skiing	
69.	Being helped	
70.	Wearing informal clothes	
71.	Combing or brushing my hair	
72.	Acting	
73.	Taking a nap	
74.	Being with friends	
75.	Canning, freezing, making preserves, etc.	
76.	Driving fast	
77.	Solving a personal problem	

(continued)

Pleasant Events Schedule *(page 3 of 8)*

	Activity	Like or Want to Try
78.	Being in a city	
79.	Taking a bath	
80.	Singing to myself	
81.	Making food or crafts to sell or give away	
82.	Playing pool or billiards	
83.	Being with my grandchildren	
84.	Playing chess or checkers	
85.	Doing craftwork (pottery, jewelry, leather, beads, weaving, etc.)	
86.	Weighing myself	
87.	Scratching myself	
88.	Putting on makeup, fixing my hair, etc.	
89.	Designing or drafting	
90.	Visiting people who are sick, shut in, or in trouble	
91.	Cheering, rooting	
92.	Bowling	
93.	Being popular at a gathering	
94.	Watching wild animals	
95.	Having an original idea	
96.	Gardening, landscaping, or doing yard work	
97.	Jumping rope	
98.	Reading essays or technical, academic, or professional literature	
99.	Wearing new clothes	
100.	Dancing	
101.	Sitting in the sun	
102.	Riding a motorcycle	
103.	Just sitting and thinking	
104.	Social drinking	
105.	Seeing good things happening to my family or friends	
106.	Going to a fair, carnival, circus, zoo, or amusement park	
107.	Talking about philosophy or religion	
108.	Gambling	
109.	Planning or organizing something	
110.	Smoking marijuana	
111.	Having a drink by myself	
112.	Listening to the sounds of nature	
113.	Dating, courting, etc.	
114.	Having a lively talk	
115.	Racing in a car, motorcycle, boat, etc.	
116.	Listening to the radio	
117.	Having friends come to visit	
118.	Playing in a sporting competition	
119.	Introducing people I think would like each other	

(continued)

Pleasant Events Schedule *(page 4 of 8)*

	Activity	Like or Want to Try
120.	Giving gifts	
121.	Going to school or government meetings, court sessions, etc.	
122.	Getting massages or backrubs	
123.	Getting letters, cards, or notes	
124.	Watching the sky, clouds, or a storm	
125.	Going on outings (to the park, a picnic, a barbecue, etc.)	
126.	Playing basketball	
127.	Buying something for my family	
128.	Photography	
129.	Giving a speech or lecture	
130.	Reading maps	
131.	Gathering natural objects (wild foods or fruit, rocks, driftwood, etc.)	
132.	Working on my finances	
133.	Wearing clean clothes	
134.	Making a major purchase or investment (car, appliance, house, stocks, etc.)	
135.	Helping someone	
136.	Being in the mountains	
137.	Getting a job advancement (being promoted, given a raise, or offered a better job; getting accepted at a school, etc.)	
138.	Hearing jokes	
139.	Winning a bet	
140.	Talking about my children or grandchildren	
141.	Meeting someone new of the opposite sex	
142.	Going to a revival or crusade	
143.	Talking about my health	
144.	Seeing beautiful scenery	
145.	Eating good meals	
146.	Improving my health (having my teeth fixed, getting new glasses, changing my diet, etc.)	
147.	Being downtown	
148.	Wrestling or boxing	
149.	Hunting or shooting	
150.	Playing in a musical group	
151.	Hiking	
152.	Going to a museum or exhibit	
153.	Writing papers, essays, articles, reports, memos, etc.	
154.	Doing a job well	
155.	Having spare time	
156.	Fishing	
157.	Loaning something	
158.	Being noticed as sexually attractive	

(continued)

Pleasant Events Schedule (page 5 of 8)

	Activity	Like or Want to Try
159.	Pleasing employers, teachers, etc.	
160.	Counseling someone	
161.	Going to a health club, sauna bath, etc.	
162.	Having someone criticize me	
163.	Learning to do something new	
164.	Going to a "drive-in" (Dairy Queen, McDonald's, etc.)	
165.	Complimenting or praising someone	
166.	Thinking about people I like	
167.	Being at a fraternity or sorority	
168.	Planning a skit	
169.	Being with my parents	
170.	Horseback riding	
171.	Protesting social, political, or environmental conditions	
172.	Talking on the telephone	
173.	Having daydreams	
174.	Kicking leaves, sand, pebbles, etc.	
175.	Playing lawn sports (badminton, croquet, shuffleboard, horseshoes, etc.)	
176.	Going to school reunions, alumni meetings, etc.	
177.	Seeing famous people	
178.	Going to the movies	
179.	Kissing	
180.	Being alone	
181.	Budgeting my time	
182.	Cooking meals	
183.	Being praised by people I admire	
184.	Outwitting a "superior"	
185.	Feeling the presence of the Lord in my life	
186.	Doing a project in my own way	
187.	Doing "odd jobs" around the house	
188.	Crying	
189.	Being told I'm needed	
190.	Being at a family reunion or get-together	
191.	Giving a party or get-together	
192.	Washing my hair	
193.	Coaching someone	
194.	Going to a restaurant	
195.	Seeing or smelling a flower or plant	
196.	Being invited out	
197.	Receiving honors (civic, military, etc.)	
198.	Using cologne, perfume, or aftershave	
199.	Having someone agree with me	
200.	Reminiscing, talking about old times	

(continued)

Pleasant Events Schedule *(page 6 of 8)*

	Activity	Like or Want to Try
201.	Getting up early in the morning	
202.	Having peace and quiet	
203.	Doing experiments or other scientific work	
204.	Visiting friends	
205.	Writing in a diary	
206.	Playing football	
207.	Being counseled	
208.	Saying prayers	
209.	Giving massages or backrubs	
210.	Hitchhiking	
211.	Meditating or doing yoga	
212.	Seeing a fight	
213.	Doing favors for people	
214.	Talking with people on the job or in class	
215.	Being relaxed	
216.	Being asked for my help or advice	
217.	Thinking about other people's problems	
218.	Playing board games (Monopoly, Scrabble, etc.)	
219.	Sleeping soundly at night	
220.	Doing heavy outdoor work (cutting or chopping wood, clearing land, farm work, etc.)	
221.	Reading the newspaper	
222.	Shocking people, swearing, making obscene gestures, etc.	
223.	Snowmobiling or dune-buggy riding	
224.	Being in a body-awareness, sensitivity, encounter, therapy, or "rap" group	
225.	Dreaming at night	
226.	Playing ping-pong	
227.	Brushing my teeth	
228.	Swimming	
229.	Being in a fight	
230.	Running, jogging, or doing gymnastics, fitness, or field exercises	
231.	Walking barefoot	
232.	Playing Frisbee or catch	
233.	Doing housework or laundry; cleaning things	
234.	Being with my roommate	
235.	Listening to music	
236.	Arguing	
237.	Knitting, crocheting, embroidery, or fancy needle work	
238.	Petting, necking	
239.	Amusing people	
240.	Talking about sex	
241.	Going to a barber or beautician	

(continued)

Pleasant Events Schedule *(page 7 of 8)*

	Activity	Like or Want to Try
242.	Having houseguests	
243.	Being with someone I love	
244.	Reading magazines	
245.	Sleeping late	
246.	Starting a new project	
247.	Being stubborn	
248.	Having sexual relations	
249.	Having other sexual satisfactions	
250.	Going to the library	
251.	Playing soccer, rugby, hockey, lacrosse, etc.	
252.	Preparing a new or special food	
253.	Bird watching	
254.	Shopping	
255.	Watching people	
256.	Building or watching a fire	
257.	Winning an argument	
258.	Selling or trading something	
259.	Finishing a project or task	
260.	Confessing or apologizing	
261.	Repairing things	
262.	Working with others as a team	
263.	Bicycling	
264.	Telling people what to do	
265.	Being with happy people	
266.	Playing party games	
267.	Writing letters, cards, or notes	
268.	Talking about politics or public affairs	
269.	Asking for help or advice	
270.	Going to banquets, luncheons, potlucks, etc.	
271.	Talking about my hobby or special interest	
272.	Watching attractive women or men	
273.	Smiling at people	
274.	Playing in sand, a stream, the grass, etc.	
275.	Talking about other people	
276.	Being with my husband or wife	
277.	Having people show interest in what I have said	
278.	Going on field trips, nature walks, etc.	
279.	Expressing my love to someone	
280.	Smoking tobacco	
281.	Caring for houseplants	
282.	Having coffee, tea, a soda, etc., with friends	
283.	Taking a walk	

(continued)

Pleasant Events Schedule *(page 8 of 8)*

	Activity	Like or Want to Try
284.	Collecting things	
285.	Playing handball, paddleball, squash, etc.	
286.	Sewing	
287.	Suffering for a good cause	
288.	Remembering a departed friend or loved one, visiting the cemetery	
289.	Doing things with children	
290.	Beachcombing	
291.	Being complimented or told I have done well	
292.	Being told I am loved	
293.	Eating snacks	
294.	Staying up late	
295.	Having family members or friends do something that makes me proud of them	
296.	Being with my children	
297.	Going to auctions, garage sales, etc.	
298.	Thinking about an interesting question	
299.	Doing volunteer work, working on community service projects	
300.	Water skiing, surfing, scuba diving	
301.	Receiving money	
302.	Defending or protecting someone; stopping fraud or abuse	
303.	Hearing a good sermon	
304.	Picking up a hitchhiker	
305.	Winning a competition	
306.	Making a new friend	
307.	Talking about my job or school	
308.	Reading cartoons, comic strips, or comic books	
309.	Borrowing something	
310.	Traveling with a group	
311.	Seeing old friends	
312.	Teaching someone	
313.	Using my strength	
314.	Traveling	
315.	Going to office parties or departmental get-togethers	
316.	Attending concert, opera, or ballet	
317.	Playing with pets	
318.	Going to a play	
319.	Looking at the stars or moon	
320.	Being coached	

HANDOUT 7.2

Pleasant Events I Want to Try

Activity	Currently Doing	Tried in Past	Like to Try
1.			
2.			
3.			
4.			
5.			
6.			
7.			
8.			
9.			
10.			
11.			
12.			
13.			
14.			
15.			
16.			
17.			
18.			
19.			
20.			

From *Stress Management for Teachers: A Proactive Guide* by Keith C. Herman and Wendy M. Reinke. Copyright 2015 by The Guilford Press. Permission to photocopy this handout is granted to purchasers of this book for personal use only (see copyright page for details). Purchasers can download and print additional copies of this handout from *www.guilford.com/herman-forms*.

HANDOUT 7.3

Pleasant Events Goals and Weekly Schedule

Time	Sunday	Monday	Tuesday	Wednesday	Thursday	Friday	Saturday

My goal is to do _____ pleasant activities each day and _____ pleasant activities for the whole week. When I reach my daily goal I will reward myself with _____ [smaller reward]. When I reach my weekly goal I will reward myself with _____ [bigger reward].

From *Stress Management for Teachers: A Proactive Guide* by Keith C. Herman and Wendy M. Reinke. Copyright 2015 by The Guilford Press. Permission to photocopy this handout is granted to purchasers of this book for personal use only (see copyright page for details). Purchasers can download and print additional copies of this handout from www.guilford.com/herman-forms.

HANDOUT 7.4

Adding Fun to My Classroom

I would like to add more fun to my classroom. The main reasons I would like to do this include the following: _____

_____

_____

_____

_____

Here is a list of fun things I would like to continue to do or do more in my classroom. _____

_____

_____

_____

_____

_____

_____

_____

_____

_____

_____

_____

_____

_____

_____

_____

_____

I commit to doing at least _____ fun activities in the classroom this week.

From *Stress Management for Teachers: A Proactive Guide* by Keith C. Herman and Wendy M. Reinke. Copyright 2015 by The Guilford Press. Permission to photocopy this handout is granted to purchasers of this book for personal use only (see copyright page for details). Purchasers can download and print additional copies of this handout from *www.guilford.com/herman-forms*.

HANDOUT 7.5

Incentives for Me

Daily (easy, inexpensive)

_____
_____
_____
_____
_____
_____
_____
_____
_____
_____
_____
_____

Weekly (more elaborate or valuable)

_____
_____
_____
_____
_____
_____
_____
_____
_____
_____
_____
_____
_____

From *Stress Management for Teachers: A Proactive Guide* by Keith C. Herman and Wendy M. Reinke. Copyright 2015 by The Guilford Press. Permission to photocopy this handout is granted to purchasers of this book for personal use only (see copyright page for details). Purchasers can download and print additional copies of this handout from *www.guilford.com/herman-forms*.

HANDOUT 7.6

Interpersonal Support Evaluation List

	Definitely False	Probably False	Probably True	Definitely True
1. If I wanted to go on a trip for a day (for example, to the country or mountains), I would have a hard time finding someone to go with me.	1	2	3	4
2. I feel that there is no one I can share my most private worries and fears with.	1	2	3	4
3. If I were sick, I could easily find someone to help me with my daily chores.	1	2	3	4
4. There is someone I can turn to for advice about handling problems with my family.	1	2	3	4
5. If I decide one afternoon that I would like to go to a movie that evening, I could easily find someone to go with me.	1	2	3	4
6. When I need suggestions on how to deal with a personal problem, I know someone I can turn to.	1	2	3	4
7. I don't often get invited to do things with others.	1	2	3	4
8. If I had to go out of town for a few weeks, it would be difficult to find someone who would look after my house or apartment (the plants, pets, garden, etc.).	1	2	3	4
9. If I wanted to have lunch with someone, I could easily find someone to join me.	1	2	3	4
10. If I was stranded 10 miles from home, there is someone I could call who could come and get me.	1	2	3	4
11. If a family crisis arose, it would be difficult to find someone who could give me good advice about how to handle it.	1	2	3	4
12. If I needed some help in moving to a new house or apartment, I would have a hard time finding someone to help me.	1	2	3	4

From Cohen, Mermelstein, Kamarck, and Hoberman (1985). Reprinted with permission from the authors and Brill/Nijhoff.

From *Stress Management for Teachers: A Proactive Guide* by Keith C. Herman and Wendy M. Reinke. Copyright 2015 by The Guilford Press. Permission to photocopy this handout is granted to purchasers of this book for personal use only (see copyright page for details). Purchasers can download and print additional copies of this handout from *www.guilford.com/herman-forms*.

CHAPTER 8

Competence and Self-Efficacy

Teaching is a complex profession. It involves many activities that often occur simultaneously, including classroom management; lesson preparation and organization of teaching and learning activities; creating and maintaining a certain climate; and assessing, evaluating, and providing feedback to students. Keeping up your skills across these many domains is an important aspect of effectively managing stress. When we feel competent in what we are asked to do, we feel less stress. For instance, teachers who have a strong sense of efficacy, meaning they feel competent and believe that they are effective at their job, exhibit greater levels of planning and organization, are more open to new ideas and more willing to experiment with new methods, work longer with students who are struggling, and exhibit greater enthusiasm for teaching (Tschannen-Moran & Hoy, 2001). Figure 8.1 provides a visual of how improving skills can lead to self-efficacy which then leads to competence. One way to stay on top of your game is to engage in ongoing professional development and lifelong learning.

We begin this chapter with an overview of effective classroom management practices and a discussion of challenging student behavior because many teachers report feeling less efficacious in these areas, feel undertrained in these topics, and because many teachers leave the field, citing challenges with managing student behavior as the main reason for leaving. Next we discuss the key components of professional development and describe coaching or consultation models for your consideration.

Effective Skills → Higher Self-Efficacy → Improved Performance

FIGURE 8.1. The relationship between skills, efficacy, and performance.

CLASSROOM MANAGEMENT AND CHALLENGING STUDENT BEHAVIORS

One area in which many teachers express that they wish they had more training or support is managing classroom behaviors. We have surveyed hundreds of teachers about their top concerns for their job and classroom management, and challenging student behaviors were at the top of their list. Many teachers who encounter challenges in managing student behaviors feel isolated or helpless in the situation. Classroom management can be very personal. When students are disruptive and disrespectful, many teachers feel ineffective and internalize the problem. In fact, many teachers leave education as a result of the challenges they face in managing student behaviors. One elementary teacher we worked with to help improve her classroom management revealed that she went home each night and cried because of the ongoing misbehavior of students in her classroom and lack of support from others. When teachers feel in control of their classrooms and respected by their students, they have greater efficacy. Having greater efficacy is linked with less stress and being more effective at your job. The following sections provide ideas for developing an effective classroom management plan that can reduce disruptive and challenging behaviors in your classroom.

Authentic Relationships with Students

Foundational to effective classroom management is having positive, authentic relationships with your students. Without these relationships, praise, reprimands, and other strategies to manage student behavior will be less effective. Consider the student who feels disconnected from you. When you praise this student, the student may not feel that the praise is genuine. When you attempt to correct misbehavior, this student may feel a lack of concern with the reprimand or loss of points. Being connected to students and having an authentic positive relationship with each of them is important.

Think about your relationship with students as a bank. You need first to have money in a bank to be able to later withdraw it. Having a positive, authentic relationship with students will put money in the bank (positive/caring interactions) that can then be withdrawn when needed (correcting misbehaviors). Keeping a higher positive to negative ratio is one goal toward ensuring you have enough "money in the bank." In addition, having clear, consistent expectations and structure in the classroom will support a positive classroom climate. Other strategies include making a point to greet students daily, connecting with each student, asking about their likes and dislikes, expressing when you truly enjoy spending time with them, finding ways to make learning fun and enjoyable, and sending them off at the end of the day. Make your classroom comfortable, yourself approachable, and your interactions with students positive and unemotional when challenging situations occur. Let learning be fun, but with structure and limits. Keep the classroom organized, functional, yet inviting. Consider the cultural backgrounds of the students in your classroom, integrate different viewpoints and cultural perspectives in your teaching, what you display in your classroom, and how you interact with your students. Make efforts to communicate with the parents or caregivers of the students in your classroom regularly about accomplishments and positive qualities of their child. Being aware of your relationships with students and putting effort toward connecting to all students, particularly those whom you may discipline more or interact with less, can help you to determine when and if you need to "make a deposit" toward improving your relationship with students.

Handout 8.1 provides some questions you might consider that can guide you toward improving your relationship with students and creating a positive classroom climate. The questions tap into different aspects of authentic relationships, but they do not capture all that goes into making a relationship positive and productive. First, the questions are intended to make you aware of your relationships with your students. Second, if you find that you are unsure about the answer or are missing information for one or more students, then you can work to better know the information through strengthening your relationships. You may want to revisit the questions or ask related questions of yourself throughout the school year, working toward continuous improvement of your relationships with your students.

Using Proactive Classroom Management Strategies

Proactive strategies are helpful because they emphasize preventing problem behavior rather than waiting to respond to behaviors after they occur. Consistently using proactive strategies such as having clear rules and expectations, teaching expectations, and praising or reinforcing students when they exhibit appropriate classroom behaviors can help create learning environments that prevent problems and increase the time available for learning by reducing the time spent correcting misbehavior. Proactive strategies allow teachers to spend more time teaching and less time putting out fires. You can begin building a proactive classroom management plan by asking yourself the following questions, and by planning, and implementing a classroom management system that you employ from the first day of classes.

> **Proactive strategies allow teachers to spend more time teaching and less time putting out fires.**

What are the expectations and rules for your classroom? One of the best proactive things that teachers can do to make it less likely that classroom management will be an issue in their classroom is to start with clear rules and expectations from day one. Expectations are global qualities that we would like students (and adults) to uphold. For instance, we would like students to be responsible. A rule, on the other hand, is specific and observable. For example, coming to class with completed homework is the specific and observable form of being responsible. Begin each year with three to five brief expectations that are stated positively (e.g., Be Respectful, Be a Good Learner, Be Kind). Many schools employ schoolwide behavior support systems (e.g., positive behavior interventions and supports [PBIS]). Your school may encourage you to use the same expectations in your classroom. This does not reduce your ability to clearly articulate how these expectations play out in your classroom. Specifically, rules that demonstrate what each expectation means in your classroom can be developed, taught to students, and displayed for students to review. For each expectation you will have multiple classroom rules that correspond. See Figure 8.2 for examples of expectations and corresponding rules.

Expectation	Classroom Rule
Be respectful.	• Raise hand before talking. • Keep the classroom neat and clean. • Listen to the teacher and others when they are talking.
Be safe.	• Keep hands, feet, and objects to yourself. • Follow directions the first time. • Line up one at a time.
Be kind.	• Share classroom materials with others. • Use kind words. • Use an inside voice when talking to the teacher or others.

FIGURE 8.2. Examples of expectations and corresponding classroom rules.

How will students know what they need to do to successfully meet the classroom expectations? Once you are clear about the specific expectations and rules for your classroom, you need to plan for how to effectively teach your students these expectations. You should start teaching expectations at the start of the school year. Spending some time up front on making sure your students understand how they can be successful will save time in the long run. Teaching behavioral expectations is most effective when you give students opportunities to understand the expectation and then to practice it successfully. The next section provides suggestions for how you can use the plan with students.

Teach, Model, Practice, and Praise

Begin by teaching the expectation. State the rule and then explain briefly how the rule will be useful. For instance, one expectation in the classroom might be that students are safe. To be safe, students will keep their hands and feet to themselves (rule). Being safe in the classroom keeps others from being hurt and allows everyone to give attention to learning (reason for rule). After describing and explaining the rule, demonstrate what the rule would look like to be successful. This can be done by modeling positive examples of the rule. For being safe, you might demonstrate walking slowly with your hands to your side, not touching others or objects. It is also a good idea to model negative examples of the rule. This can be particularly useful for demonstrating slightly incorrect versions as well as obviously incorrect ones. For being safe, you might demonstrate poking a student in the back, pushing someone in line, and kicking an object. Ask students after each demonstration whether you did it correctly or incorrectly. Next, ask a student, group of students, or the whole class to show you the appropriate behavior. We do not suggest having students practice negative examples of the rule. It is best if they rehearse positive examples only. Praise appropriate behaviors related to the rule at that time and throughout the day on a regular basis. Depending on the rule, this proactive classroom management strategy often takes less than 10 minutes to complete. Figure 8.3 gives an example of teaching a rule using a guide to help in the planning. A blank version of this form is provided in Handout 8.2.

What routines and daily tasks do students need to complete in your classroom? In every classroom students need to figure out how to navigate many routines and tasks.

Expectation: Be responsible	Rule: Enter the classroom quietly and ready to learn.
Teach by providing a verbal explanation of the rule.	When we enter the classroom quietly and ready to learn we are able to begin right away, getting more done in the time we are together.
Model a positive example of the rule.	Demonstrate coming into classroom from hallway quietly, sitting at a desk, putting math book on top of desk, and looking to front of classroom.
Model a negative example of the rule.	Demonstrate coming into classroom, but talking to students, stopping at another student's desk to talk more, and then finally coming to seat, but not pulling out book. Have students comment on what was incorrect and how to do it differently.
Practice by having a student or students demonstrate the rule.	Ask a student to model the correct way. Have other students comment on what the student did to demonstrate the rule. Have a table of students demonstrate the correct way.
Praise students when they demonstrate the rule correctly.	Provide behavior-specific praise to students as they come into the classroom: "Thank you for being ready to learn," "Nice job, coming into the room quietly and getting ready to start class," "You are all ready to learn! Great job."

FIGURE 8.3. Example of a completed Plan for Teaching Classroom Rules.

These often differ from one classroom to another. Think about your classroom and the types of routines or tasks that students are required to navigate throughout the day. Next, envision what successful completion of the task looks like. For instance, students in your classroom may be required to sharpen a pencil. What does that look like? Perhaps you want the student to (1) raise his or her hand; (2) ask permission after you call on them; (3) stand up, push in his or her chair, and walk, using the most direct route, without talking to or touching other students, to the sharpener with his or her pencil; (4) sharpen the pencil for only the amount of time necessary to produce a point; (5) remove the pencil from the sharpener; (6) walk back to his or her seat using the quickest route to their desk (not taking a tour of the classroom), without talking to or touching other students; (7) pull out the chair and sit down at his or her desk; and (8) resume working. These eight steps would be what it means to "be responsible" when sharpening a pencil. This may seem like an overly nuanced way to think about an activity like sharpening a pencil—however, there are many ways that a student could be unsuccessful in this task. For instance, a student could disrupt other students by talking with them, touching them, or sharpening his pencil excessively, making too much noise. Being proactive means thinking about all the things that could go awry with a task and teaching students what the behavior should look like instead. Figure 8.4 provides a list of common student routines or tasks that may happen in your classroom. Identify the major routines and tasks you require of students and then determine what successfully completing this task looks like when in your classroom. Each of these tasks can be broken into small steps that can then be linked to the classroom expectations. Teaching students how the routines and tasks in the classroom should look will prevent many disruptive behaviors.

How will I gain the attention of students when needed? Getting and holding students' attention is an important management tool for any teacher. Developing and using an attention signal will decrease the amount of time and number of disruptions that occur during transition periods in your classroom. Attention signals are useful prior to a transition, during times that noise or disruptions are higher than normal, and when clarifications are required. Without the signal it could take several minutes of yelling over the noise in the classroom to get everyone's attention.

Begin by deciding what your attention signal will be. Combining an audible and visible component to the signal can help because if students miss one cue, they may notice the other. One effective method for gaining attention is saying in a firm, loud voice (but not shouting), "Class, your attention please," while swinging your right arm in an arc straight out from your side and holding your arm above your head until all students are looking at you with their hands raised. Another popular attention signal used by teachers is rhythmic clapping. For this attention signal, you clap out a rhythm and the students clap back the same rhythm in response while looking quietly toward you. Other attention signals that we often see teachers use include flicking the lights in the classroom on and off, using a bell, a harmonica, or music. The signal should be developmentally appropriate. For instance, high school students may consider clapping back as part of the signal to be childish, whereas elementary students might find it fun and easy to acknowledge.

Regardless of the signal used, you should be able to get the entire class's attention within 5 seconds. First, introduce the signal and explain when it will be used. Next, tell the students what the expectation is after the signal has been given (e.g., raise their hands and quietly look at the teacher). Last, practice the signal with students, providing them with feedback and praise as appropriate. Continue to practice until the signal results in the

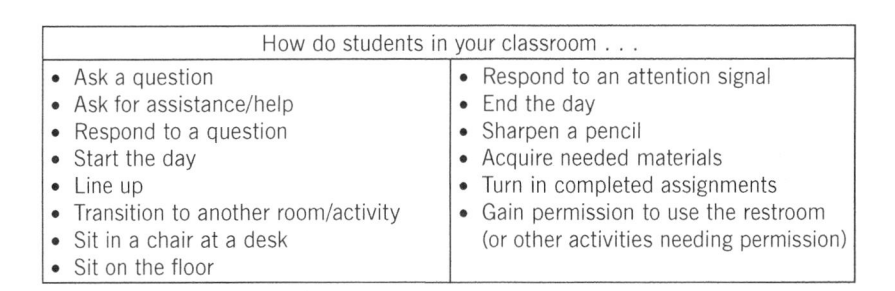

How do students in your classroom . . .	
• Ask a question	• Respond to an attention signal
• Ask for assistance/help	• End the day
• Respond to a question	• Sharpen a pencil
• Start the day	• Acquire needed materials
• Line up	• Turn in completed assignments
• Transition to another room/activity	• Gain permission to use the restroom
• Sit in a chair at a desk	(or other activities needing permission)
• Sit on the floor	

FIGURE 8.4. List of common routines and tasks in classrooms.

attention of the entire class within 5 seconds. A well-practiced signal will help students to transition quickly between tasks, creating additional time for instruction.

How will the students in your class know how to successfully complete daily tasks and routines? Similar to teaching your classroom expectations and rules, time spent directly teaching routines and tasks, particularly those for which students often struggle, is time well spent up front. Using a similar guideline to Figure 8.3, you can plan and teach students exactly how to complete a task or routine. Figure 8.5 provides an example of teaching students a morning routine. A blank version of this form is also available in Handout 8.3.

Precorrective Statements

Precorrection is a strategy for preventing predictable problem behaviors by reminding students of the appropriate behavior or response prior to the situation in which the error typically occurs. This strategy can help children learn how to succeed in situations in which they repeatedly make social, behavioral, or preacademic errors (Colvin, Sugai, Good, & Lee, 1997; DePry & Sugai, 2002; Lewis, Colvin, & Sugai, 2000). This strategy can be used

Routine/Task: Morning Routine	
Teach by providing a verbal explanation of the routine or task.	"Beginning our morning smoothly will help us all get ready to be good learners. Each morning when we come to school, we will put our personal items in our cubby space, place completed work in the completed work folder, sit down at our desks, take out our morning folders, and begin working on our daily math problems."
Model a positive example.	Demonstrate what this looks like by doing it in front of the class.
Model a negative example.	#1: "OK, class. What if I walked into the room and dropped my backpack next to my desk and started doing my daily math, would that be correct?" Class responds no. "What would I need to do differently?" Prompt class to describe first leaving materials in cubby, then turning in completed work, then sitting to begin daily math. #2: "What if I put my materials in my cubby, turned in work, and then started talking to my friends I had not seen since yesterday? What is wrong with that?"
Practice by having a student or students demonstrate the routine or task.	Have a table of students demonstrate what the routine looks like in the morning. Ask class, "What did they do well?"
Praise students when they meet expectations.	Catch students coming in each morning by greeting them and stating, "Thank you for using the morning routine," "You remembered the morning routine, great work!," or "I like how you show me you are ready to learn by using the morning routine."

FIGURE 8.5. Example of a completed Plan for Teaching Classroom Routines and Tasks.

with the whole class when students struggle with a specific task, or with one or two students who struggle. A precorrective statement reminds students of the expectations to successfully complete a task. These statements may be necessary earlier in the year as students learn exactly what behaviors are appropriate in the classroom. For instance, in a kindergarten class where the expectation was to move to the carpet for morning meeting, the teacher may first teach the routine to the students as described above. Then, prior to moving to the carpet in subsequent days, the teacher might say, "OK, class, remember when we move to the carpet you push in your chair at the table, walk to your spot on the carpet without talking to others, and sit cross-legged in your carpet square. Ready? Let's move to the carpet for morning meeting." Another method for precorrecting unsuccessful behavior is to ask the students what they need to do as they transition.

> **A precorrective statement reminds students of the expectations to successfully complete a task.**

TEACHER: OK, class, we are going to move to the carpet for morning meeting. Candice, tell me what we need to do to get there safely.

CANDICE: We push in our chairs and walk to our spot.

TEACHER: Do we talk to our friends as we walk to our spot?

CLASS: No.

TEACHER: Do we touch others when we get to our spot on the carpet?

CLASS: No.

TEACHER: How do we sit when we get to our spot?

CLASS: Crisscross with our hands in our lap.

TEACHER: You know exactly what to do. Great. Let's go to the carpet for morning meeting.

Following a precorrective statement, it is important to let students know that they did the task appropriately by providing praise: "Look how everyone got to the carpet and sat correctly. Nice work!" However, if students continue to struggle despite the precorrective statement, then you might consider reteaching the task until the students are consistently successful.

How will you reinforce students for successful behaviors? One of the most effective and simple strategies a teacher can use to increase appropriate behaviors in the classroom is to reinforce students when they successfully meet expectations. If you give attention to successful behaviors in your classroom you will see more of them. One way to reinforce students for meeting expectations is to praise them. Research demonstrates that praise is effective in reducing disruptive behaviors and increasing student engagement (Reinke, Lewis-Palmer, & Merrell, 2008). Having more positive than negative interactions with students is a useful goal. Being more positive on a regular basis in your classroom means you are reinforcing students more for meeting expectations. Teachers who are more positive also have better relationships with their students, are less stressed, and are likely to experience improvements in their mood. You may have heard that teachers should strive for a 4:1 positive-to-negative ratio in their classrooms. Increasing the praise that you use in classroom will improve your relationship with the students as well as give more attention to the behaviors you want to see more of. Figure 8.6 provides some ways to increase the positive-to-negative ratio in your classroom.

Behavior-Specific Praise

It's important to note that effective praise needs to be genuine, developmentally appropriate, and specific. This means that when you praise your students you specify exactly what they are doing that warrants the praise (e.g., "Thank you for quietly and calmly coming to the carpet"). To use praise proactively, think about the behaviors that you would like to see more of. Perhaps you would like students to raise their hands more frequently to avoid calling-out. To increase this behavior, you might first reteach the expectation: "I will be calling on people who raise their hand." Next, call on students who raise their hand, ignoring those who call out, and praise them for raising their hand: "Melissa, thank you for raising your hand. What would you like to say?"

Giving attention to appropriate behavior does not always have to be verbal praise. The use of stickers, nonverbal gestures (e.g., thumbs up, high five), or earning points all encourage students to continue the behaviors that you reinforce. Some students may respond better to less public displays of reinforcement. Therefore, coming alongside a student and whispering to her that she is doing a great job or providing some form of nonverbal reinforcement

---

1. Place a reminder somewhere in your classroom that will prompt you to praise students.
2. Have clear expectations, teach them directly, and praise students regularly who meet these expectations.
3. Place coins, paperclips, or other small object in your pocket (e.g., 8 pennies). Each time you praise a student, move one object from your pocket to the other side. Each time you reprimand a student, move an object back over. Set a goal for having more objects in the praise pocket than the reprimand pocket.
4. Select a student behavior you want to see more often (e.g., getting right to work), then "catch" students when you see the behavior. Provide them praise or other form of reinforcement (e.g., sticker, star, high five, pat on the back).
5. Greet students as they come into your classroom. This is a form of attention not tied to a behavior, but it is a very positive way to interact with students.
6. Praise or provide positive attention to each student who answers an academic question correctly (e.g., "You are correct. Nice answer!").
7. Use sticks with student names on them or another method to randomly call on students, providing more opportunities for students to respond to academic questions. Praise students for correct answers.
8. Use tickets that students can turn in for a reinforcer (e.g., PBIS tickets).
9. Use a bingo marker to easily and unobtrusively mark dots on a paper on each student's desk throughout the day. When students get a certain number (e.g., 10 dots), they earn reward.
10. Each time you provide a reprimand (or think about providing a reprimand), use it as a prompt to praise two students exhibiting successful behaviors.

FIGURE 8.6. Ideas for ways to increase positive interactions with students.

may be more appropriate for students who do not like to be singled out. Your relationships with your students and knowledge of their personalities will help you determine what types of praise will be best.

Some teachers find it hard to keep a high rate of praise or reinforcement for successful behaviors. It can be challenging because as a teacher you are required to do many things at once. At times praise may fall to the back burner. Teachers we have worked with over the years have come up with some great strategies to help remind themselves to praise. For instance, one teacher we worked with placed a sticky note on the overhead projector she used during math instruction. This sticky note said, "Look up and praise two students." She was able to significantly increase the amount of praise she provided with this simple reminder. As a result the disruptive behavior in her classroom decreased. Another teacher placed a smiley face under the clock in her room. She often looked up to check the time of day. The smiley face reminded her to look around and praise a few students who were doing their work.

In addition, some teachers have selected certain times of the day, those times when the students seem to struggle behaviorally (e.g., immediately after lunch, following a transition, end of day), to target for increased praise. For instance, if you want students to have a seat and get right to work following lunch you could specifically target this time of day to praise students you "catch" doing the behavior (e.g., "Oh, Marvin got right to work without wasting a moment," "I see Tawney is working hard at her desk," "Thanks to everyone who came in and got right to work"). You may be able to come up with some very feasible and simple ideas to help remind yourself to praise and reinforce students. Do you have ideas for how you can remind yourself to catch students being successful? If so, put them into action. As you become more fluent in your use of reinforcement or praise, it will become easier to keep a higher positive-to-negative ratio in your classroom.

Rewards or Incentives

Another way to reinforce successful student behaviors is to develop and utilize a reward system. Reward systems can be particularly helpful when you are working with students to learn a new behavior or when they struggle repeatedly with certain classroom tasks or activities. Some people express concern about rewarding behaviors that students are supposed to be doing, citing the potential for students to lose their intrinsic motivation, or their own interest in performing a task, for doing the rewarded task. Student motivation is more complicated than this. The research suggests that rewarding behavior can increase, decrease, or have no effect on intrinsic motivation (Eisenberger, Pierce, & Cameron, 1999). If rewards are provided for ill-defined or minimal performance of a task, they are more likely to reduce intrinsic motivation because this conveys that the task is trivial; providing rewards for specific high task performance can actually increase intrinsic motivation by conveying the task's personal or social significance. Think of yourself: perhaps you have set a goal you hoped to achieve for which you rewarded yourself in the end. If you set a specific goal that

Reward systems can be particularly helpful when you are working with students to learn a new behavior or when they struggle repeatedly with certain classroom tasks or activities.

is attainable, but challenging, and you select a reward that matched the significance of meeting this goal and one you would like to attain, you are likely to feel more motivated to meet this goal. The same applies to students. Students in your classroom can step up to the challenge to earn a well-deserved reward for meeting important classroom goals.

Another consideration with regard to using rewards or incentives is to make them feasible (e.g., not expensive or beyond your resources) and reinforcing to students. You may think your ideas for rewards are perfect, but if the students in your classroom don't find them appealing, then the reward system will be less effective. One way to ensure that you utilize incentives that students find truly rewarding is to ask them what they like. You can ask your students to rank-order a list of potential rewards or simply spend 10 minutes brainstorming ideas for rewards they would like to earn for successful completion of the specific tasks. You could develop your own survey or list of rewards. Figure 8.7 provides an example of such a list. Include items on the list that you are willing to provide, have the resources to provide, and that you think most students will find enjoyable. There are many examples and forms available for this purpose (see *www.pbis.org* for some). For younger children you could provide a list of rewards and have them vote, tallying the vote on a whiteboard for all to see.

Group Contingencies and Token Economies

Group contingencies and token economy systems are often used in combination and are most frequently implemented at the elementary and middle school levels. A token economy

Please place an **X** by your top five choices for a reward for meeting the classroom goal.
Free time in class
Leave class 1 minute early
Reduced homework assignment
5 points extra credit on assignment
Small snack or candy
Sticker
Choice to sit or stand at desk
A good note home to parents
Pencil, paper, small notebook, pen
Lunch with teacher or other favorite adult
Listen to music
Extra computer time
Go to library
Extra recess time
Be class helper

FIGURE 8.7. Example of a student survey of reward preferences.

system occurs when students exchange earned tokens (e.g., sticker, chips, marbles) for a reinforcer. Group contingencies occur when the teacher provides a group of students with reinforcement that is contingent on appropriate behavior for the entire group. Typically, group contingencies are established to increase positive behaviors by attending to the behavior that you would like to see increase in your classroom (e.g., raising hand, completing assignments on time). However, group contingencies have also been used to reinforce the absence of problem behaviors. This form of group contingency teaches students to inhibit problem behaviors while increasing on-task behaviors.

One example of a group contingency intervention that works to inhibit behavior is the Good Behavior Game. The Good Behavior Game was developed in 1969 by a classroom teacher and has an extensive research base showing that it increases on-task behavior and decreases disruptive behavior (see Embry, 2002, for a review). To set up the Good Behavior Game, you split the classroom into small groups or teams. For instance, if the students are seated in tables clustered together, each cluster would be a team. Next, explain that each time someone from within their group misbehaves the group will earn a point. For the game to be effective, you will need to clearly explain what constitutes misbehavior. In an area of the classroom easily accessible to you and visible to students, post the name of each team and provide a space where tallies of misbehavior can be marked. Then inform the class that teams who earn five or fewer points (this can be adjusted according to what makes the most sense for students in your classroom) during a specified period will earn a reward. You may want to gather baseline information about the number of misbehaviors that occur regularly in your classroom and set a goal for the classroom so that fewer occur during the game. For instance, if you count that 15 or more misbehaviors occur in a 10-minute period, then setting the goal for 7 (approximately half of the current rate) or fewer points initially and reducing this amount over time may be more appropriate.

Next, announce the start of the game and how long it will last. It is most effective if the game starts out in relatively short intervals (e.g., 5 minutes) and builds up to longer games. During the game, you continue teaching as you normally do. However, when you notice misbehavior, calmly and briefly announce it (e.g., "Blue team, that's talking out") and mark a tally for the offending team. After the designated time lapses the game ends, then proceed to count the points for each team. Teams that meet the goal (e.g., 5 or fewer points) earn a brief and immediate reward that is reinforcing (i.e., students enjoy them) and is developmentally appropriate. Teams who have points in excess of the goal (e.g., 6 or more) do not earn a reward. Brief, simple prizes allow you to pause instruction for only 30 seconds to 1 minute to provide the winning teams with the prizes (e.g., dancing at your desk for 30 seconds, talking to your peers for 1 minute). Developing a list of brief, simple prizes and verifying that students like them will be helpful prior to implementing the game.

How will students know what will happen if they display inappropriate behaviors? Students will make mistakes or intentionally violate a classroom rule on occasion. Having strategies for letting them know they have done so is as important as acknowledging when they are successful. The following provides some suggestions to ensure students understand when they have done something inappropriate in the classroom and what will happen when an inappropriate behavior occurs.

Explicit Reprimand

The simplest way to let students know that a behavior is not appropriate is to provide a calm, brief, and explicit reprimand. This type of reprimand indicates that students need to correct their behavior and what they should do instead without disrupting the flow of instruction (e.g., "Nick, you are calling out; please raise your hand before answering," "Chris, you are out of your seat without permission, please sit down at your table"). These brief interactions are delivered in a neutral tone. As soon as the student corrects the behavior, give attention to the student (e.g., "Nick, thank you for raising your hand. What is the answer?"). This type of reprimand is qualitatively different than simply telling a student to stop what they are doing because it tells them what to do instead. Of course, explicit reprimands are not the only way to let students know when they need to correct their behavior. The next section outlines an effective method for identifying how you will respond to different classroom misbehaviors that you may encounter.

> **The simplest way to let students know that a behavior is not appropriate is to provide a calm, brief and explicit reprimand.**

Predetermined Consequences for Inappropriate Behavior

Another proactive strategy toward decreasing disruptive classroom behaviors is to be consistent with how you handle student infractions of classroom rules and expectations. Much like setting up the rules and expectations, it can be extremely helpful to think about what inappropriate behaviors look like in a classroom and how they will be handled when they occur. One way to go about this is to create a list of possible student misbehaviors. Next, for each misbehavior write how you will respond to each behavior should it occur. Being prepared before you encounter student disruptions will decrease the likelihood that you are caught off guard. It can be helpful to begin the list with minor infractions and move toward major behavior problems. Include behaviors that you have encountered before as well as those that you have only heard about from others. Figure 8.8 provides an example of this activity for an elementary classroom. This list is not all inclusive, nor does it indicate how you would handle the situation in your classroom. Rather, it is an example of how you can proactively determine your response to student behaviors.

Once you develop the list, it is important to share early in the year with your students what happens if certain behaviors occur. For instance, if you use a thinking chair (i.e., time-out) as a strategy in your classroom for misbehaviors, teach the students when and how this occurs. This can be done much in the same way you teach classroom rules and expectations. Start by stating the rule, "If you hit, kick, or throw an object at anyone, you are not being safe and you will have to go to the thinking chair. This will help keep everybody safe." Next, model what it looks like and does not look like by going to the thinking chair yourself. You could also have a few students practice while having the other students comment on what they did well when they went to the thinking chair. This ensures that when an incident occurs to which you need to respond, neither you nor the students are surprised by the consequence.

Student Behavior	Response to Behavior
Leaving seat without permission	Provide explicit reprimand; thank student for returning to seat. Praise other students who are seated.
Talking out during instruction	Provide explicit reprimand the first time; ignore further talk-outs following the reprimand; call on students at first opportunity that they raise their hand; praise the students for raising their hands.
Talking to peers when not appropriate	Provide explicit reprimand; if behavior continues following reprimand, separate students by moving seats for remainder of activity.
Off task/not completing work	Walk to the student's desk, prompt the student to begin working. If student begins working, praise student. If student does not begin within 2 minutes, provide explicit reprimand. Require the student to complete required work during recess time.
Hitting a peer	Provide explicit reprimand; send student to the thinking chair for 5 minutes; send an e-mail to the student's parent about the incident.
Hitting an adult	Provide explicit reprimand; send student to the thinking chair for 5 minutes; send an e-mail to the student's parent about the incident.
Throwing objects	Provide explicit reprimand; send student to the thinking chair for 5 minutes; send an e-mail to the student's parent about the incident.
Noncompliance/defiant behavior	Provide explicit reprimand; if noncompliance continues give the student a choice to make (e.g., you can either come to the carpet or go to the thinking chair); if student refuses to do either provide an if–then statement (e.g., "If you don't come to the carpet or the thinking chair, then I will send you to the office").
Severe aggression—hitting peers and throwing objects	Provide explicit reprimand; remove other students from the area; call the office for assistance; make parent aware of the incident.

FIGURE 8.8. Example of proactively determining responses to student misbehaviors.

How will you discourage inappropriate behaviors? There are many strategies available to help discourage student misbehavior. We review a few in this section, but we suggest that you consult other resources (some are provided at the end of this chapter) to develop other strategies as well. Importantly, when you implement any strategy to discourage inappropriate behavior, the method should be consistent, fair, respectful of the student, and done in an unemotional manner. While some students or some misbehaviors will likely irritate you or rub you the wrong way, responding with a neutral voice is more effective. Emotional responses can undermine your relationship with the students in your classroom, and for some students can increase the likelihood they display a similar behavior in the future.

Distinguish between "Won't-Do" and "Can't-Do" Behaviors

Understanding the relationship between academics and behaviors is important when helping to support students who display disengaged or even defiant behaviors in the classroom. For instance, a student who struggles with reading may become noncompliant during reading instruction or disengaged during quiet reading time. These behaviors may seem like "won't-do" behaviors. In other words, you may become frustrated with the student because he or she refuses to complete a task or participate in an academic activity. However, the behaviors may be a way for that student to cover up or deal with a "can't-do" problem. The student may be unable to complete the task or activity and uses the behavior to compensate for this deficiency. Therefore, it is important to evaluate whether the student needs to be completing academic tasks that match his or her ability level. In addition, finding additional academic supports may be warranted. If we treat "can't-do" behaviors as "won't-do" behaviors the student is likely to fall further behind academically. Identifying ways to allow all students to succeed academically is important and can reduce challenging classroom behaviors.

Similarly, some social situations present challenges for students. For instance, a student who lacks the necessary skills to join peer groups or interact confidently with adults may display disruptive behaviors. Students who are unable to successfully navigate situations in which they must share materials with others may become aggressive, taking materials from others or arguing. They may also become disengaged during opportunities to pair up with partners or when asked to participate in small groups. Understanding how social skills deficits can lead to disruptive classroom behaviors will allow you to support these students better. These students may be displaying "can't-do" behaviors because they have never learned how to enter a group or share materials.

Treating academic or social skills deficits as "won't do" in a manner that punishes students for not using skills they don't have will only exacerbate the problem, whereas setting these students up for success and taking the time to teach them the skills needed to effectively and appropriately complete these tasks will reduce the likelihood of future problems and provide them with skills they will use throughout their life.

> **Treating academic or social skills deficits as "won't do" in a manner that punishes a student for not using skills they don't have will only exacerbate the problem.**

Planned Ignoring

Planned ignoring, or not giving attention to certain behaviors, can be an effective strategy to decrease disruptions and the number of negative interactions you have with students. This strategy is particularly helpful for minor behaviors that seem like they occur to gain your attention (e.g., calling out, tantrums, acting silly). However, it is not a good strategy for more severe behavior problems or behaviors that are not to gain your attention (e.g., not completing work, walking around the classroom to avoid doing work). Ignoring attention-seeking behaviors and praising students exhibiting appropriate behaviors also helps you to have a higher rate of positive interactions and fewer negative interactions.

Begin by making a list of misbehaviors that can be ignored, keeping in mind that it is not effective to ignore behaviors that students use to avoid activities. We asked teachers to develop a list of behaviors they could ignore. Figure 8.9 shows a list of examples they came up with.

Planned ignoring sounds fairly simple until you try to do it. This strategy is an extinction strategy; in order for it to work, the behavior must be completely ignored (i.e., never acknowledged). Planned ignoring can be challenging because when first implemented, the target behavior will actually get worse before it gets better. As odd as this sounds, it is true. This is called an extinction burst. It is important to continue through this period in which it seems like the behaviors are getting worse. Take the instance of a student who has been calling out answers and has been acknowledged by the teacher for more than a month. Then, suddenly, the teacher no longer acknowledges the student when he calls out. The student becomes confused, thinking, "Perhaps the teacher didn't hear me," and calls out again and again, looking for the teacher to acknowledge him. Eventually, the student figures out that calling out no longer works and instead raises his hand when he has an answer, but this takes time. If the teacher gives in and acknowledges the student who calls out at the height of his increased calling-out, then this student learns that he just needs to call out more often and perhaps more loudly, making the behavior worse.

> Ignoring attention-seeking behaviors and praising students exhibiting appropriate behaviors also helps you to have a higher rate of positive interactions and fewer negative interactions.

In order to employ this strategy, (1) explain to the students what behavior you will ignore, why you are ignoring, and what they should do instead; (2) consistently ignore the behavior, even if it gets worse; (3) give attention/praise to students who behave correctly; and (4) provide precorrections to students who continue to struggle prior to challenging times of the day.

Response Cost

A response-cost system is one in which students lose a point or token as a result of misbehavior. If you use a token economy system, response-cost procedures can be put into place

- Calling out my name
- Interrupting
- Make noises when raising hand
- Following me around
- Interrupting guided reading
- Pouting, mini-tantrums
- Sighing
- Calling out
- Mumbling

FIGURE 8.9. Examples of behaviors teachers identified to ignore.

Coping Thoughts for Planned Ignoring

Using planned ignoring or extended ignoring strategies like time out can be taxing for teachers. When a behavior problem has persisted for a long time and it is suddenly put on extinction (ignored) the behavior will usually escalate initially. Sometimes these behaviors are very difficult to ignore because they are disruptive or because they push a teacher's buttons. To be effective, though, ignoring must be complete and must continue until the behavior stops and the student presents a new behavior that the teacher can acknowledge or praise. Teachers are sometimes surprised at how long some instances of ignoring can go on and how much a behavior consultant would advise them to ignore. If the student is safe and not harming others, it is best to continue ignoring.

Given these challenges, when using planned ignoring it can be helpful to use positive coping thoughts. For instance, when you are working at ignoring behaviors, you could think to yourself, "I can do this!," "This won't last forever," and "If I give my attention now, he will just learn that if he does it long enough he will get my attention." Some other examples of positive coping thoughts teachers have used to cope when ignoring misbehavior include the following.

An expert behavior consultant we know uses the mantra "It's all just behavior." By this she intends to remind herself not to take misbehavior personally. It also reminds her about her theory of behavior that tells her that all behavior has been learned and serves a purpose for the individual. It is simply a misrule that the environment has supported, and it is her task to help the student learn a new behavior and a new rule for when and how to get attention. By remembering that *it's all just behavior* she can focus on what she can do to change the environment rather than on feeling hurt or annoyed by the behavior.

"Time is on my side" is another excellent reminder for teachers. It is easy to feel pressured to act immediately in moments of ignoring or conflict in a classroom. In fact, being patient and giving students time to make better choices rather than demanding immediate compliance is a well-established effective approach to gaining compliance. Students are much more likely to be reactive and make poor decisions when they feel intimidated and pressured to act quickly. Waiting 5 seconds after giving a command, walking away rather than hovering over students, and then coming back to them gives them space and time to do the right thing. In a similar way, reminding yourself that *time is on your side* when ignoring keeps your attention focused on the endgame, and that eventually a new, more positive behavior will emerge for you to give attention.

Some other positive coping thoughts we have heard teachers use over the years include the following. Try one or more and see how it works for you.

- "All I need to do is figure out what is maintaining his behavior."
- "I might be the only positive model for these kids."
- "If I'm calm, kids are calm."
- "If I give up now he will just learn to persist longer than me."
- "I will focus on noticing and praising students who are meeting expectations."

to discourage student misbehavior. However, it is important to ensure that strategies for responding to appropriate behavior are in place before establishing a response-cost system, as this is a punitive strategy that is fairly intrusive. To begin, expectations for earning and losing points and rewards must be clear and precise. Second, reinforcers must be selected—the reward must be truly reinforcing. One of the main reasons that token economies with response cost do not work effectively is because the students do not care if they earn the reward (review using rewards and incentives above). Third, a system for informing the student or group of students when they have lost a point needs to be devised to avoid confusion. For instance, when students do not begin work right away following a signal to start, the teacher will simply say, "Please remember to get started right away; that's one point." The teacher will then cross off a point on the behavior management chart that is visible to the class. It is helpful to anticipate possible problems that will occur, such as students trying to explain their behavior or denying that they engaged in the problem behavior. You don't want to engage in lengthy explanations about these issues during instruction. To avoid this problem, devise a lesson plan to actively teach, model, practice, and praise students for behaving appropriately following removal of a point. Fourth, don't set up a system that allows students to go into debt or owe points back. Having students go into debt will increase the likelihood that students will feel like the system is impossible, will not find it reinforcing, and then will not care about earning points.

Importantly, if response cost is used excessively, to the point that the students feel like there is no way to earn the reward in a timely manner, then the students will give up and stop caring about losing points. In fact, it may increase disruptive behavior because the student will view the system as unfair and may lead them to retaliate. Given these important considerations, we suggest that response cost be used sparingly in classrooms and only after positive, proactive classroom strategies are solidly in place.

Time Out

Time out has been used across elementary and secondary settings. Although it has many different names depending on the setting ("thinking chair," "quiet space"), the underlying principles are the same. The purpose of time-out is to remove a misbehaving student from an opportunity to earn positive reinforcement. The overall goal is to communicate that if students disrupt the class, they do not get to participate in the interesting, productive, and enjoyable classroom activities that will continue without them. One important implication here is that classroom activities need to be interesting, productive, and enjoyable. If students behave inappropriately to get out of doing something, then time-out is much less effective because you are giving them what they want.

To set up this strategy in the classroom, identify a low-traffic area in the classroom. It can be as simple as a chair or desk set off to the side of the room. Next, develop a plan for how to teach the use of time-out to the students in the classroom. Include the rationale for time-out, how long the student will be expected to remain in time-out, and what will happen afterward. A successful time-out is one in which the student goes quietly to the area, completes the time-out without further disruption, and rejoins the class with no additional consequences.

For younger children, it can be helpful to have them practice going to time-out when they are not misbehaving. Older students may find the idea of time-out to be too childish. The teacher may want to use a sports example to show how adults use time-out. For instance, during hockey games if the player breaks the rules, there is a penalty box. In other sports, coaches use time-outs to help players regroup, calm down, and come up with a new plan. When teaching the students about time-out, it is important to explain what will happen if they continue to be disruptive or refuse to go to the time-out location (e.g., they will be sent out of the classroom and receive a disciplinary referral). As with all strategies to discourage behaviors, use a calm voice when sending students to time-out. When the time-out is over, it's over. We do not recommend having students apologize or explain to you what they did wrong that sent them to time-out. Instead give the signal to return (e.g., "China, come back to your desk; thank you") and continue with the activity at hand.

The purpose of the sections above is to help you develop a proactive plan for managing student behavior in your classroom. Having a solid plan will lead to successful student behaviors. This in turn will help you to feel more competent and efficacious in your teaching. Furthermore, reducing the number of disciplinary issues in your classroom will reduce stressful and negative interactions with students. The strategies we outlined above are universal, meaning that they will work with the majority of students in your classroom. However, there are often students in who do not respond to universal strategies. These students will need additional supports from you, and you may need additional support from

GROUP EXERCISE: Angel-Thought Role Plays

We have found that many teachers overestimate their skills at ignoring. It sounds simple, but when we ask them to demonstrate the skill, they are surprised at how completely they must ignore the student who is engaged in attention-seeking behavior. One of the best strategies for getting better at ignoring is to do role-play practices. In a group setting, ask a teacher about a student for whom she thinks ignoring would be an effective strategy. Have the teacher describe the specific behaviors she would like to ignore, then ask for a volunteer to play the part of the student. Ask the teacher to set up the role play, including when and where the behavior is most likely to occur. The teacher's task is to go about her routine without giving attention to the problem behavior and to persist until the student emits a new behavior. To help the teacher, ask for another volunteer to play the part of an angel who whispers coping thoughts to her while she is ignoring. The angel uses any or all of the coping statements described earlier to help keep the teacher calm and focused ("You're doing great," "Keep it up," "This will work," "Stick with it," etc.). These practices give the teacher ideas for coping in the moment and make it more likely these coping statements will become part of her repertoire. This strategy was developed by Carolyn Webster-Stratton in her Incredible Years series. Although role plays can feel uncomfortable at first, teachers nearly always love them after they try a few. The key is making them fun and focused on learning. They are an excellent teaching tool.

others in your schools for helping these students. The following section discusses students with challenging behaviors and offers a guide for more effectively managing these students in your classroom.

STUDENTS WITH CHALLENGING BEHAVIORS

Some students, despite your best proactive classroom management, will display persistent challenging behaviors. What we know about the science behind human behavior can help you cope better when students seem unmanageable. Key to understanding students with challenging behavior is that all behavior has a purpose. Behaviors not appropriate for the classroom persist or reoccur because they allow the student to meet a particular need.

To figure out how to intervene or prevent a challenging behavior, the first thing you can do is ask yourself, "What is the purpose of this behavior?" For instance, you may have encountered students who refuse to do work or who are always calling out the answer to questions before everyone else. The student who refuses to work is most likely trying to avoid a task she dislikes or struggles to complete. The student who constantly calls out is most likely trying to gain your attention. It is natural to want to avoid things we dislike or where we lack efficacy. Rather than thinking to yourself, "This student is being defiant or intentionally trying to upset me by not following directions," you can instead think to yourself, "This student needs something and that is why he or she is behaving this way." As noted in prior chapters, the way we think about a situation can affect the way we feel and behave. When students in your classroom act out and you take it personally or feel like they are intentionally trying to make you upset, you are more likely to have an emotional reaction to the situation. However, if you consider the behavior as a way for the student to gain something that they need, you will be a better problem solver. Consider the following examples:

> **Behaviors not appropriate for the classroom persist or re-occur because they allow the student to meet a particular need.**

> **Think to yourself, "This student needs something and that is why he or she is behaving this way."**

> Devon is a third-grade student who lives with his biological mother and four siblings. He often comes to school late. During teacher-led instruction, he frequently asks questions while the teacher is talking. During independent work, he has difficulty working alone. Instead, he will walk to the teacher asking questions and gaining assurances that his work is correct. His teacher notes that his work is accurate and that he is at grade level across subjects. However, his teacher finds that she spends a significant portion of her time interacting with Devon. She is concerned that he is taking time away from other students who truly need additional support in her classroom. When she redirects Devon and tells him that he can do the work on his own, he will begin to whine and cry, sometimes falling to the floor and disrupting the classroom.

What might be the purpose of Devon's needy behaviors?

Catherine is a very bright sixth-grade student. During class she often talks to peers, walks around the classroom, and disrupts others. This happens across academic subjects. Her teachers state that she is not engaged when they teach. Instead, during lessons she will often write and pass notes. Several of her teachers have sent her to the office for her disrespectful behaviors. They are frustrated by her behaviors because they disrupt other students. They report that she has no trouble keeping up with the assignments and turns in all work on time. Therefore, her grades are not affected by her behavior, but they feel she is a bad influence on other students and keeps them from learning at their potential.

What are some possible ideas for why Catherine is so disengaged in the classroom?

Sophia is a first-grade student and only child. In a recent parent–teacher conference, the teacher informed Sophia's parents that she is often defiant and refuses to transition from one task to another. In addition, the teacher reported that Sophia has trouble in writing. The drawings in her writing book are very elaborate, but she does not write more than five words. The teacher said she directs Sophia to write more words, but Sophia will tell the teacher that she doesn't know what to write or that she is still working on her drawing. The teacher showed several pages of writing in which the students were asked to write about what they did over the weekend to which Sophia has written, "I don't know." The teacher noted that other students in her class are writing two or three sentences at this point in the year. The parents were surprised to hear that Sophia was being defiant toward her teacher.

What are some reasons that Sophia is writing less than her classroom peers?

Each of these students presents behaviors that can disrupt classroom instruction and take away the teacher's time from doing other things. Handling persistent misbehavior in the classroom can be stressful, particularly if you are unclear about how to address the behavior. The first step to figuring out the best approach to working with students displaying challenging behaviors is to determine the purpose or function of their behavior. Once you understand what the student needs or wants, you can devise and employ strategies to help support the student. The most likely reasons for a student to exhibit challenging behaviors are (1) to gain attention from an adult or peers, (2) to avoid or escape something (e.g., academic work, uncomfortable social interaction), and (3) to obtain a tangible item (e.g., student pushes down a peer on the playground to get the ball). Some students display behaviors as a function of self-stimulation, but for most normally developing students, behaviors fall into the other three categories. The following provides a step-by-step guide for determining the function of challenging student behaviors. A blank version of the steps is provided in Handout 8.4.

- ***Step 1: Define the problem behavior(s).*** What does the challenging behavior(s) look like in your classroom? Give the behavior objective, specific qualities that describe it so well that if someone visits your classroom they will easily notice the behavior. Avoid terms like *disrespectful*, *irresponsible*, or *power struggle*, because they do not provide specifics about what the behavior looks like when the student is engaging in the behavior. The following are objective descriptions of the behaviors seen in the examples:

Devon: He interrupts the teacher. He repeatedly asks questions of the teacher and asks the teacher to review his work. He will cry, whine, and drop to the floor.

Catherine: She is off task. This behavior often looks like her talking to peers or passing notes to peers during inappropriate times.

Sophia: She will verbally complain or ignore teacher requests.

- **Step 2: Determine when this is most likely to happen.** What happens right before the behavior occurs? What time of day does it occur? Whom does it occur with? For behaviors that seem to occur all the time, when are they truly the worst?

Devon: During teacher-led instruction, he will interrupt the teacher. During independent work he will ask questions excessively. He will cry, whine, and drop to the floor when the teacher tells him to work on his own. It is more likely to happen in the morning than the afternoon.

Catherine: During academic instruction across all subject areas, she will engage in off-task behaviors with peers.

Sophia: She will complain and ignore requests from the teacher during writing time and when she is asked to transition from one activity to another.

- **Step 3: Determine when the behavior is least likely to happen.** When and with whom is the student less likely to exhibit the behavior?

Devon: He is less likely to ask questions, request reassurances, whine, cry, or drop to the floor when he is working with the teacher independently or with the teacher in a small group of students. His school counselor indicated that he does not display these behaviors when he meets with her individually to discuss his behaviors.

Catherine: One teacher noticed that she was more engaged when the topic was new and challenging. Another teacher noticed the behaviors were less likely to occur when she was working with a small group of peers and helping them to understand the content.

Sophia: She is less likely to complain or ignore teacher requests to transition during math, reading, and science, particularly when they do not involve illustrating or drawing.

- **Step 4: Determine what happens after the behavior.** What happens when the student uses the behavior in the classroom? What do you do? What do peers do? What does the student get out of doing it? What does the student obtain?

Devon: When he asks questions, requests reassurance, or cries, the teacher provides him with attention either through answering questions, providing him feedback, or reprimanding him for the behavior.

Catherine: When she engages in off-task behaviors, she avoids academic tasks and gets attention from her peers.

Sophia: When she complains or ignores her teacher's requests to transition from drawing to writing, she avoids writing. She also is able to continue with a preferred activity.

- *Step 5: Determine the function based on the information in Steps 1 to 4.* Is the behavior most likely attention seeking, to escape something or someone, or to get obtain something tangible/physical?

Devon: His behavior most likely serves the purpose of gaining adult attention.

Catherine: Her behavior is slightly more complex in that she is escaping tasks that she does not prefer while gaining peer attention.

Sophia: Her behavior is avoiding tasks she prefers less than others.

- *Step 6: Develop a function-based plan.* Now that you know the purpose of the behavior, come up with a plan that will allow the student to meet this need without using the challenging behavior. One important component typically is teaching the student a new behavior that serves the same function as the challenging behavior. There is no one-fit solution for all students. Therefore, it is helpful to consider what is known about the students, the resources available at your school, and what strategies will fit best with you and your classroom. For some students, it can help to engage a team of individuals in the planning and execution of the plan. This is particularly true for students who are aggressive or display dangerous behaviors. Your school may have a behavior support team or student assistance team to which you can refer more challenging students or those not responding to your initial plans to support their behaviors.

There is no one-fit solution for all students.

Devon: When you think about Devon's case, one thing to consider is that he lives with his single mother and four siblings. He may be seeking attention from his teacher because his mother has limited time to give him individual attention at home. Thus he comes to school seeking out this needed attention. A few ideas come to mind when working with him. Since his behavior is worse in the morning, the teacher could set aside 5 minutes in the morning to meet individually with Devon and ask him about his day and teach/remind him to raise his hand and wait for her to come to him when he needs her help, encourage him to do his best work, and share with him times when he was successful in the past. The teacher could also send a note home to his mother at the end of the day describing the things that he did well, asking that she praise him for his success. In addition to giving him individualized attention, the teacher needs to ignore times when he does not raise his hand or asks for feedback too frequently, which teaches Devon that these behaviors do not result in attention. The teacher can also try to provide him with unsolicited attention by praising him for working alone, listening quietly, and doing his best work.

Catherine: Unusual aspects of Catherine's case were that the behavior occurred across subjects and that she had no problems in completing her assignments, and she still earned good grades despite being disengaged. Additionally, she seemed to be more engaged when the topic was new or she was helping small peer groups learn the content. Her behavior of avoiding instruction could indicate that she is bored and not challenged by the content. A possible solution would be for the teachers to develop more challenging assignments for Catherine to complete. She could have the option of working on these tasks during instructional times rather than engage with peers. In addition, they could take advantage of her interest in peer attention by having her take on a leadership role to help others in the classroom or tutor peers or younger students. She would need to be taught how to effectively help other students. Also, finding ways to pique her interest in the content by including examples that are of interest to her could potentially increase her engagement.

Sophia: Sophia seemed to find drawing really enjoyable and writing less so. She was avoiding writing or transitioning from drawing. One strategy would be to allow Sophia to draw once she completed a certain amount of work. Initially it would be important to allow her to avoid some writing because that is the function or purpose of her behavior. The teacher could have her write one sentence and then draw. As time goes on the teacher can increase the amount of writing that must be completed before Sophia is allowed to draw (e.g., two sentences, three sentences). The teacher or other school personnel (e.g., school psychologist), could meet with her to teach her the plan of writing before drawing. In addition, the teacher may consider varying the writing content for Sophia. If she is unable to think of something to write about the weekend, perhaps she could simply write a funny story. Another option is to give a starter sentence to get her going with her writing (e.g., I had so much fun when . . .). Lastly, to support her in other transitions, the teacher could use a timer or give a 5-minute warning before the transition, making sure the Sophia is clear that the transition will be coming up and what the expectation is for the next activity (an individualized precorrection).

The purpose of this section was to give you a different way of thinking about student behaviors. Understanding why these behaviors occur can be very helpful and empowering when you strive to support the students in your classroom. Working with the school psychologists, behavior specialist, or other school personnel or school team may be warranted for some students. However, this function-based framework for thinking about student behavior can be used with any student at any time. A list of additional resources is provided at the end of this chapter for ideas of classroom management strategies and tailored or individualized interventions for students with more challenging behaviors.

PROFESSIONAL DEVELOPMENT

Staying abreast of the most up-to-date methods for supporting student emotional, behavioral, and academic success can be stressful in itself. Knowing how to discern innovative and effective practices can be difficult. Furthermore, figuring out how to incorporate new practices into your classroom also is challenging. The following section provides a brief overview of things to look for when you have options in the type of professional development you receive. In addition, we discuss some models for helping you translate what you learn in professional development trainings to your classroom.

What we know about professional development is that one-shot training sessions are not the most effective way for teachers to learn a new skill or strategy (see Fixen, Naoom, Blase, Friedman, & Wallace, 2005). Teachers who receive training by attending one workshop are less likely than teachers who received training with ongoing support (e.g., coaching) to use new strategies in their classrooms. In addition, trainings that are interactive (e.g., use role play, encourage dialogue) and allow time for practice and reflection are more effective than trainings that do not use these strategies. While a lot of good information can be gained from attending a workshop, particularly on a relevant and useful topic, it can be difficult to translate the information learned into classroom practices. Any new skill takes practice and rehearsal to fully develop. In addition, anything new introduced in the classroom affects not only you, but also the students. Students will also need time to adjust to new strategies or ideas. The complexities of the classroom create challenges for beginning and maintaining new skills in the classroom.

Consultation and Coaching

One promising method for supporting teachers in their use of new skills and strategies in their classroom is coaching or ongoing consultation. There are at least three key reasons underlying the need for coaching. Newly learned skills are (1) crude compared to performance by a master practitioner; (2) fragile and need to be supported in the face of reactions from students, parents, and others; and (3) incomplete and need to be shaped to be most functional in the actual classroom setting (Fixen et al., 2005). The form coaching takes varies, but it tends to include a combination of the following: planning, teaching, modeling, and practicing new skills; observation of implementation of targeted practices in the classroom; feedback on implementation performance; and reflection.

Peer Coaching

Some school districts have coaches who work with teachers to develop new skills (e.g., instructional coach, PBIS coach). School psychologists are also trained in consultation and can be utilized to help support new practices in the classroom. However, if your school does not have coaches readily available, you can consider peer coaching.

Teaming up with someone in your building can be an effective way to improve your classroom management and instruction while feeling supported. Teachers can learn from one another by visiting one another's classrooms. Observing in one another's classrooms during a time of the day when you are working to develop a new skill (e.g., new instructional strategy or during a time when students are difficult to manage behaviorally) can produce ideas for overcoming challenges. Having a second set of eyes can be very helpful in spotting your strengths and areas that would benefit from improvement. Both teachers commit to supporting one another in implementing new practices in their classrooms by observing one another, providing feedback on what went well and what could be improved, and problem solving around challenges to implementing new strategies in the classroom. The approach can reduce the feelings of isolation and stress by allowing for time to reflect with someone who knows the challenges you face and goals you have for your classroom and students.

> **Teaming up with someone in your building can be an effective way to improve your classroom management and instruction while feeling supported.**

One of the most important aspects of coaching is the use of performance feedback. To be helpful, this feedback needs to be specific, objective, and delivered shortly after the observation. Thus, prior to visiting the classroom it is important to discuss exactly what you will observe (e.g., use of behavior-specific praise and planned ignoring of calling out). Next, when visiting one another's classrooms take notes, gather data, and notice strengths as well as areas to improve. The data should be specific to the skill and associated outcomes. For instance, if you were trying to increase your use of behavior-specific praise and increase your ratio of positive to negative statements in your classroom, you would have the peer coach tally the number of times you use behavior-specific praise and the number of times you reprimand or correct a student. These data could be used to determine your ratio during that observation period. In addition, your peer coach could give your feedback on the quality of your praise and interactions with students. Your partner could also give you feedback on the types of disruptions that occurred in the classroom, including how often they occurred. Using a form to guide the observation can be helpful. Figure 8.10 provides a very general form that can be adapted according to the purpose of the observation. Such a form can be delivered to you immediately after the observation or used to guide feedback to one another either verbally in person, via e-mail, or in a note.

Goal Setting

Goal setting is an effective practice for improving your competence and efficacy. Identifying areas of your teaching (or personal life) that you want to improve and setting goals toward making these improvements is an aspect of professional development that you can institute with or without the support of a coach or training. Attaining important goals can be fulfilling. You want to ensure your goals challenge you but are also feasible. To begin, identify an area you want to improve, determine the ultimate goal for this area (e.g., "I want to have a 4:1 positive-

> **Identifying areas of your teaching (or personal life) that you want to improve and setting goals toward making these improvements is an aspect of professional development.**

What went well?	What could be improved?	Data (tallies for frequency, duration, time between occurrences)
General comments:		

FIGURE 8.10. Peer coaching observation form.

to-negative ratio every day of the week"), and work backward from this goal with smaller, feasible goals (e.g., "I will have a 2:1 ratio in my classroom at least three days a week"). Once the smaller goal is met, celebrate! Next, create another small goal toward the ultimate end goal (e.g., "I will have at least a 2:1 ratio in my classroom each day"). Be sure to celebrate and enjoy your successes. Often we are well aware of our faults. Spend time with your successes. Reward yourself for meeting goals. Keep developing feasible smaller goals toward meeting your end goal. When you realize the ultimate goal, be sure to reinforce yourself, just like you would your students.

> ### IF YOU DO ONLY ONE THING: What Went Well in Your Classroom
>
> In Chapter 2 we introduced "Building Positive Emotions—What Went Well." Here, we ask you to do that exercise again, but focus specifically on what went well in your classroom. For the next several nights before you go to bed, take a moment to reflect back on the day. Keep a tablet, piece of paper, journal, or an electronic device you are comfortable writing on next to your bed. Write down three things that went well in your class that day and why; why it went well, why your enjoyed it, and why you experienced it in a positive way. You don't have to write for long, but it is important that you spend time thinking deeply about what happened, why, and what caused it to happen. Within a few days, you will notice a difference in your ability to tune your feelings to be more positive. Give it a try!

> **GROUP ACTIVITY: Setting Goals for Improvement**
>
> Lead a group activity in which each person writes down three areas they would like to receive additional support or training. Then have a group discussion where each person tells the group one or more of the areas he or she would like to target. Write the areas on a white board or flip chart. Note any common areas across teachers, then have teachers group up by areas they would like to target for additional training and support. Have the groups brainstorm goals and potential strategies for improving their skills in the target area. Have the groups share their ideas with the full group. Take turns having teachers describe how they feel improving their skills in a particular area will support their wellness and reduce stress.

SUMMARY

Feeling competent and efficacious are important aspects of reducing your stress. Because so many teachers identify classroom management and challenging student behaviors as major stressors, this chapter focused on ideas for planning and improving skills in these areas. An important aspect of managing student behavior is also providing relevant and effective instruction. Therefore, professional development focused on instruction is as important. We discussed professional development, coaching to support transfer of new skills to the classroom, and goal setting. Taking the time to plan, learn, and improve as a professional will keep you at the top of your game, which in turn can help toward reducing job-related stress.

RESOURCES

There are many other resources that you may find helpful in expanding your knowledge and repertoire of evidence-based classroom management practices that support teachers with students who exhibit challenging behaviors. Below we list additional resources you may wish to consult.

Crone, D., Hawken, L., & Horner, R. (2010). *Responding to problem behavior in schools: The Behavior Education Program* (2nd ed.). New York: Guilford Press.

Crone, D., & Horner, R. (2003). *Building positive behavior support systems in schools: Functional behavioral assessment.* New York: Guilford Press.

Doll, B., Brehm, K., & Zucker, S. (2014). *Resilient classrooms: Creating healthy environments for learning* (2nd ed.). New York: Guilford Press.

Good, T., & Brophy, J. (2003). *Looking in classrooms* (9th ed.). New York: Allyn & Bacon.

Rathvon, N. (2008). *Effective school interventions: Evidence-based strategies for improving student outcomes.* New York: Guilford Press.

Reinke, W. M., Herman, K. C., & Sprick, R. (2011). *Motivational interviewing for effective classroom management: The Classroom Check-Up.* New York: Guilford Press.

Sprick, R., Knight, J., Reinke, W., Skyles, T., & Barnes, L. (2010). *Coaching classroom management: Strategies and tools for administrators and coaches.* Eugene, OR: Pacific Northwest.

Sprick, R., Booher, M., & Garrison, M. (2009). *Behavioral response to intervention: Creating a continuum of problem solving and support.* Eugene, OR: Pacific Northwest.

Sprick, R. (2008). *CHAMPS: A proactive and positive approach to classroom management* (2nd ed.). Eugene, OR: Pacific Northwest.

Sprick, R., & Garrison, M. (2008). *Interventions: Evidence-based behavioral strategies for individual students* (2nd ed.). Eugene, OR: Pacific Northwest.

Sprick, R. (2006). *Discipline in the secondary classroom: A positive approach to behavior management* (2nd ed.). Eugene, OR: Pacific Northwest.

Stormont, M., Reinke, W. M., Herman, K. C., & Lemke, E. (2012). *Academic and behavior supports for at-risk students: Tier 2 interventions.* New York: Guilford Press.

Webster-Stratton, C. (1999). *How to promote children's social and emotional competence.* Los Angeles: Sage.

HANDOUT 8.1

Assessment of Teacher–Student Relationships

Question	Answer
What are the first and last names of all the students I teach?	
Can I describe one thing that each student in my classroom likes and dislikes? Create a list of likes and dislikes for each student.	
How are students different and alike in my classroom? How might their cultural backgrounds be different from my own/from each other?	
How do I show that I value the perspectives of my students?	
How do I make learning fun in my classroom?	

(continued)

From *Stress Management for Teachers: A Proactive Guide* by Keith C. Herman and Wendy M. Reinke. Copyright 2015 by The Guilford Press. Permission to photocopy this handout is granted to purchasers of this book for personal use only (see copyright page for details). Purchasers can download and print additional copies of this handout from *www.guilford.com/herman-forms*.

Assessment of Teacher–Student Relationships *(page 2 of 2)*

Question	Answer
How do my students know that I care for them?	
How do I encourage students to cooperate with one another/be supportive of each other?	
Which students have friendships with one another? Which students have fewer friends?	
How do I communicate with parents/caregivers the positive accomplishments of their child?	
How often do I communicate with parents/caregivers of the students in my classroom?	

HANDOUT 8.2

Plan for Teaching Classroom Rules

Expectation:	
Teach by providing a verbal explanation of the rule.	
Model a positive example of the rule.	
Model a negative example of the rule.	
Practice by having a student or students demonstrate the rule.	
Praise students when they demonstrate the rule correctly.	

From *Stress Management for Teachers: A Proactive Guide* by Keith C. Herman and Wendy M. Reinke. Copyright 2015 by The Guilford Press. Permission to photocopy this handout is granted to purchasers of this book for personal use only (see copyright page for details). Purchasers can download and print additional copies of this handout from *www.guilford.com/herman-forms*.

HANDOUT 8.3

Plan for Teaching Classroom Routines and Tasks

Routine/Task:	
Teach by providing a verbal explanation of the routine or task.	
Model a positive example.	
Model a negative example.	
Practice by having a student or students demonstrate the routine or task.	
Praise students when they meet expectations.	

From *Stress Management for Teachers: A Proactive Guide* by Keith C. Herman and Wendy M. Reinke. Copyright 2015 by The Guilford Press. Permission to photocopy this handout is granted to purchasers of this book for personal use only (see copyright page for details). Purchasers can download and print additional copies of this handout from *www.guilford.com/herman-forms*.

HANDOUT 8.4

Step-by-Step Guide for Determining the Function of Student Behavior

Student Name: _____ **Date:** _____

Step 1: Define the problem behavior(s). What does the challenging behavior(s) *look like* in your classroom?
Step 2: Determine when this is most likely to happen. What happens right before the behavior occurs? What time of day does it occur? Whom does it occur with? For behaviors that seem to occur all the time, when are they truly the worst?
Step 3: Determine when the behavior is least likely to happen. When and with whom is the student less likely to exhibit the behavior?

(continued)

From *Stress Management for Teachers: A Proactive Guide* by Keith C. Herman and Wendy M. Reinke. Copyright 2015 by The Guilford Press. Permission to photocopy this handout is granted to purchasers of this book for personal use only (see copyright page for details). Purchasers can download and print additional copies of this handout from *www.guilford.com/herman-forms*.

Step-by-Step Guide for Determining the Function of Student Behavior *(page 2 of 2)*

Step 4: Determine what happens after the behavior. What happens when the student uses the behavior in the classroom? What do you do? What do peers do? What does the student get out of doing it? What does the student obtain?

Step 5. Determine the function based on the information in Steps 1 to 4. Is the behavior most likely attention seeking, to escape something or someone, or to obtain something tangible/physical?

Step 6. Develop a function-based plan. Remember to teach the student a new behavior that meets the same purpose or function as determined in Step 5. Include information about who will be responsible for implementing the plan.

CHAPTER 9

Beyond Survival
Getting to Good

Prior chapters have focused on the nuts and bolts of managing stress and getting through difficult times. Of course, life is about more than survival and just getting by. Over the past several decades, much attention has been directed toward exploring optimal human functioning. This work has emerged from the field of positive psychology, but many of these ideas have taken shape over the past century as an outgrowth of humanistic approaches to the world. In fact, the foundation for much of the work can be traced to ancient approaches to mindfulness and meditation. In this chapter, we explore these ideas and present strategies for experiencing optimal functioning, life satisfaction, happiness, and contentment on a regular basis, a goal we refer to as *getting to good*.

GETTING TO GOOD

By now, we hope you have found some useful strategies for reducing your stress and coping better with adversity. This was likely a goal you set for yourself in an earlier chapter. If so, celebrate and acknowledge your accomplishment. Continuing to use these skills, and remembering to use them, will be another goal you may set for yourself.

At some point, you may decide you are coping well enough and you want to focus on personal growth and optimizing your functioning. Just like the absence of illness is not the same as health, reduced stress is not equivalent to happiness and well-being. If experiencing happiness and contentment on a more regular basis is important to you, the topics and skills of this chapter will be of interest to you.

Getting to good refers to that elusive concept of the *good life*, immortalized by the philosophical writings of Aristotle. The good life encompasses a sense of life satisfaction and happiness. Essentially, the good life implies living the life one hopes to live in the fullest sense of the word—morally, spiritually, and as part of the larger world. Popular definitions of the term have focused more on the material aspects of having all the modern luxuries one could hope to accumulate. Such definitions are far astray from the meaning intended here.

> **Essentially, the good life implies living the life one hopes to live in the fullest sense of the word—morally, spiritually and as part of the larger world.**

Abraham Maslow referred to this process of optimizing self as self-actualization many decades ago. His ideas emphasized the importance of a hierarchy of needs that must be satisfied before humans are capable of this higher level of fulfillment and purpose. In a similar way, the TCM emphasizes the basic aspects of coping that form the foundation for higher levels of functioning. For Maslow, these needs included basic needs like food and shelter and social needs for love and belonging. Only when these are met are we capable of actualizing our full selves. One could argue about the cultural variability of these concepts, especially the notion of self-actualization, which is a Western ideal that may not fit well with collective cultural values of harmony and connectedness to family and society. That is, optimal functioning is partly defined by the cultural context in which it occurs.

The eminent positive psychology scholar Mihaly Csikszentmihalyi described a particular type of optimal human experience that he called *flow*. He based his theory of flow on observations of artists who were fully immersed in their work. He extended these observations to other human activities and discovered this distinct type of human experience. It occurs when we are completely immersed in an activity, when our attention is entirely focused on the moment and the activity, and time is distorted, seemingly moving faster or slower during the experience. Flow can occur during any activity, although is most likely to happen when we are doing things we most enjoy and that involve action rather than being passive (like when we take a bath or watch TV). It is also more likely to occur in activities that we are good at, as one component of flow is a strong sense of perceived control over the outcome of the activity. Csikszentmihalyi suggested flow experiences were most likely to occur in activities that involved an intersection between a high level of challenge and a high level of skill. In this sense, flow emerges when we are engaged in an activity that we do well and it is at the edge of our skill level.

> ***Flow*** **occurs when we are completely immersed in an activity, when our attention is entirely focused on the moment and the activity, and time is distorted.**

Perhaps you have experienced moments of flow in your teaching, where you become fully involved in a challenging teaching task that you are mastering, lose track of time, center your entire awareness in the moment without self-consciousness, and experience a deep sense of enjoyment and fulfillment in the experience. You may have experienced flow in other activities of your life, such as your hobbies or relationships. Moments of flow can be rich and highly desirable human experiences that bring us great fulfillment and satisfaction.

Martin Seligman (2002, 2011) was deeply influenced by the work of Csikszentmihalyi in his efforts to broaden the scope and influence of positive psychology. Seligman articulated the aspects of these ideas in his own research and several popular books. The terms he has used to describe similar phenomena include *authentic happiness* and *flourishing*. Seligman and his colleagues have developed methods for achieving these states and experiences, several of which we describe below.

In his original conceptualization of positive psychology, Seligman focused on the concept of *authentic happiness*, by which he meant achieving a state of engagement with the self and the world of life satisfaction, and pursuit of self and world happiness. He later realized this concept excluded some other critical aspects of well-being and optimal functioning, which he came to refer to as *flourishing*. Flourishing encompasses five dimensions: positive emotion, engagement, relationships, meaning and purpose, and accomplishment.

Positive emotion refers to the domain we have spent much time focusing on in this book. Increasing your experience of calmness and happiness while reducing stress and anxiety are the elements of positive emotion. By *engagement*, Seligman means attending to your strengths and virtues and using them as resources in your daily life. *Relationships* refer to our social being and having a sense of connectedness and bonding with others. *Meaning* is the aspect of flourishing whereby we come to view ourselves as being connected to and serving some greater purpose beyond ourselves. Finally, *achievement* means goal-centered flourishing.

In Seligman's view, humans are more likely to attain a state of flourishing when they attend to all five of these domains. They are able to attain a higher level of life satisfaction and contentment, more frequent moments of flow, and a sense of well-being that goes well beyond simply surviving.

MINDFULNESS

Many of these modern conceptions of optimal human functioning can be traced to ancient ideas about mindfulness, a concept that comes from Eastern meditative approaches. It refers to a state of fully being in the moment of one's life, centered in thought and action in the now, rather than in the past or future. In this chapter, we focus on mindfulness as the next building block in *getting to good*. It is, as you will see, an elusive concept that represents both the end and the beginning of higher states of being. All of this will be familiar, and all of this will be new. Approach this section of the book with new eyes, learning it for the first time, and also bring all your skills and virtues to bear in achieving even higher states of functioning. To begin, try the exercise involving mindful eating on the next page.

> **Mindfulness refers to a state of fully being in the moment of one's life, centered in thought and action in the now, rather than in the past or future.**

Mindful eating is often an enlightening experience for people. First, it helps dispel some common myths about mindfulness. People often picture mindfulness involving secluded mediation in a dark and quiet place. While this can be the case, mindfulness can be incorporated into every life experience. Second, many people notice things about raisins

> **Mindfulness Eating Exercise for Individuals or Groups**
>
> Mindfulness is a way of being you can enter at any time and with any activity. To experience it, try this exercise developed by Jon Kabat-Zinn (2013) as part of his acclaimed stress and coping program at UMass Hospital. You will need a box of raisins for this activity. Pour a few raisins into the palm of your hand and study them. Feel them in your hand and note how heavy or light they feel, how rough or smooth they are, and any other aspects of their texture. Examine each of them with your eyes, noting their color and any unusual aspects of them that you may have never noticed before. Do this for several minutes. Then bring them closer to your nose and smell them. Notice the aroma and any distinct smells about them. Place one on your lip and note the texture and smells again. Bring one into your mouth and let it rest on your tongue. What flavors do you taste without biting it? Move it around to different spots on your tongue. Are there places on your tongue where the flavors are stronger or weaker? Now bite it and chew it slowly, noticing any changes in texture and taste with each bite. After a dozen or more chews, swallow it and repeat the process with the remaining raisins.

for the first time, even though they may have eaten them their entire lives. For instance, were you surprised to discover that many raisins have stems on them from their earlier form as grapes? Perhaps you noticed new tastes and textures to a raisin that you had not been aware of before. We can use this type of mindful reflection to notice all aspects of our experience in new ways. Third, people often have an "a-ha" experience or realization that they can do this mindfulness thing. It is simply a matter of learning to pay attention. You've already made great progress in that regard. Now let's layer your awareness with an attitude of acceptance.

Paradox

In many ways, everything you have learned to this point in the TCM is the foundation for mindfulness. In another sense, though, you will have to unlearn everything in the TCM to be fully mindful. It is this paradox that is at the core of truly mindful being. The awareness habits that you have cultivated to this point will continue to serve you well as you become even more mindful. Awareness habits are the foundation for all aspects of mindfulness and well-being. At the same time, the intentionality and goal setting focus that we have encouraged you to take in this book are antithetical to a truly mindful way of being. In fact, some mindfulness training programs ask participants to set specific goals at the start of the program and then tell them to spend the rest of the program *not* trying to achieve them. Purposefulness and intentionality serve us well in many aspects of life, including when we are intending to make important changes in our life. Acceptance, another key element of mindfulness, serves us better for many of the challenges we endure. In mindfulness, we combine a heightened sense of awareness with an attitude of acceptance and nonjudgment to achieve fuller states of being.

Mindful Breathing

As before, mindfulness practice usually begins with the breath. To enter a state of mindfulness, you will need to approach your breathing in a different way than we have taught you thus far. Try the following practice.

Close your eyes and take a moment to attend to your breathing. Unlike before, do not try to influence it, just observe it and breathe naturally. Study your breathing, noticing how the air enters your nose or mouth, how it feels in your lungs, how your stomach or chest expands, how it sounds and tastes, and any other experiences that go along with your breathing. Do this now for several minutes. If your mind starts to wander simply redirect it back to your breath.

What was this experience like for you? Was it easy or hard to simply focus on your breath for this amount of time? Most people find this task very challenging. If you have been doing some of the relaxation and imagery exercises along the way, we suspect it may have been easier for you. Regardless, most people find their thoughts drifting away from their breath to other thoughts, other demands on their time, or worries.

Aspects of Mindfulness

This experience contains all of the elements of mindfulness. A fundamental aspect of mindfulness is an ever-present awareness of the now and a focus on this moment rather than on the past or future. By focusing on your breath, you are training yourself to attend to the here and now of existence. Too often in life, we ignore or miss the present with our attention focused on all that we have to do or on the worries of the future and hurts of the past. This ongoing mental turmoil can take an enormous toll on our bodies and well-being, as we have established in earlier chapters. Quite often this translates into a lack of awareness of our own body and how it is being affected by our environment and our interactions with others.

In addition to awareness, mindfulness also involves a willingness simply to observe how things are without trying to change them. Learning to let go and allow things to be without trying to control or influence them as we observe brings us closer to a mindful way of being. It is often this struggle to control and shape all aspects of our lives that creates the most enduring stress for us. In being mindful, we learn to let go and truly relax as we come to see the world and its challenges with fresh eyes.

In his book *Full Catastrophe Living*, Jon Kabat-Zinn (2013) identified seven attitudes that go along with a mindful orientation: nonjudging, patience, beginner's mind, trust, nonstriving, acceptance, and letting go. As we observe and pay attention to the moment, we bring these seven attitudes to our awareness. The first of these is *nonjudging*. As you pay attention to your own breathing and life experience through a mindful lens, it may surprise

> **Learning to let go and simply allow things to be without trying to control or influence them as we observe brings us closer to a mindful way of being.**

you to notice how much judgment we bring to most of our daily observations. Perhaps you became aware of this habit to some extent when you learned more about common types of maladaptive thinking, most of which involves some form of judgment. We judge ourselves and others, our experiences, places, and things as good, bad, helpful, or neutral. Becoming more aware of this habit is a first step to allowing yourself to suspend these types of judgments in mindfulness practice.

Patience is a virtue and a type of wisdom. In mindfulness, it is a practice that reminds us that mindfulness will come in time and with practice. *Beginner's mind* refers to a willingness to see and experience things as if for the first time. When we live our lives on autopilot, we often gloss over daily experiences and ignore or miss the subtleties of existence. With beginner's mind, we tell ourselves to try to see and experience things anew and discover what we may have missed. In the mindful eating exercise, perhaps you never noticed before that raisins have stems; by approaching your eating mindfully and with beginner's mind, you discover all sorts of aspects of existence that have been flowing beneath your awareness.

Trust involves trusting yourself and your experience, that they are guiding you where you need to be. *Nonstriving* is an important aspect of mindfulness. When we are mindful, our only goal is to be more fully ourselves. It does not work to say, "I'm going to be more mindful so that I can lose weight or so that I can be a better person." Mindfulness is nondoing. It is simply being in the moment.

Acceptance refers to learning to accept things as they are, including yourself. In mindfulness it serves no purpose for us to be angry with ourselves for being overweight or for some other malady. Quite often, it is this angst and judgment about ourselves that keeps us in the same place. When we learn to accept ourselves as we are, we often only then are able to change. Acceptance includes taking the "shoulds" and "musts" out of our vocabulary and simply allowing things to be. Finally, *letting go* refers to a form of nonattachment in which we allow our thoughts to flow without trying to hold on to some and push others aside.

Practicing Mindfulness

You can be mindful in any activity, at any time of day. As you begin cultivating this way of being, however, it is a good habit to set aside a time and space for mindful meditation. Plan on devoting 10 to 20 minutes each day where you allow yourself to be mindful. You can do this by finding a quiet and comfortable space, getting into a comfortable position, closing your eyes, and paying attention to your breathing. Bring your full awareness to your breath and practice the seven attitudes as you allow yourself simply to be for the entire practice session. At first, this will be challenging for you if you have never done it before. As with any skill, you will find it becomes easier with practice. As you begin to acquire the skill and you get better at adopting the seven attitudes, you will find yourself using it during your daily routines. Expand your mindfulness habits outside of your daily practice sessions to include mindful walking, eating, sitting, and other routines.

VALUES, VIRTUES, AND AFFIRMATIONS

Getting to good also involves becoming more mindful of who you truly are in the fullest sense. Your values and your virtues define some of your most important attributes, but we sometimes lose sight of what those are. In this section, we ask you to take some time to get to know yourself better.

Values Card Sort

Values card sort activities involve taking time to reflect on the values that are most salient for you and then thinking or talking about why each is important to you. Your values encompass many aspects of who you are and who you want to be. Held within each of our values are passions and energy that we can call forth to move ourselves to do better and more in life. Often we let our values sit beneath the surface, guiding us. By calling them forth and bringing them into awareness we can find a spark to energize us.

Read over the following list of values and sort them into the following categories: Most Important, Important, and Not Important. You can write these on separate pieces of paper and sort them that way or simply use a coding system. For instance, you put an "X" next to the most important ones, a " / " through those that are important, and leave the not important ones blank.

> **Often we let our values sit beneath the surface, guiding us. By calling them forth and bringing them into awareness we can find a spark to energize us.**

- ☐ Accepting differences in people
- ☐ Being a good teacher
- ☐ Working hard
- ☐ Taking time for myself
- ☐ Being organized
- ☐ Being happy
- ☐ Not giving up
- ☐ Being healthy
- ☐ Being honest
- ☐ Being responsible
- ☐ Being liked by everyone
- ☐ Being a leader
- ☐ Being respected by others
- ☐ Doing the right thing
- ☐ Being a lifelong learner
- ☐ Being a role model
- ☐ Having fun
- ☐ Having a safe classroom
- ☐ Feeling good about myself
- ☐ Being a good colleague
- ☐ Communicating effectively
- ☐ Being aware of personal biases
- ☐ Being self-reflective
- ☐ Relating to students
- ☐ Understanding others
- ☐ Being a good listener
- ☐ Being fair
- ☐ Taking care of my family
- ☐ Helping others
- ☐ Staying in control
- ☐ Making a difference in the world
- ☐ Being real/genuine
- ☐ Being patient
- ☐ Being kind
- ☐ Being flexible

After reading, sort all of them into one of these three categories, and look back over the ones you rated most important. Read each of these again and select the three most important values to you. It can be challenging to narrow your values down in this way, but it is a useful exercise. If you cannot select just the top three, choose any three of your most important values.

Now, take a moment to write down why each of these three values is important to you. Be specific. Carry these values with you throughout the day. Write them somewhere where you will see them and be reminded about them. Think about how you can use these values in your daily life as resources.

Exploring Your Virtues

What are your virtues? What do you do well, and even more, what do you contribute to the world? How often do you take time to seriously contemplate these virtues? If you haven't done so already, take time now to complete the VIA test described in an earlier chapter. Go to *www.viame.org/survey/Account/Register* and complete the VIA Inventory of Strengths (developed by Christopher Peterson and Martin Seligman). You will need to register your name and create a password, but the survey and results are free. The survey will ask you a series of questions about qualities and whether these qualities are like you or not. At the end of the survey, you will receive a strengths profile. These will be the qualities that most define your virtues.

Values and Virtues Affirmations

Research has shown that taking time to reflect on your values and ways that you demonstrate them can lead to real and lasting positive changes for people. In particular, Reed

---

GROUP ACTIVITY

Do the values card sort in your groups. Pair off and take turns with one of you as the sorter and the other as the listener. For this exercise, it is best to write the values on separate cards that can be sorted into the three categories. Follow the steps above, with the person assigned as sorter placing each of the values into one of the piles: Most Important, Important, or Not Important. Pick up the Most Important pile and then sort these again until you have your final three most important values. Now tell the listener why each of those final three values is important to you. The role of the listener is to listen! Reflect back what you hear the person saying ("You get energized when you recall what led you to become a teacher in the first place"). Offer affirmations ("That makes sense" or "I can see why that is important to you") and ask clarifying questions as needed to fully understand what they are saying ("Tell me more about that"). Finally, summarize what you hear the person saying ("So making a difference, doing good in the world, and helping children are your most important values. And these values have shaped who you are as a person and professional").

and Aspinwall (1998) and Armitage, Harris, Hepton, and Napper (2008) have developed some self-affirmation manipulations to encourage adaptive functioning. Essentially, they ask participants in their studies to elaborate on their past acts of kindness. Read and answer the statements in Handout 9.1. For each statement that you respond "yes," write a specific example that illustrates the point. Make your response as detailed as you can. The point is to encourage you to actively think about specific instances when you were kind to others.

Immediately after completing this activity, set a goal for yourself of something you would like to change or improve. Self-improvement goals like "I want to increase my positive interactions with students/parents/colleagues," "I want to quit smoking or drinking," or "I want to do some form of exercise every day" work well. Research suggests that you will be more likely to achieve goals you set after reflecting on your virtues than you would without reflecting on them. See if it works for you!

GRATITUDE AND GENEROSITY

A helpful exercise is to take time expressing your gratitude toward others. In earlier chapters we wrote that it is helpful to think about things that make you feel grateful and to take time to personally express gratitude to significant others in your life. The more sincere and active you are with this, the more effective it will be for you and whomever you express yourself to.

Altruism and generosity are also associated with health and happiness (see Lyubormirsky, 2008). It turns out that giving to others not only makes us feel better about ourselves, it also changes our perceptions of others by making us more compassionate. It helps us feel more connected and can also trigger positive reactions from others, a cycle of altruism. A recent study even showed that generosity predicted mortality by buffering stress (Poulin, Brown, Dillard, & Smith, 2013). Researchers asked people whether they had helped a friend or family member during the prior year and then followed them over time to determine predictors of longevity. They found that people who had not helped others in the prior year and who had higher levels of stress were at greater risk of death compared to others who had provided assistance. One warning, though, too much of a good thing can be harmful. If you are overextended by giving of yourself to others it can be damaging to your health. As with everything, the key is balance.

USING STORIES

We all have a narrative about our lives and our world that we tell ourselves. We spend most of our lives describing ourselves and experiences through stories. When we go home at the end of the day, we tell our loved ones about our day with small stories. We understand ourselves and our lives through story. Yet we may not often think about the stories that comprise us. Sometimes, unedited stories can come to dominate our lives and our view of ourselves. We have stories that define us. For instance, if we perceive ourselves as unlovable in some way, we carry within us a series of stories from our past that contain that theme and narrative. Similarly, if we perceive ourselves as competent, we have stories that go along with that idea.

What we do not often take time to do is to realize that we literally are the authors of our life story. Much as we wrote in the chapter about adaptive thinking, the stories that comprise the narrative of who you are, who you were, and who you will be are within your control.

So how do you begin to take control over the story of your life? First, it begins with awareness that you have within you stories about yourself and your world that define you. Second, change requires spending time actually writing your story. If you spend any time writing a journal, consider writing it not just as a series of events that happened in your day but rather as a story. Give your story a title. Literally, what do you want the title of your life story to be? Write it down, recall aspects of your life that fit within that title, and more important, live it. Next, think of your life as a series of chapters, each with its own title, that you want to define you. You choose the words. Choose ones that strengthen and empower you. Finally, choose titles of chapters that you want to lead in the future.

IF YOU DO ONLY ONE THING: Walking Meditation

There are many different ways to meditate, some involving physical activity. Some people find it challenging to keep their focus while doing nonactive variations of sitting meditation. As a way to extend your thinking and your experiences with meditation give walking meditation a try. There are several variations of this method, but the basic one involves finding time to walk outside and tune into your inner world. For this activity, set aside 20 minutes where you can walk outside, not to a particular destination and without any other pressing demands (e.g., to run an errand). Begin, as usual, by taking several deep breaths and turning your awareness inward. Scan your body and notice how it feels to stand. Pay attention to your muscles and how they contract and release in subtle ways to keep you upright. As you begin walking, keep your focus inward and notice the details of your walking movements. Notice how your arms sway and how you lift and drop each leg. For most of us, walking has become an automatic movement that we barely notice. Bring your attention to your feet. Notice how your foot strikes the ground with each step and how it feels in your ankle, sole, arch, and toes. Scan your body as you continue walking and notice the movement and sensations in your calves, knees, and thighs. Feel your stomach muscles and their involvement in your movement; feel your buttocks, lower back, chest, and upper back. What do you feel in your neck and shoulders, your biceps, forearms, and fingers? What sensations do you experience in your face? Continue this inward focus for your entire walk. Many people find the activity of walking helps maintain their focus in ways that sitting meditation cannot. Once you have tried this a few times, see if you can bring this mindful attention to other daily routines.

SUMMARY

In this chapter, we asked you to move beyond the concepts of daily coping and immerse yourself in higher levels of human adaptation and functioning. Mindfulness can encompass all that we are and all that we do. There is growing evidence to support the benefits of mindful coping. In this way, the Western concepts of self-improvement that were discussed in earlier chapters meld with Eastern concepts of non-doing meditation. Within this broad array of coping approaches, you can find what works for you.

RESOURCES

There are many resources that you may find helpful in going deeper with mindfulness and positive psychology. Below we list additional resources you may wish to consult.

Csikszentmihalyi, M. (1990). *Flow: The psychology of optimal experience*. New York: Harper & Row.
Hanh, T. N. (1995). *The miracle of mindfulness*. New York: Harper Audio.
Hanh, T. N. (1992). *Peace is every step: The path of mindfulness in everyday life*. New York: Bantam Books.
Kabat-Zinn, J. (1994). *Wherever you go, there you are: Mindfulness meditation in everyday life*. New York: Hyperion.
Kabat-Zinn, J. (2013). *Full catastrophe living: Using the wisdom of your body and mind to face stress, pain, and illness* (rev. ed.). New York: Bantam.
Lyubormirsky, S. (2008). *The how of happiness*. New York: Penguin Books.
Seligman, M. E. P. (2002). *Authentic happiness*. New York: Free Press.
Seligman, M. E. P. (2011). *Flourish*. New York: Free Press.

HANDOUT 9.1

Self-Affirmation Manipulations to Encourage Adaptive Functioning

	Yes or No	Specific Example
1. Have you ever forgiven another person who has hurt you?		
2. Have you ever been considerate of another person's feelings?		
3. Have you ever been concerned with the happiness of another person?		
4. Have you ever put another person's interests before your own?		
5. Have you ever been generous and selfless to another person?		
6. Have you ever attended to the needs of another person?		
7. Have you ever tried not to hurt the feelings of another person?		
8. Have you ever felt satisfied when you have helped another person?		
9. Have you ever gone out of your way to help a friend, even at the expense of your own happiness?		
10. Have you ever found ways to help another person who was less fortunate than yourself?		

Based on Reed and Aspinwall (1998) and Armitage, Harris, Hepton, and Napper (2008).

From *Stress Management for Teachers: A Proactive Guide* by Keith C. Herman and Wendy M. Reinke. Copyright 2015 by The Guilford Press. Permission to photocopy this handout is granted to purchasers of this book for personal use only (see copyright page for details). Purchasers can download and print additional copies of this handout from *www.guilford.com/herman-forms*.

PART III

APPLICATIONS AND EXTENSIONS

CHAPTER 10

Specific Applications

Now that we have reviewed the entire TCM approach and all the tools, the purpose of this chapter is to illustrate the application of these methods to the wide variety of stressors teachers commonly encounter in school settings. In Chapter 2, we described several categories of stressors that teachers reported experiencing. Chapter 8 described methods for dealing with classroom management and disruptive behaviors. In this chapter, we focus on applying the TCM to administrative pressures, peer conflicts, parent–teacher interactions, and work–life balance.

ADMINISTRATIVE PRESSURES

In our consultation work with teachers, the most common daily stressors teachers vent about are an array of administrative pressures. Many teachers report conflict with principals over a variety of matters. A common stressor is the perception that administration, principals, and superintendents are judging them harshly and viewing their efforts and performance in an overly negative light. Many teachers express a sense that there is always someone looking over their shoulder evaluating, judging, and second-guessing them.

Planned or unplanned walk-throughs by building or district administrators create stress and burden for nearly all teachers, even those with high skill levels. Those with lower skill levels come to dread these walk-through observations, and many report concerns about being targeted by administration. This creates another layer of stress for them. Clearly, one crucial aspect of coping with the stress of performance evaluations is to focus on improving skills. The content of Chapter 8 was designed to focus on this aspect of stress.

However, even the best teachers may experience stress about walk-throughs, so how do the skills in this book apply to this common stressful situation? As we have commented throughout, when under duress, we really only have two options for improving our stress load: change what we are doing or change what we are thinking.

> **We really only have two options for improving our stress-load: change what we are doing or change what we are thinking.**

Adaptive Behaviors

If you think the circumstance can be improved, one option is to talk with the administrator about your concerns or experience. Depending on your relationship with your administrator and your comfort and willingness to express your concerns, you may schedule a meeting to discuss your concerns. To be effective, use your assertive communication and listening skills.

You might begin the conversation by stating the obvious: it is a difficult topic and you are only willing to take the risk because your job is so important to you. It is also a good idea to begin with something positive about the principal, their effort, their passion, and the shared goal of improving education for children. Then concisely state your concern, using "I" statements, and expressing your feelings while focusing on the facts (refer back to Chapter 7 if needed). Examples of assertive expressions include the following:

> "I feel uncomfortable when you criticize my teaching. One thing that would help would be if you could say one or two specific positive things about my work before telling me about what I'm doing wrong."
>
> "Walk-throughs make me feel very uneasy. I feel like I'm being judged."

Relaxation skills are other behaviors that can help manage the stress of walk-throughs. For instance, you can remind yourself to take deep breaths prior to and during the observation. In addition, you can take a moment to visualize yourself being effective prior to the observation. Using these behaviors will help to calm you when walk-throughs occur, and they can reduce any anxieties that might interfere with your performance.

Adaptive Thoughts

Another option is to focus on how you are thinking about the situation. Use the ABC method to determine whether you are overreacting and if you can find new, more adaptive thoughts about the walk-through. You might also use one of the strategies of the positive/negative thoughts method to prompt more positive thoughts. For instance, you might use the entry of an observer in your classroom as a cue to prompt specific adaptive thoughts you have planned in advance. When they enter the room, you might tell yourself to think, "I'm a good teacher," and come prepared to quickly visualize a time in the past when you felt especially effective as a teacher (e.g., when you delivered a great lesson, supported a child, or handled a child's disruptive behavior well).

Remind yourself that administrators act in a system themselves. Their behavior is usually strongly influenced by pressures from their superiors. It is easy to forget this in the moment. The irony is that teachers and administrators often experience the same types of stressors, but in the moment they blame each other. Administrators, like teachers, feel judged and expected to perform miracles. They often have unrealistic expectations put on them and in turn feel a need to pressure teachers to bring these unrealistic expectations to fruition.

Practice

Now we will use the ABC method with a sample administrative situation. In this example, a new principal comes into a school and wants the staff to adopt a new practice. Mr. Ellis, a sixth-grade teacher in the building, has a strong reaction to the announcement.

> Dr. Hangler, the school administrator, was recently hired from a nearby school district. He wanted to introduce some practices that he used in his last elementary school with the teachers in his new building. In particular, he wanted the school to adopt a universal classroom management program that he had found to be effective in the past. To begin, he bought each teacher a book that outlined the program. In addition, the program had a DVD training program that he planned to use during weekly faculty meetings across the school year so that all teachers would be using the same approaches in each classroom. Between the weekly faculty meetings where the video was reviewed, teachers were expected to read book chapters and implement the newly learned practices in the classroom. He also planned to conduct walk-throughs regularly to give teachers feedback on how they were doing with implementing the program. He announced his plans at the start of the year in the first meeting. Upon hearing the news, Mr. Frank slammed his fist on the table and let out a heavy sigh.

Many districts and schools seem to chase every new fad in education. It seems every year or two the existing curriculum or behavior approach is thrown out and a new one is adopted. This can be very frustrating for teachers, given that learning any new approach requires time and effort on top of all their other responsibilities. Follow along as we complete an ABCDE Worksheet as an example of developing more adaptive thoughts about such an event (Figure 10.1).

In this example, after hearing the principal's announcement Mr. Frank experienced three powerful emotions. He became enraged and felt indignant and vulnerable. He identified several maladaptive thoughts that were fueling these emotions, including ideas that the principal was wasting his time, that the principal only cared about himself, and that he was trying to weed out bad teachers. By examining these one at a time, Mr. Frank identified new, more productive ways of thinking that lessened the intensity of his overreaction and made him better able to do his job with less stress.

Activating Event	**B**eliefs	**C**onsequences (Emotions)
Mr. Hangler announced that he was adopting a new classroom management program and would be doing observations.	1. This is a total waste of time. We do this every year and nothing changes. He's wasting my time.	1. Enraged
	2. He has no idea what he is doing. He just wants to look and act important without concern for how he affects us.	2. Indignant
	3. He is going to use this to get rid of bad teachers.	3. Vulnerable

Disprove/Dispute/Debate	**E**valuate
1. We do have a high rate of referrals, so something needs to be done.	1. Annoyed but tolerant
2. I don't know what his motives are, but I do think he means well. I will give him the benefit of the doubt.	2. More open
3. I am a good and honest teacher. I will try my best and things will work out.	3. Empowered

FIGURE 10.1. Sample completed ABCDE Worksheet for Mr. Ellis.

PEER CONFLICTS

Colleagues can be a source of support and/or a source of ongoing aggravation. It is not uncommon to find that you enjoy spending time with some colleagues and not so much with others. Having a positive relationship with others in your workplace can provide you with a source of support when challenges arise; however, maladaptive relationships are also a possible source of stress.

> **Having a positive relationship with others in your workplace can provide you with a source of support when challenges arise; however, maladaptive relationships are also a possible source of stress.**

Gossip

A common but ineffective coping response to peer conflicts is to engage in workplace gossip. Psychologist Amanda Rose has termed this maladaptive response as co-rumination and has showed that it is associated with risk for depression. In this situation, teachers may gather to discuss negative qualities of colleagues or the school administration. This venting leads to a powerful focus on the negative and little to none on problem solving or seeing the positive in the situation. Seeing how co-rumination can lead to feelings of depression makes perfect sense within the TCM. Thinking and spending time talking (behavior) about the negative qualities of others or the situation will have a negative effect on your mood, whereas thinking about the situation or person differently can lead to behaviors that may help solve the problem. Solving the problem can make you feel more empowered or included as well as feel and behave more compassionately toward your colleague(s).

Bullying

Much has been written about student bullying. However, there has been less emphasis on workplace bullying. We have worked with several teachers over the years who describe stress associated situations with what can only be labeled as workplace bullying—both as bullies and victims. Bullying among adults may look different than it does among students. For instance, your colleagues may not be demanding that you give them your dessert or lunch money, nor hit, kick, or throw objects at you. Instead, bullying in the workplace may be less overt and take the form of relational aggression. In fact, gossiping about colleagues is a form of relational aggression. Therefore, if you are participating in workplace gossip about a colleague(s), you are being a bully. Other examples of relational aggression include isolating colleagues (e.g., not sitting with them during lunch or faculty meetings, not inviting them to activities or meetings, not returning a greeting), laughing or taunting an individual when they make a mistake or need support or help, limiting access to resources (material or otherwise), ensuring that the unpleasant or less preferred work activities are unequally burdened on one or more teachers, using sarcasm or jokes targeting an individual, and ignoring or discouraging input on important topics during meetings from certain individuals.

Recently, several organizations have been developed in response to workplace bullying. One organization, the Workplace Bullying Institute, conducted a national survey of employee experiences of workplace bullying. They found that 35% of individuals have been victims of workplace bullying. Furthermore, they noted that bullying is four times more likely to occur than illegal harassment. Interestingly, they found that both men and women bully, but 80% of bullying is same-gender harassment, which is mostly legal according to anti-discrimination laws and workplace policies.

Think about how your school handles bullying among students. It certainly should not be tolerated or seen as a normative part of development, nor should individuals have to come to work in an environment where they are feeling bullied. Bullying has serious and significant negative outcomes for students and adult victims, including stress-related physical ailments (e.g., headaches, digestive problems), feelings of depression, helplessness, and in some instances, suicidal ideation. Everyone deserves to feel connected and supported. We certainly will not have close relationships with everyone in our lives, but ensuring that our behaviors are supportive and not purposefully detrimental to others is a positive life goal. The following provides some suggestions for responses to bullying in the workplace.

Victim of Bullying

Many schools have policies to address bullying among students but not necessarily among coworkers. This presents challenges to individuals who are targets of workplace bullying and becomes even more so if direct supervisors are involved in the bullying. If you feel that you are a target of bullying in the workplace, there are resources available online and information about strategies that you can employ to protect your right to work in a safe environment. In this next section we discuss a few potential strategies that you could utilize in the event you are a victim of bullying. However, you should consult workplace policies and other resources, as workplace bullying is a serious situation that can be challenging to resolve.

When students are bullied, we tell them to get help. This is true for adult situations as well. Particularly if you are a victim of recurrent, serial bullying, you should discuss the issue, giving specific details of the incidents to your supervisor and/or human resources office. Also, documenting each time an incident occurs over time can be useful if you need to file a formal complaint to gain the support needed to resolve the issue.

Depending on the situation, it may be useful to confront the individual or group of individuals who are targeting you. Using effective communication skills, approach the individual, make it clear that you are feeling bullied, give examples of situations in which this has occurred, and assertively express that you would like the behaviors to stop. You may want to practice what you would like to say before approaching the individual. When confronting the person, you want to appear confident and assertive. Some ways to demonstrate these assets are to make eye contact, stand or sit tall, provide concise statements using a strong (but not angry or emotional) voice, and listen to any response provided (whether sarcastic, taunting, or not) without displaying an emotional reaction. It can also help to have an exit phrase to leave the situation. For instance, after describing the issues using "I" statements, expressing your feelings, and providing objective specific information, state, "I wanted to let you know how your behavior was affecting me," or "I needed to let you know how I felt," or simply, "I wanted you to know this." There is no need to shake hands and say that you will be friends in the future (this also not a good idea to require of students), but if the issue is a miscommunication or the individual was unaware of how his or her behavior was affecting you, then confronting the situation can help.

Another strategy is to find allies within or outside the school. An ally could be another teacher or someone in human resources who can work toward problem solving in the situation. Victims of bullying often feel very isolated and finding individuals with whom you can share information about bullying incidents and who can help garner support and potentially advocate on your behalf can be very useful. Bullies can be very socially skilled and good at covering their attacks. Therefore, having another set of eyes to see and ears to hear your perspective will not only help you feel less isolated but may also help legitimize your case and support problem-solving challenges faced in resolving the situation.

Witness of Bullying

According to the Workplace Bullying Institute, 15% of individuals have witnessed workplace bullying incidents. Many anti-bullying curricula for schools discuss the issue of bystanders, or individuals who witness bullying and do nothing to intervene. Do not be a workplace bully bystander. First, become informed of what constitutes workplace bullying. Then, if you witness a situation that appears to be bullying, intervene. Today, we discuss with students that if they witness bullying, one thing they can do is to intervene by coming alongside the victim and removing them from the situation. Finding ways to intervene in a similar vein at work when bullying occurs is an option. For instance, when you hear gossip or negative comments about others, you could offer a different perspective that disputes or counters the comment. If you are aware that a colleague is being isolated during meetings, you can choose to sit next to him and ask him for input about the meeting topic. If you see that individuals are withholding resources from others, you could confront them on your observation. While intervening in bullying can increase your initial stress as the situations may feel conflicting, helping others who are being victimized can also be gratifying.

Do not participate in workplace gossip or other forms of relationally aggressive behavior. It can be challenging when the workplace environment is hostile or toxic. Toxic environments that promote gossip or other forms of bullying are harmful to everyone. You have control of your own behaviors and reaction to others' behaviors. Using the TCM to counter negative discussions or meetings by changing how you choose to react to the gossip or co-rumination is an effective way to avoid becoming sucked into the negativity of others. In addition, your counterbehaviors may actually help to improve the workplace environment. You could also work with the school administrator to develop an environment that is positive and productive. Using similar strategies to those discussed in Chapter 8 for creating a positive classroom climate, administrators, teachers, and school personnel can employ clear expectations for meetings, recognize the assets of individuals, and use high rates of positive to negative interactions to create a positive workplace environment.

> **Toxic environments that promote gossip or other forms of bullying of one another are harmful to everyone.**

WORKING WITH PARENTS

"Why bother even trying with these parents? They don't care." —Third-Grade Teacher

Parents can be a major source of stress for teachers. Not all families cause stress, of course. In fact, teachers have neutral to positive relationships with most families. In our work with teachers, we have asked them to rate the type and quality of relationships they have with parents of their students. In one study, we found that there were three patterns of teacher–parent relationships (Stormont, Herman, Reinke, David, & Goel, 2013). One pattern, about 20% parents, was characterized by frequent contact and high level of comfort between teacher and parent. The second and most common pattern (69%) was a low level of contact and a moderate to high level of comfort. For these parents, teachers had limited contact, but they still reported feeling comfortable with the parent and that their goals were aligned with those of the parent. The last pattern, which we observed in 11% of cases, involved a low level of contact and comfort. It is really these families, the ones with whom teachers report less comfort, that are the source of stress.

We asked the next question: What is different about these families and the students of these families compared to those with whom the teachers reported greater comfort? We were especially intrigued to note that teachers reported the same amount of contact with the families with whom they felt less comfortable as those with whom they felt more comfort. We wondered what else was driving these perceptions, if not the amount of contact. What we found was that the group of families that teachers reported as low-comfort were different in certain ways from the low-contact, high-comfort families. Children of families in the low-comfort group were more likely to have behavior and academic problems and were more likely to qualify for free and reduced lunch. We are speculating a bit here, but it does not seem like much of a stretch to connect the dots by suggesting that teachers were less comfortable with families if their children were experiencing problems at school and the parents were not increasing their contact and involvement with school. It may also suggest that teachers, as is probably true for all humans, report less comfort with families who they perceive as different from themselves.

What do these findings imply about coping with stressful families? First, checking your perceptions at the door is critical to being effective with families. In our work with parents surrounding virtually any parenting issues, be it academics or behavior management, parents expect to be judged by society, especially parents of children with academic or behavior problems. We blame parents (much like teachers are blamed) for their child's behavior. In our experience, parents have their antennae up to sense any sort of judgment from other adults about their parenting, and if they perceive even a hint of evaluation, they will not return for services, and they will avoid that person. For the families who have students who are struggling, it is especially critical for you to withhold judgment about the parents in your interactions with them.

Checking your perceptions at the door is critical to being effective with families.

Just like your thoughts influence your behaviors and mood in general, your thoughts about parents will have direct effect on how you behave toward them. Consider the following quotes we have overheard teachers saying about parents:

"Why bother reaching out to them? It's hopeless. They're not gonna change."
"These parents care more about themselves and their gadgets than their children."
"These kids act this way because of their parents."

Are these beliefs true? Are they accurate? Who knows for sure? It is possible that some parents really are beyond help and really do not love their children. The key questions are the same ones you used in earlier chapters to assess the value and validity of any of your beliefs. What is the evidence for and against these beliefs? Is it helpful in any way to believe these things? Are there alternate explanations for the parents' behavior? Are there more helpful ways to think about the situation?

Given that parents will only work with you if they believe you are trustworthy and that you will not judge them in harsh and critical ways, it is very unlikely that these types of beliefs are going to be helpful in any effort to engage a parent in education. If these beliefs are in your head when you interact with a parent, they will influence your behavior and your mood, and the parent will be able to sense this. It then becomes a self-fulfilling prophecy whereby a teacher expects parents not to be involved and parents respond in kind because they feel they are not welcome or that they will be judged if they do become involved.

What are some more adaptive ways to think about parents, even the most difficult and disengaged ones? We encourage teachers to adopt a mantra or a belief about parents that they truly believe and that they can repeat to themselves during times of discomfort with a parent. Some examples of adaptive mantras teachers have used include the following:

"All parents want their children to be happy and successful."
"All parents want the best for their children."
"All parents are doing the best they can."
"It's easy to judge and much harder to take time to truly understand."
"If I'm going to help these parents, I need to truly believe they have good intentions."

Second, since most humans are most comfortable with and seek out other humans that are more like themselves, we need to take extra steps to be sure we are reaching out to those who are different than ourselves. When you feel uncomfortable with a parent, take time to reflect on why. What is it about the parent that makes your interaction uncomfortable? Do they have a different communication style? Do they look different than you? Do they have different values than you? How much of your discomfort is simply due to cultural differences? How can you make yourself more comfortable?

> **Since most humans are most comfortable with and seek out other humans that are more like themselves, we need to take extra steps to be sure we are reaching out to those who are different from ourselves.**

Third, use the communication skills described in Chapter 7 and apply them to conversations with parents. In our work with parents, we advise teachers to use the following strategies to engage parents.

Using Your ABCs

The ABC method applies very well to parent challenges. We will practice again.

198 APPLICATIONS AND EXTENSIONS

Ms. Thompson has agreed to meet with DeVaugn's parents after school to discuss his progress. She has had problems with DeVaugn all year and has had no luck involving his parents. When they do not show on time, she is not surprised. Fifteen minutes pass and she is about to go home when they finally arrive. She is flustered and unsure of how to proceed.

Let's work through the ABCDE Worksheet for Ms. Thompson (Figure 10.2) to help get her centered and on track for a productive meeting. Ms. Thompson caught herself feeling very strong negative emotions in anticipation of meeting with DeVaugn's parents. She uncovered some maladaptive beliefs behind her emotions that were laden with social judgments about the parents. By challenging these assumptions, she derived new ways of thinking about the situation that lessened her emotional reaction and made it more likely she could connect with the parents in positive ways.

Activating Event	**B**eliefs	**C**onsequences (Emotions)
I was waiting for DeVaugn's parents and they arrived 15 minutes late.	1. His parents don't care about anyone but themselves.	1. Furious
	2. They are rude and disrespectful and wasting my time.	2. Frustrated
	3. They are awful parents.	3. Disgusted

Disprove/Dispute/Debate	**E**valuate
1. They showed up. That's half the battle. All parents want the best for their kids.	1. More compassionate
2. I don't know their situation. Maybe there is another explanation for their lack of involvement. Maybe they don't know my expectations.	2. Curious; open to learning
3. I have not seen them parent outside of the school context. I am in no position to judge them.	3. Empowered

FIGURE 10.2. Sample completed ABCDE Worksheet for Ms. Thompson.

High Positive-to-Negative Ratio of Interactions

Just like with students, you are more likely to have functional relationships with parents if you ensure that you have more positive interactions with them than negative. This is difficult to do with a classroom of 20–30 or more parents, so effective teachers identify creative methods to reach this goal. Home notes with more positive than negative feedback about children is one way teachers have found to do this. Scheduling brief calls, or if parents prefer, e-mails, at regular intervals (weekly, bimonthly) to note something positive about the child is another method. Weekly newsletters with positive information about each student also work well. Finally, when you do have to deliver negative feedback to a parent, be sure to start with something positive and be sure it is sincere and specific about the child.

Starting the Year Off Right

Effective teachers invest a lot of time and energy in setting up expectations and routines for their students at the beginning of the year. This works equally well with parents. Scheduling a parent night early in the year at which you orient parents to your classroom, expectations, and routines is a good way to do this. Many parents do not have a clear understanding of their role in education or expectations that a teacher has of them. Keep in mind each teacher may have somewhat different expectations about what they want parents to do. The only way parents will know your expectations is if you are clear about them to yourself and if you communicate them clearly to the parents. Creating a parent booklet with bullet points about how they can be most helpful to you and to the students during the year can accomplish this as well. Parents who do not read or who do not read English will need accommodations to be able to access this information. Finally, consider home visits at the start of the year. While these may appear challenging or unfeasible due to time constraints, when teachers find ways to do this, without exception they report the effort they put in pays huge dividends over the course of the year.

Parent–Teacher Conferences

Perhaps no other event at school sets the tone for parent–teacher interactions than the routine conferences that occur several times a year. For the students who are doing well, these meetings are brief and fun interactions for both teachers and parents. For the parents of struggling students, however, the ones we described above as being the least comfortable for teachers to interact with, these can be challenging. One of the problems is that few teacher training programs prepare teachers for these difficult encounters.

Fortunately, much is known about what makes it more or less likely that delivering difficult feedback will be met with resistance or openness. For one, prior interactions will set the tone of the meeting, so if you have not built up your "piggy bank" of positive interactions with a parent before now, you need to make a withdrawal based on negative feedback, and it is likely the news will not be received well. Second, prepare all parents for the possibility of receiving negative feedback at some point during the year. Convey this in your parent orientation or information packet and be sure to normalize it as part of learning and growing. All children have strengths and areas for growth. Third, prepare what you want to say to the parents prior to the meeting. Decide on the most important piece of information you want them to hear and highlight that and repeat it. Sometimes, our message is lost in too much information. Choose one thing you want the parent to know that can make a difference and focus on that.

Fourth, create a feedback form where you give student ratings on a range of domains that are important in your classroom. Report cards carry a history and set of personal experiences and biases for everyone—parents have their own associations to report cards. For this reason, we find it helpful to use a different sort of feedback form like the one depicted in Handout 10.1. You can change the categories and choose the ones that fit best for your classroom. The idea is to have a range of skills that every student will have—some in which they excel and some in which they may need more work. The other idea conveyed in this form is that all of these behaviors occur on a continuum; they are not something you either have or do not have. Place an X on each domain and go through them one at a time. Tell parents these ratings are based on objective data.

Begin the meeting with a statement about some of the student's positive qualities. Then explain the form and note that you have placed an X for each important area of development on the form. Ratings in the green area indicate proficiency and that the student and parent should keep doing whatever they are doing, because it is working. Ratings in the yellow indicate emerging skills that should be monitored and considered for improvement. Any ratings in the red are areas the parent will want to give special attention and work with the teacher to develop a plan for improvement.

As you deliver the feedback one section at a time, monitor the parents' reaction. For any items on which the parent gives nonverbal agreement, disagreement, or surprise, comment on the emotion they express. For instance, if a parent seems surprised at a student's area of success, you could state, "You seemed surprised to see Juan's reading skills are in the green." At the end of each section, be sure to check in with parents and ask them for their reactions to any of the feedback. Listen to their response, be open to their perceptions, and reflect back what you hear them saying. It is also a good idea to give brief summaries of what you said in the feedback, what you heard them saying, and any take-home messages you want them to leave with.

We have found that delivering feedback in this way serves several useful functions. For one, it can help lessen your anxiety about delivering the feedback because it is preplanned and you simply have to walk through the form. Second, it tends to make the feedback more about the findings and less about the reporter of the findings (you), so it lessens the opportunity that the parent will be angry with you. Much like a lab report from a doctor's office, the conversation focuses on factual findings and what to do about them, rather than an interpersonal disagreement.

Finally, be sure to end the meeting with a plan for next steps. Ask parents to summarize what they will take from the meeting and then ask them what if anything they want to do about it. Remind yourself that it is ultimately the parents' choice and responsibility as to how they use the information you provide them. Try not to become too attached to a particular outcome. Instead, trust that the parents will make the best decisions for themselves and their family based on their life circumstances. If the parents are not sure how best to proceed or address the problem, ask whether they want your advice. We always ask permission before giving advice because in this way, it is much more likely to be heard. If the parents are open to it, ask them to set a goal about what they would like change, especially something that they have control over rather than something about the child. Parents may have control over how much time their child spends on homework or how often they communicate with the teacher; they have less direct control over what the student ultimately decides to do in the classroom.

Based on the goal they set, develop a plan of steps for achieving it. Help come up with a menu of options based on your experiences with other parents. Parents are much more likely to do things if they feel they have choices. You might tell them, "I've worked with a lot of parents on similar issues and have found several different things that can be helpful. Would you like to hear about these and then decide which one might work best for you?"

Be sure to have a role for yourself in the plan. Ask the parent what you can do to help. Document the plan and a timeline for when things get enacted, including a time for checking back in with each other to see if the plan is working. At any follow-up reviews, if the plan is not working, you may need to work through the steps again and identify new potential solutions.

WORK–LIFE BALANCE

Many students are surprised to learn that teachers have lives outside of school. Teaching is a demanding profession, and it can be challenging to keep a healthy balance between work and home. The demands and pressures from work can seep into our interactions with our family members at home. Therefore, taking the time to be mindful of how workplace stressors affect our life outside of work is important. Equally important is determining whether stressors at home are leaking into your classroom in ways that make your teaching less effective. Becoming aware of all the roles you play in your life and the demands associated with each can be useful toward becoming more balanced.

My Life Pie

Sometimes we find ourselves stretched very thin by all of the demands or roles that we play in our life. Use the circle in Handout 10.2 to create your life pie. What are the roles you play, and how much time do you spend in each role? Be sure to include all roles that take up your time, space, and energy. Figure 10.3 provides an example pie from the life of a teacher. Once you have identified the multiple roles outlined on your life pie, consider where you are spending the most and least time. Are you happy with the time you spend in each role? Do you have any areas you would like to spend more or less time and effort? How can you

FIGURE 10.3. Example of a completed life pie.

go about making changes so that you are giving time and effort to all the important areas of your life? Given the many roles and demands in your life, consider how much time you spend on taking care of yourself. Where does that fit into your life pie? How might you adjust the current demands in your life to ensure you are in fact spending time on taking care of yourself?

Taking Care of Yourself

To be effective in all you do, it is important that you take time to care for yourself. Many of us neglect taking time for ourselves. There never seems to be enough time in the day, given our many demands. If you do not make it a priority, it is unlikely that the time will ever be found. Therefore, we suggest that you deliberately schedule time in your day to take care of yourself. It is also important to figure out what you enjoy. What are the pleasant activities you identified in Chapter 7 that you hope to increase? Use Handout 10.3 to determine how you plan to take care of yourself. Write down which activities you will do and how often you plan to do them. At the bottom, write down what needs to happen to ensure you are able to take these times for yourself. For instance, if you list reading a book for 1 hour a day on your Taking Care of Myself Worksheet, then designate the hour of day you would like to read. Say you want to read for 1 hour before you go to bed. In order for this to happen, you might need to put all the children to bed by 9:00 P.M. so that you can go to your room and read for one hour before you go to bed at 10:00 P.M. If you plan to take a nice long bubble bath once a week, can you negotiate with your partner to spend time with your children during your bath? Thinking through possible barriers or challenges to taking care of yourself is important.

> **We suggest that you deliberately schedule time in your day to take care of yourself.**

> **IF YOU DO ONLY ONE THING: Values Affirmations**
>
> If you have not tried the values affirmation exercise described in Chapter 9 yet, try it now. You will need to complete the questions that appear in Handout 9.1. Read and answer each statement. For each statement that you respond "yes," write a specific example that illustrates the point. Make it as detailed as you can. The point is to encourage you to think actively about specific instances when you were kind to others in specific ways. Immediately after completing this activity, set a goal for yourself of something you would like to change or improve. Self-improvement goals like "I want to increase my ratio of positive interactions with students/parents/colleagues," "I want to quit smoking or drinking," or "I want to exercise daily" work well. Research suggests that you will be more likely to achieve any goal you set after reflecting on your virtues than you would without reflecting on them. See if works for you!

SUMMARY

In this chapter we focused the TCM on specific areas of stress that teachers commonly experience. The principles and strategies are the same: awareness, adaptive behaviors, adaptive thoughts, goal setting, and problem solving. Teaching is a demanding job. In addition, workplace hassles or stressors outside the workplace can affect your performance and health if you allow it. Use the TCM principle and strategies throughout all aspects of your life.

HANDOUT 10.1

Parent–Teacher Conference Feedback Form

Academic Skills

Reading skills	
Math skills	
Writing skills	
Science skills	

Proficient   Emerging   Needs Attention

Global Skills

Persistence	
Work completion	
Organization	
Preparation and planning	

Proficient   Emerging   Needs Attention

Social Skills

Friendship skills	
Respectful	
Adaptive	
Communication	

Proficient   Emerging   Needs Attention

From *Stress Management for Teachers: A Proactive Guide* by Keith C. Herman and Wendy M. Reinke. Copyright 2015 by The Guilford Press. Permission to photocopy this handout is granted to purchasers of this book for personal use only (see copyright page for details). Purchasers can download and print additional copies of this handout from *www.guilford.com/herman-forms*.

HANDOUT 10.2

My Life Pie

What are the current roles that take up time, energy, and space in my life?

In what areas would I like to spend more time?

What are some strategies I can use to make this happen?

In what areas would I like to spend less time (prioritize, delegate some things)?

How much time do I currently spend taking care of myself?

From *Stress Management for Teachers: A Proactive Guide* by Keith C. Herman and Wendy M. Reinke. Copyright 2015 by The Guilford Press. Permission to photocopy this handout is granted to purchasers of this book for personal use only (see copyright page for details). Purchasers can download and print additional copies of this handout from *www.guilford.com/herman-forms*.

HANDOUT 10.3

Taking Care of Myself Worksheet

What activities will I do?	How often will I do them?	What needs to happen to make sure I can do them?

From *Stress Management for Teachers: A Proactive Guide* by Keith C. Herman and Wendy M. Reinke. Copyright 2015 by The Guilford Press. Permission to photocopy this handout is granted to purchasers of this book for personal use only (see copyright page for details). Purchasers can download and print additional copies of this handout from *www.guilford.com/herman-forms*.

CHAPTER 11

Coping with Serious Symptoms

Stress is a common human experience and, as we have shown throughout this book, there are many well-established methods for managing it. Stress is also related to and a precursor for various other problems that can involve serious symptoms and consequences. In this chapter, we review four common types of potentially serious complications of prolonged or intense stress: anxiety, depression, anger, and substance abuse. This chapter provides some suggestions for identifying and self-treating minor concerns in these areas. However, for serious problems you should seek professional help. At the end of this chapter we provide some general information about how you might access professional help when needed.

ANXIETY

Anxiety disorders are the most common type of emotional or behavioral disorders in the United States. Forty million Americans experience an anxiety disorder in a given year, and nearly half the population will meet criteria for one or more of these disorders at some time in their lives (Kessler, Chiu, Demler, & Walters, 2005). Common anxiety disorders include specific phobias (e.g., fear of spiders, flying, heights), social phobias (e.g., public speaking, social interactions), generalized anxiety disorder (GAD; chronic worrying), panic disorder, agoraphobia, obsessive–compulsive disorder (OCD), and posttraumatic stress disorder (PTSD). Some indications that you may be experiencing anxiety include physical symptoms (e.g., sweating, racing heart, stomachache, headache, shaking), emotional symptoms (e.g., fear, nervousness, agitation) and behavioral symptoms (e.g., avoiding situations due to feeling afraid).

> **Forty million Americans experience an anxiety disorder in a given year, and nearly half the population will meet criteria for one or more of these disorders at some time in their lives.**

A Caveat

As you reflect on your emotional life and symptoms, be mindful of the goal of this chapter. We included it because it is likely that some people who read this book will benefit from additional counseling or other mental health services. On the other hand, we want to be careful not to pathologize every aspect of our emotional lives. We all experience a wide range of emotions, including upsetting ones from time to time. Experiencing negative emotions or other symptoms by themselves do not constitute a "disorder." The key in determining whether you are experiencing a condition that could be labeled a disorder is whether the symptoms are interfering with your life either by causing extended suffering or by contributing to distress in your work, school, or social life. So as you complete any self-assessments in this chapter, do so not simply to discover whether you have a psychiatric disorder (this type of evaluation would be reserved for a clinical setting); instead, focus on determining whether you would benefit from additional professional consultation and support. We happen to believe that seeking counseling can be adaptive, even in the absence of severe symptoms, as a tool to foster personal growth and awareness. We also believe that anyone experiencing thoughts of harming self or others should consult with a professional. National hotlines that we list in this chapter are a good place to start if you or a loved one ever experience such symptoms.

Self-Assessment

In Chapter 3, you completed a four-item screening assessment of your anxiety and mood symptoms. These yes/no questions came from the Patient Health Questionnaire–4 (PHQ-4) part of the suite of brief measures developed by Robert Spitzer, Janet Williams, and Kurt Kroenke to screen anxiety and depressive symptoms. The PHQ-4 is composed of two shorter subtests: the GAD-2 (for detecting GAD) and the PHQ-2 (for detecting depression).

Take a moment now to complete the GAD-2 below by rating how often you have experienced each of the following symptoms during the past 2 weeks.

Over the *last 2 weeks*, how often have you been bothered by the following problems:	Not at All	Several Days	More Than Half the Days	Nearly Every Day
1. Feeling nervous, anxious, or on edge	0	1	2	3
2. Not being able to stop or control worrying	0	1	2	3

To get your anxiety total, sum the two items on the GAD-2. Scores of 3 or higher suggest an anxiety disorder. One study found that 86% of people with GAD (diagnosed by clinical interview) scored 3 or higher on this test and 83% of people who did not have GAD scored lower than 3 (Kroenke, 2007). Moreover, this cutoff score was fairly accurate at detecting other types of anxiety disorders (such as panic disorder and PTSD). Thus if you scored 3 or higher on these two anxiety items, it would be a good idea for you to complete more in-depth screening measures, and/or consult a mental health professional for testing or treatment.

Given the various types of anxiety disorders, a single rating scale would not be able to capture all aspects of these conditions. Rather than include a barrage of separate tests for each type of anxiety disorder, we refer you to several online resources where you can complete more in-depth assessments of your other anxiety symptoms. A well-established test for evaluating OCD symptoms is the Yale–Brown Obsessive Compulsive scale. The free test is available at *www.healthyplace.com/psychological-tests/yale-brown-obsessive-compulsive-scale*. A free test for you to evaluate panic and agoraphobic symptoms is available at *http://psychology-tools.com/pas*.

One general resource that will allow you to assess a range of symptoms discussed in this chapter (including depression, GAD, PTSD, eating disorders, alcohol disorders) is provided by the Michigan State University Counseling Center. You can access these screening tests at *www.mentalhealthscreening.org/screening/screening/default.aspx*.

Understanding and Treating Anxiety Symptoms and Disorders

The good news is that anxiety disorders are among the most treatable and preventable social and emotional conditions. Even better news is that most of the well-established treatments for anxiety disorders are based on the very principles you have been practicing in this book. Tracking your mood, behaviors, and thoughts in relation to anxiety symptoms is an important step. Then learning to alter your thoughts that trigger anxious feelings and incorporate more adaptive behaviors can gradually lessen your symptoms.

> **The good news is that anxiety disorders are among the most treatable and preventable social and emotional conditions.**

One added element that we have not discussed in relation to stress is that all effective treatments for anxiety disorders involve some type of exposure to the feared object or situation. Exposure can occur in real life (*in vivo*) or in imagination. Additionally, exposure usually occurs in a step-by-step sequence from least-feared aspects to most-feared aspects. Occasionally exposure can occur all at once in the most-feared situation, a process called flooding. Flooding should only be attempted in consultation with a professional.

If you are looking for a therapist to treat an anxiety disorder, look for someone with expertise in behavioral and/or cognitive-behavioral therapies. These approaches have the strongest research support for treating nearly every type of anxiety disorder including phobias, OCD, and panic disorder.

Self-help books work well for many anxiety symptoms and disorders (Hirai & Clum, 2006). Here's a list of several self-help books that are been rated favorably by professionals and/or that have strong research support.

- Antony, M. M. (2000). *The shyness and social anxiety workbook*. New York: New Harbinger.
- Barlow, D., & Craske, M. (2006). *Mastery of anxiety and panic: Workbook*. New York: Oxford University Press.

- Clum, G. (1990). *Coping with panic: A drug-free guide to coping with dealing with anxiety attacks.* New York: Thomsen/Cole.
- Ellis, A. (1997). *A guide to rational living* (3rd ed.). New York: Wilshire Books.
- Foa, E. B. (2001). *Stop obsessing!* New York: Bantam.
- Hyman, B. M. (1999). *The OCD workbook.* New York: New Harbinger.
- Markway, B. (1992). *Dying of embarrassment: Help for social anxiety and phobia.* New York: New Harbinger.

Some additional resources for anxiety can be found at *www.apa.org/topics/anxiety/index.aspx*. Although these are excellent resources, be aware that if you are experiencing anxiety symptoms that significantly interfere with your life, we recommend that you consult a professional in addition to using these self-help resources.

DEPRESSION

The World Health Organization has identified major depression disorder as one of the world's most burdensome disorders, including all physical and emotional ailments (Üstün, Ayuso-Mateos, Chatterji, Mathers, & Murray, 2004). Depression earned this designation because it has increasingly affected younger and younger persons (whereas other major diseases often strike later in life) and it is often chronic, which means its burden can accrue over a lifetime. Teachers are not immune to these trends. In fact, epidemiological studies have identified teachers among the professionals most prone to experiencing serious depression. One study demonstrated that teachers were nearly three times as likely to experience a major depressive episode compared to persons in other occupations (Eaton, Anthony, Mandel, & Garrison, 1990). Signs of depression include feeling down or blue, losing interest in things you used to like to do, feeling tired or sluggish, overeating (or undereating), feelings of restlessness, feelings of hopelessness, and thoughts of hurting yourself. The following is a brief self-assessment that you can use to determine whether you may be experiencing depression.

> **In fact, epidemiological studies have identified teachers among the professionals most prone to experiencing serious depression.**

Self-Assessment

Take a moment now to complete the PHQ-2 below to assess your depressive symptoms.

Over the *last 2 weeks*, how often have you been bothered by the following problems:	Not at All	Several Days	More Than Half the Days	Nearly Every Day
1. Feeling down, depressed, or hopeless	0	1	2	3
2. Little interest or pleasure in doing things	0	1	2	3

To get your depression total, sum these two questions. One study found that 86% of people with severe depression scored 2 or higher on the depression items of the PHQ-4 and 78% of nondepressed people scored lower than a 2 (Arroll et al., 2010). This is reasonably accurate especially for a two-item test. So if you scored 2 or higher on the depression items, it would be worth your time to complete a longer test and/or to consult a professional for more extensive consultation or treatment on your symptoms.

A widely used and longer depression screening instrument is the Center for Epidemiologic Studies Depression Scale (CES-D; Radloff, 1977). The CES-D is a 20-item measure designed to assess the level of depressive symptomology in a nonclinical population. It is freely available and accurate. A newly revised version is available online (*http://cesd-r.com*), with electronic scoring and additional depression resources provided. The online resource will generate your total score and indicate whether it falls in the range of mild, moderate, or severe depression. A high score would confirm your high score on the PHQ-2 as significant and suggest the need for you to seek professional help. This is especially true if you are having any thoughts of harming yourself or someone else.

Understanding and Treating Depression Symptoms and Disorders

Aaron Beck and colleagues (Beck, Rush, Shaw, & Emery, 1979) offered one of the most influential and supported theories and interventions for depression called cognitive therapy. They described the common types of maladaptive thinking that occurs in depression as being composed of three elements: negative view of self, world, and future. That is, people who are prone to serious depression come to develop enduring perceptions of themselves as flawed, their world as unenjoyable, and their future as hopeless.

The same methods we have applied throughout this book also apply to depression. In fact, research has shown that in cases of mild to moderate depression, bibliotherapy (reading and doing activities like the ones in this book) and exercise therapy (developing a daily exercise habit) can be just as effective as more intensive psychotherapy or medication regimen (Cuijpers, 1997, 1998). For more serious symptoms, it is a good idea to consult with a mental health professional, especially one trained in cognitive-behavioral therapy, and/or to consult with a psychiatrist about medication.

If you decide to look for a therapist, again, your best bet is to look for one who specializes in treating depression using cognitive-behavioral methods or an approach called interpersonal therapy. You can find some resources for depression, including tools for finding a psychologist near you at *www.apa.org/topics/depress*.

The two books listed below are excellent, well-studied self-help books that focus on depression:

- Burns, D. D. (1999). *Feeling good: The new mood therapy* (rev. and updated). New York: New American Library.
- Lewinsohn, P. M., Muñoz, R. F., Youngren, M. A., & Zeiss, A. M. (1992). *Control your depression*. New York: Simon & Schuster.

ANGER

Another common consequence of chronic stress is irritability and severe anger. If you find yourself regularly irritated and having angry outbursts, this section applies to you. The coping methods discussed in this book apply to anger management as well. The key thing to pay attention to with anger is the types of attributions you are making in response to negative events in your life. People prone to anger tend to have hostile attributions. That is, when something goes wrong their thoughts tend to drift toward blaming others and inferring hostile intent in others for whatever happens. Not surprisingly, these types of assumptions and beliefs bring about anger, frustration, and rage.

"He did that on purpose."
"He's out to get me."
"She's trying to ruin this for me."

These types of beliefs can occur in response to even seemingly innocuous events like being bumped in the hall or someone forgetting to say hello. In addition to seeking individual counseling for intense and recurrent feelings of anger, you can also access resources for anger management at *www.apa.org/topics/anger/index.aspx*.

SUBSTANCE ABUSE

"How do I cope with stress? Usually with a glass of wine after work." —Fifth-Grade Teacher

Substance abuse is common. It is also often an ineffective coping response to high levels of stress. In our work, when we ask teachers what coping strategies they use for their stressful jobs, we often hear comments like, "Drink a bottle of wine after work." While these comments are made partly in jest, it is clear that many teachers use alcohol as a form of escape from the challenges of their days. If you drink, it is up to you to assess whether it is something you want to change.

If you decide to make a change, look for skills-based approaches that include strategies for coping, contingency management, self-monitoring, goal setting, and relapse prevention. These approaches are usually labeled behavioral or cognitive-behavioral thearpies. Many people also benefit from 12-step programs, which exist in most communities in the United States. In addition, research strongly supports the benefits of motivational approaches, so look for clinicians with expertise in a technique called motivational interviewing. Local

> **Look for skills-based approaches that include strategies for coping, contingency management, self-monitoring, goal setting, and relapse prevention. Local universities and health clinics may offer brief assessments and interventions designed to gather information from you and then help you come up with a change plan.**

universities and health clinics may offer brief assessments and interventions called checkups (e.g., the Drinker's Check-Up), which are designed to gather information from you and then help you come up with a change plan if you are so inclined.

If you prefer the self-help route, several studies have supported the effectiveness of bibliotherapy for those with mild to moderate drinking problems. As we mentioned in an earlier chapter, be sure to choose a high-quality book if you go this route. The three books below are among those that have been studied and shown to be helpful.

- Miller, W. R., & Munoz, R. F. (1982). *How to control your drinking.* Albuquerque: University of New Mexico Press.
- Sanchez-Craig, M. (1993). *Saying when: How to quit drinking or cut down.* Toronto: Addiction Research Foundation.
- Sobell, M. B., & Sobell, L. C. (1993). *Problem drinkers: Guided self-change treatment.* New York: Guilford Press.

> If you prefer the self-help route, several studies have supported the effectiveness of bibliotherapy for those with mild to moderate drinking problems.

Finally, the National Institute on Alcohol Abuse and Alcoholism (NIAAA) has an excellent website with resources for understanding alcohol abuse and effective ways to treat it: *http://rethinkingdrinking.niaaa.nih.gov/toolsresources/Resources.asp*.

SEEKING PROFESSIONAL HELP

Mental health is an essential part of wellness. We mentioned on several occasions the importance of seeking professional help for the issues discussed in this chapter. This is particularly true if you have wondered whether seeking help from a mental health professional would benefit you or if you have encountered times when feelings of depression, anxiety, anger, or substance use have interfered with your ability to function. For instance, if you have gotten into repeated arguments with a loved one over your substance use or stayed home from work due to symptoms of depression or anxiety, these are indications that you could benefit from additional supports. Likewise, if you have any thoughts of harming yourself or others it is very important that you seek additional services. Luckily, mental health services can be beneficial, particularly if you seek support from professionals who have specialized training in the area where you are experiencing difficulty.

If you are unsure of how to find a mental health professional in your community who can provide the supports you need, there are a few strategies that you can try. First, if you have health insurance, it can be very useful to call your insurance to ask whom they endorse for providing services for your condition. If you turn over your health insurance card there is typically a member services phone number listed. Call this number and tell them what you are seeking help for (e.g., symptoms of depression) and that you would like to see an individual with expertise in that area. Another method is to call local or national lifeline

> **IF YOU DO ONLY ONE THING: Seek Help**
>
> Without a doubt, if you are experiencing any of the serious symptoms described in this chapter, the one thing you need to do is seek help. If you identified yourself as having any serious symptoms based on the scales in this chapter, or even if you have some lingering doubts about having such symptoms, if you do only one thing be sure you choose to seek additional help and support. The tools in this book may be helpful supplements to those with serious symptoms, but there is no substitute for more intensive services such as individual or group counseling and even medication. Use the resources in this chapter to learn more about your symptoms and resources in your community that can help you.
>
> **If you identified yourself as having any serious symptoms, or even if you have some lingering doubts about having such symptoms be sure to seek additional help and support.**

centers. Often when you call these centers, your call is routed to the one closest to your area code. The local crisis center may have resources such as counseling or treatment centers to which they provide you a referral. The centers are actively involved in providing referrals to mental health professionals who can help you work through whatever issues you are dealing with, no matter how large or small. The Suicide Prevention Lifeline (1–800–273–TALK [8255]) is a national hotline that you can call when you are in crisis or when you are looking for an appropriate referral. The website associated with the Suicide Prevention Lifeline (*www.suicidepreventionlifeline.org*) is also a valuable resource.

SUMMARY

Serious emotional and behavior symptoms are alarmingly common in our society. Be alert to these symptoms; awareness of any times you start to experience them frequently or intensely can allow you to catch them early and intervene. Stress is a precursor for all of these problems. When we allow stress to fester and grow, we can eventually start to experience some of these problems. Managing your stress in the ways we describe in this book can thus serve a preventive function for avoiding these types of symptoms. In addition, the skills we describe all build off the same basic premise and are useful in any treatment approach for these more serious symptoms.

> **Serious emotional and behavioral symptoms are common in our society. Managing your stress can thus serve a preventive function for avoiding these types of symptoms.**

CHAPTER 12

For School Administrators and Other School Professionals

School administrators have many of the same stressors as teachers, and they also have responsibility for setting the tone of their entire building or district. With this added burden comes the possibility for positively influencing the culture of a school to make it more likely the adults in it will manage stress effectively. In this chapter, we explore how school administrators can use the tools and ideas in this book to establish a positive coping culture. Many of the ideas are also relevant for other school professionals, school psychologists, and counselors, who are interested in helping support teachers cope with stress.

AWARENESS

As always, effective coping begins with cultivating awareness. Schoolwide awareness involves establishing coping and wellness as priorities. Priorities are demonstrated both in words and, most important, in actions. Actions that highlight staff wellness as a priority include devoting effort and resources to it.

> **Schoolwide awareness involves establishing coping and wellness as priorities.**

How can administrators devote time and money to staff wellness when they are already strapped for resources to fulfill their mission of educating children? One way to justify it is to recognize that all administrative decisions can be thought of in terms of their cost effectiveness. Research has shown that stress, anxiety, and depression are some of the most costly conditions that affect the workplace and worker productivity. When workers are under stress

> **Research has shown that stress, anxiety, and depression are some of the most costly conditions that affect the workplace and worker productivity.**

and not coping, they are less efficient and more toxic in their social interactions. Obviously, in schools, this can undermine instruction, reduce time spent on teaching, increase behavior problems in the classroom, and ultimately increase administrative time spent managing disruptive behaviors and disaffected faculty. More serious and enduring symptoms of stress and internalizing problems exacerbate all of these issues. Thus one way to justify spending time and resources on staff wellness is that it comes with a return on investment in the form of greater productivity, better staff relationships, fewer conflicts, and better classroom management and instruction. Ultimately, promoting staff wellness allows schools to better fulfill their mission of educating children.

> Ultimately, promoting staff wellness allows schools to better fulfill their mission of educating children.

Assessing Current Perceptions

It is important for administrators to assess their own behaviors and how teachers perceive them. There are, of course, many very effective administrators who are positively viewed by their staff. On the other hand, there are also many administrators who struggle with the balance of meeting school and district expectations while supporting their staff. One of the most common stressors we hear from teachers is about their relationships with their building principal. Many teachers feel administrators are overly punitive, overly focused on the negative, have unrealistic expectations, and do not provide enough support to meet those expectations. These perceptions are just that: perceptions. They may be inaccurate and unfair. Regardless, if they exist in your building, these undermine the goals of education. Importantly, there are actions that can be taken to change any negative perceptions of school personnel.

> It is important for administrators to assess their own behaviors and how teachers perceive them.

If you are an administrator, it is a good idea to gauge teacher and staff perceptions about your performance. You can do this with quarterly or biannual anonymous surveys about several specific dimensions:

- Are you satisfied with the school climate?
- Do you feel supported by the school administrator(s)?
- Do you feel supported by your colleagues?
- Do you receive enough positive recognition for your work?
- Do you feel respected?
- Do you feel like meetings are productive and result in meaningful outcomes?
- Do you feel that the school administrator communicates effectively?
- Do you receive constructive feedback from your administrator?
- Do you feel like there are people in your school you can come to when you face challenges in the workplace?

While you cannot always please everyone, gathering feedback about the perceptions of your staff allows you to be more proactive in handling issues that can contribute to loss of productive time or that are detrimental to morale. We have observed occasions when very well-intentioned principals were unaware of how they were perceived by their faculty or how their well-intentioned actions were undermining their impact and credibility. Consider the following example:

> **Gathering feedback about the perceptions of your staff allows you to be proactive in handling issues that can contribute to loss of productive time or that are detrimental to morale.**

Principal Bridgewater was charged with addressing the behavior problems in his school that had increased during the prior year. He asked for and received extra support from the district to have more time from a behavior consultant to help his teachers improve their classroom management and behavior support plans. Although teachers were pleased with the added support and there were some observable reductions in discipline referrals, after a week Principal Bridgewater was not satisfied. Several students continued to display very disruptive and aggressive behavior. He decided to become more actively involved in the behavior support plans created for individual students and overrode several of the plans created by the behavior consultant. Principal Bridgewater replaced them with more punitive consequences, believing that this would result in more immediate behavior change. His revisions actually undermined the progress made to that point and teachers in his building became dispirited and disgruntled.

Like many principals, Dr. Bridgewater was under a lot of pressure to turn around his school and facilitate immediate improvements in behavior and, ultimately, academic scores. Unfortunately, he lost sight of the big picture in his effort to make something happen quickly. First, he failed to notice that his staff felt empowered and engaged after meeting with the behavior consultant, which is an important outcome in itself. Second, he forgot that creating lasting changes in well-established behavior patterns requires setting a new foundation of positive interactions. The first several days or even weeks of a new behavior plan, even an effective one, can involve some fluctuations in behavior as the children will test the new rules and revert to old behaviors to see whether the new rules really apply. When old behaviors are extinguished, we expect there to be some extinction bursts—brief, exaggerated increases in the problem behavior—before the behaviors diminish. By failing to consider this well-established law of behavior, Principal Bridgewater quickly returned the behavior plans to the old methods that had not worked in the first place, and simply intensified them. If, as an administrator, you perceive a problem or you collect data that reveal a problem, you would be wise to attend to some of your behaviors that may influence these perceptions before making drastic changes.

> **The first several days or even weeks of a new behavior plan, even an effective one, can involve some fluctuations in behavior as the children will test the new rules.**

Adaptive Behaviors

As an administrator and leader of your school, it is important that you model the behaviors you would like to see more of among your faculty and staff. For instance, if you would like adults in the school to use effective communication and problem-solving skills, you should demonstrate them yourself. In fact, you could openly outline the problem-solving steps that you use to determine the best solutions to problems you encounter. Having open discussions about how problems are identified and resolved provides an effective framework that everyone in the school can use and, thereby, support effective communication and problem solving. Some basic problem-solving steps are provided in Handout 12.1 along with an example of how they can be used to support productive conversations among school personnel, leading to positive outcomes.

> As an administrator and leader of your school, it is important that you model behaviors you would like to see more of among your faculty and staff.

Furthermore, providing structure and consistency to faculty meetings is a way to reduce stress among all involved. When meetings are predictable, faculty and staff are less likely to act defensively or feel caught off guard around an issue or topic. In addition, you would be modeling a practice that you would like to see in your classrooms—clear structure and expectations for participants.

The following case provides an example of using the problem-solving framework within a potentially stress-inducing workplace problem.

> Mrs. Harbor was approached by three teachers in her school, concerned about the fact that a few teachers were consistently late to meetings. Their tardiness caused the meetings to run over or made it less likely that these teachers would be asked to participate on additional committees or be assigned work. Mrs. Harbor thanks the teachers for bringing the issue to her attention and asks them to gather some data to support the claims. In addition, Mrs. Harbor herself would gather data on who arrived on time versus late for the upcoming full faculty meeting. The following week Mrs. Harbor reviews the data to see that indeed four teachers, who had been identified as the ones who often ran late to meetings, were late to the full faculty meeting and several other meetings by more than 10 minutes. Two of these meetings ran over by 15 minutes because the late teachers had to be caught up on the meeting content.
>
> - *What is the problem?* Meetings are not beginning on time or are running over schedule. This is causing some teachers to feel like their time is not valued.
>
> - *What is causing the problem?* Four teachers have been identified as being consistently late, often by more than 10 minutes. This causes the meetings to run long because they have to be updated on the content of the meeting when they arrive late.
>
> - *What can be done about the problem?* Mrs. Harbor arranges individual meetings with each of the four teachers to discuss the problem and identify solutions to the problem. During the meeting each teacher discloses either not being aware of the problem or having

challenges in reaching the meetings on time. Mrs. Harbor brainstorms with each teacher to identify ways they can make attending the start of the meetings a priority. In addition, Mrs. Harbor openly communicates to all faculty the need for being at meetings on time so that they can begin and end as scheduled. At the next full faculty meetings she hands out tickets to the teachers who arrive on time for the meeting. At the end of the meeting Mrs. Harbor raffles off a chance for one of the teachers who received a ticket to have her come to the classroom and teach a lesson for 20 minutes.

- *Was the problem resolved?* Mrs. Harbor continued to gather data about the arrival time of teachers to the meetings. She also continued the raffle at each full faculty meeting to encourage on-time behavior; other raffle rewards included coupons for dress-down days and other low- or no-cost incentives. The data indicated that no teachers arrived late without having informed her beforehand. Therefore, the problem was resolved.

While this was an example of using the problem-solving model with workplace issues, it can also be used in grade-level meetings, behavior support team meetings, and other meetings to streamline the discussion about student issues. This reduces the amount of time that personnel spend venting about the problems rather than problem solving, reducing rumination on negative topics.

Positive-to-Negative Ratio

Another important adaptive behavior that is helpful in gaining support among your staff, while modeling something you would like them to use with students, is initiating higher rates of positive to negative interactions with them. We advise teachers to have a higher rate of positive to negative interactions with their students and parents of students; thus it is critical for effective leaders to model a favorable positive-to-negative ratio in their interactions with staff. This means for every negative comment or criticism you make, you should strive to deliver three or four positive comments and interactions for every staff member. If you rolled your eyes when you read that and thought it was unrealistic, just know that is how teachers feel when we ask them to do the same with children in their classroom. Also, know that you are much less likely to be effective in your interactions with adults in your building or district if your ratio is more negative than positive.

> **It is critical for effective leaders to model a favorable positive-to-negative ratio in their interactions with staff.**

Think about relationships with others as piggy banks. Every positive comment and interaction you have with someone builds up deposits in the piggy bank. The more deposits you make, the easier it is when you have to make a withdrawal, that is, deliver negative feedback or comments. If you need to make a withdrawal from a relationship that has few or no deposits, your relationship will suffer. Figure 12.1 provides some ideas for increasing positive interactions with your staff. To create a positive school climate, it is also effective for you to interact with students and parents using similar strategies.

1. Place a sticky note on the corner of your computer or somewhere you look often as a reminder to keep your interactions positive or to trigger you to interact positively (e.g., "Everyone is doing their best," "Be positive," or a simple smiley face).

2. Greet all staff when they arrive at school or enter a meeting with you.

3. Send positive feedback to teachers about their accomplishments via e-mail.

4. When conducting walk-throughs, provide three positive remarks for each piece of feedback on what could be improved. This can be done in person, e-mail, or in a handwritten note.

5. Have lunch with your staff. Have conversations to learn about their lives outside of the school building.

6. Send cards to staff on their birthday or other special occasions.

7. Similar to strategies used in schoolwide positive behavior supports for students, you could implement a system for rewarding staff who exhibit exceptional behaviors. For example, hand out tickets to teachers who are standing in their doorways greeting and monitoring students in the hallway between classes. The tickets can be turned in for small rewards such as movie tickets, extra planning time with you as a sub in their classroom, a manicure, etc.

8. Walk through the hallways of your building throughout the day, providing genuine and meaningful positive feedback to teachers in front of their students (e.g., "Oh, Ms. Dumphey, your first graders are lined up nicely and are being very respectful. Thanks to all of you for doing your very best").

9. Identify behaviors you would like to see your staff to display more (e.g., arrive on time to meetings, use active supervision in their classrooms and hallways). Then "catch" teachers who are using this behavior by verbally providing positive feedback, sending them a note, or handing out a token that can be used for a greater reward.

10. Publicly discuss or display work-related accomplishments of teachers or staff. For instance, if a grade-level team has successfully implemented new learning strategies that resulted in higher student performance, acknowledge the hard work and commitment of this team both publicly to other staff (if appropriate), to district leaders (if appropriate), and to the individuals themselves.

FIGURE 12.1. Ideas for increasing positive interactions with staff.

Delivering Negative Feedback

One of the most stressful aspects of administrators is the need to deliver performance feedback to staff, especially when the feedback is negative. Unfortunately, few education training programs do a good job of preparing administrators for how to do this well. Poorly delivered feedback can set a tone of conflict in a relationship. It's important to note that receiving feedback is stressful to teachers. When the feedback is less than positive, it is important that you have a relationship with the teacher that allows him or her to hear the feedback in a constructive manner. Therefore, having "money in the bank" with respect to having more positive interactions than negative is particularly important when it comes time to provide negative feedback.

> **When the feedback is less than positive, it is important that you have a relationship with the teacher that allows him or her to hear the feedback in a constructive manner.**

There are ways to deliver feedback that make it more likely it will be heard. We have written an entire book about effective teacher consultation that includes specific recommendations for how to give feedback (Reinke et al., 2011). Here we highlight the big ideas of this model.

- *Make yourself approachable.* Make time for your staff. Withhold your initial judgment about issues that are brought to you. Approach delivering performance feedback as an opportunity to learn about the challenges or successes of your staff.

- *Have a collaborative spirit.* Use partnership language ("we" and "us") and convey a sense of joint commitment to wellness and improvement. Of course, there are some cases in which you ultimately need to make decisions. However, including staff in discussions around problem solving and brainstorming solutions helps to foster feelings of belonging and empowerment among those you supervise.

- *Start off the meeting with positives.* Giving a bit of time up front to reflect on the positive qualities and skills of a teacher can go a long way. The positive feedback will need to be genuine and meaningful, otherwise the teacher might perceive that you are simply placating them prior to giving your "real" feedback. So, during observations or in meetings, identify specific and important positive qualities that you can share with your teachers during a performance feedback meeting.

- *Use constructive feedback.* Feedback is most useful when it is constructive, meaning that it states the problem in specific and solvable terms. In addition, it describes how the behavior being discussed is problematic. For example, you might say, "You arrive late to meetings. On two occasions you were 15 minutes late. This causes the meetings to be delayed or requires others to catch you up on the meeting content. Ideally all faculty will come to meetings on time so that we can get through the content and end on time." A negative nonexample would be, "You hold up meetings and that makes others upset." After providing the feedback, be sure to make time to problem solve the issue so that when everyone departs there is a plan in place to make the issue less likely to occur in the future.

- *Don't avoid giving difficult feedback.* Providing negative feedback can be uncomfortable for everyone involved. However, as a leader you have to be able to overcome the predisposition to avoid problems or give negative feedback. Often the problem is really the elephant in the room or the school. Everyone is already aware of the issue, and avoiding it simply allows it to fester and grow worse, making it even more difficult to discuss. We have found that if you simply state an objective fact about the problem area in a matter-of-fact way it opens the door for effective problem solving. For example, in a calm voice, you might say: "When I walked by your classroom yesterday I noticed that you had pulled one student aside and were reprimanding him in a loud, angry voice. I am concerned about what I saw and wonder what led to the incident and how we can avoid this in the future." In our own work we find it surprising how openly discussing matters can actually be a relief to the individual receiving the feedback. Often it leads to productive conversations, particularly if you are able to maintain the focus on solving the situation.

- *Develop a menu of options.* An effective way to ensure that the individuals you work with follow through with feedback-based changes is to collaboratively develop a menu of options. More specifically, identify areas that need improvement based on the feedback you provided. Next, identify one or two of those areas that the person would like to address (or guide her to the area you need her to address first). Then, in collaboration with the teacher, come up with two or more ideas for improving skills or changing behavior in relation to the identified area. Finally, have the teacher select from the menu the strategies she will use to change. By providing teachers with a choice, you encourage their own investment in actually implementing the plan in their classroom. While it seems like it is faster just to tell people what they should or should not do, this often does not work. Whereas getting people invested by having them co-create options alongside you and pick what they think will work best for them can be faster in the long run.

- *Notice body language.* You may have been in a meeting where you give some feedback to a teacher and you see him pull back from you, cross his arms, and stop making eye contact. This is likely a sign that he feels uncomfortable with the feedback. Perhaps he doesn't find it credible. Perhaps he felt judged or mistreated. Who knows? If you notice a change in body language you may want to simply ask about the reaction. For example: "It seems like you were uncomfortable with what I just said. What was it that made you feel this way?" If we leave a meeting following an interaction in which the person disconnects, yet nods the remainder of the meeting as if in agreement with any plan of action, we can most certainly expect that the plan will not be put into place. However, if you take note and comment about the obvious, it could make the meeting more productive as you hear the other person's side with the ability to work through the challenges.

It's also a good idea to comment on positive body language. For instance, you deliver positive feedback and notice a teacher sit taller, smile, and make direct eye contact. This is likely an indication that the teacher feels proud of the accomplishment being discussed. Commenting on these moments can increase the level of support the teachers perceive as well as feeling like they are truly appreciated.

- *Drop you defenses.* It can be easy to take comments made by others as personal attacks, especially when the comments are about your school or your performance. To have productive conversations, it is important that you be able and willing to hear the other person's perspective. Also, for other people to be able and willing to express their concerns, they have to perceive that you are open to receiving the feedback and that they will not be punished for expressing their views. When you enter into a conversation that you expect to be uncomfortable, with a possibility that you will be told things you may not want to hear, it is a good idea to prepare yourself with some coping thoughts. Tell yourself that everyone is entitled to their perceptions. Listening to other people's perceptions, accepting them (not necessarily agreeing with them, just accepting that different people have different views), and showing them that you understand their concerns can itself remove one major roadblock in solving problems. Sometimes, giving people a chance to express themselves and to be heard leads them to feel better about the situation and more willing to work with you to solve the problem. On the other hand, reacting defensively by disagreeing with or rejecting what the other person says usually escalates the problem and makes it less likely to be solved. Another benefit of being able to hear criticism

> **When you enter into a conversation that you expect to be uncomfortable it is a good idea to prepare yourself with some coping thoughts.**

and negative perceptions is that it might actually lead you to new insights about the school environment and potential solutions. If we approach difficult conversations in a defensive posture, we end up retaining our original view of the situation and are stuck with our original solutions that do not work. Instead, if we truly open up and listen to different perspectives, we make it more likely that new ideas and insights will emerge.

TALKING WITH TEACHERS ABOUT STRESS AND COPING

How do you support a teacher in developing more effective coping skills? You can broach the topic by including it in performance evaluations. You can give teachers feedback about how you perceive them as coping and/or you can have them self-assess their stress and coping levels using some of the simple questions we provided in Chapters 1 and 2. You can normalize it as just being part of the job. You can make it an ongoing conversation and an important aspect of supporting your staff. The following tips provide some ideas for how you can incorporate ongoing discussion or awareness about coping with stress in the workplace. It's important to remember that you too are affected by workplace stressors and can benefit from these activities as well.

Tips for Talking with Teachers and Supporting Wellness

- *Hold a study group using this book.* Have teachers in your building read this book and meet to discuss it, the strategies they are using to improve their wellness based on the book, and the challenges they face with using some strategies. The meetings can be empowering, as the group can support each other, share experiences that make them feel stressed, and discuss how the strategies in this book can be used to better cope with these stressors. Throughout the book each chapter shares ideas for group activities that can be incorporated into a reading group, and the next chapter provides clear guidelines for running such groups.

> One idea is to have teachers in your building read this book and meet to discuss it.

- *Normalize stress and coping.* There is a host of literature that documents the negative outcomes of teacher stress. For instance, we know that nearly 50% of new teachers leave the field within 5 years of entering the profession. These teachers often leave because of challenges encountered in their work that cause them to feel stress and like they are ineffective. Furthermore, stress leads to burnout, which has negative effects on teacher health, their teaching, and student outcomes. Burnout is the accumulation of responses to extended stressors caused by one's job; characteristics of burnout are emotional exhaustion, cynicism, and low levels of self-efficacy (Maslach, Schaufeli, & Leiter, 2001). The depersonalization aspect of burnout arises from the need to protect oneself from the negative emotional stressors on the job that can negatively affect job performance (Maslach et al., 2001). The ongoing pressures school personnel face make them likely to experience stressors that can lead to burnout. Make your faculty aware of this as a possible issue that each of them can face or may be facing. Awareness is the first step to taking actions that can lead to more positive outcomes for teachers. However, it is not enough to be aware that your job may negatively affect you. This book can provide your staff (and you) with effective coping strategies. You need to learn better coping strategies to avoid the negative outcomes found in the research literature.

> The ongoing pressures school personnel face make them likely to experience stressors that can lead to burnout.

- *Form a committee of staff to organize wellness activities.* You might find that a small group of faculty or staff are willing to get together to develop activities or other strategies to promote coping and wellness strategies at the school level. This committee could develop informational handouts for all school staff on coping strategies to deal with stress. They could also organize staff events that promote healthy behaviors (e.g., after-school walks, reading groups focused on reducing stress, organizing luncheons in which staff share positive comments to one another, recognition events to celebrate accomplishments).

- *Use resources in your district or building.* If you have a school psychologist, school counselor, social worker, or other mental health professionals in your building, assess their knowledge and expertise on the topic of stress and coping. Many of them will have been trained in the methods described in this book and know how to support your efforts in implementing them. For instance, many school psychologists are trained in providing consultation to teachers and frequently support teachers who are experiencing stress and burnout. If you have one or more teachers whom you have identified as having stress-related challenges, you could ask that the school psychologist or other mental health professional meet with the teacher to provide individual consultation. In addition, you might ask for the school psychologist or other mental health professional to support your efforts by serving on wellness committees and/or by facilitating study groups on the topic.

> You could ask that the school psychologist or other mental health professional meet with the teacher to provide individual consultation.

What If the Person Doesn't See the Problem?

A common scenario is that you may observe a problem in someone else, but they disagree. How can you be helpful in these circumstances? The first rule is to avoid arguments with people about why they need to change. That is not helpful because the predictable response is that the person will tell you why they *don't* need to change. Worse, arguments about how or why people need to change will almost certainly undermine your relationship with them and make it less likely they will seek you out in the future. So begin with the assumption that other people know themselves better than you do and will make the best decision for themselves. You can, however, direct the conversation by asking questions that may lead the person to see the problem. For instance, if you are conducting an observation in a classroom of a teacher and you notice that his behaviors have changed since your last observation, perhaps he is less positive with the students or seems a bit disconnected or disorganized in comparison to other times you have visited, you might follow up with the teacher before leaving the classroom by asking, "How do you think that lesson went? Was this a typical day for you?" Perhaps the teacher will share with you that he is having a bad day for a particular reason. This could lead to a follow-up meeting in which you first describe the things that went well, and then those things you saw that could have been better. Have the teacher reflect on what might have changed since you last observed him, or what was different from times in the past when the teacher was more effective. Thus, rather than saying, "It seems like something is really bothering you" or "I noticed that you seem burnt out or stressed," the questions may lead the teacher to think about what is different. Is he experiencing personal stressors that are interfering with his normal productivity? Having him come to this conclusion, rather than you pointing it out, will make the information more effective and increase the likelihood that the teacher will work toward doing something about it.

Overall, listening and understanding is really the goal. Reflect back to the person what you hear him or her saying. Occasionally ask open-ended questions. In what ways does this worry you? How are you coping or dealing with it? How would you like things to be different? If you give advice, ask permission first. Always send the message that you recognize it is ultimately up to the other person whether he or she wants to do anything.

USING THE TCM FOR ADMINISTRATOR STRESSORS

The strategies in the TCM apply equally well to administrative stressors. Most of the examples in the book are about common teacher stressors, but it is easy to apply these to the pressures you face as an administrator. Assessing your own building blocks to *getting to good* from Chapter 9 and focusing on any blocks you do less well will improve your own efforts to cope. If you do not attend to the pleasant activities in your life, for instance, you make yourself vulnerable to stress responses and lower levels of coping. Likewise, learning to monitor your mood and attend to any overreactions you might have gives you clues and insights about more effective coping responses.

As we learned with teachers, administrators often find the strategies for monitoring and changing their thoughts to be especially helpful in dealing with daily hassles. Below we give an example of an administrator who had an overreaction and learned to use the ABC method (see Chapter 6) to manage it.

> Mr. Ellison was a new principal in an urban middle school. He had been assigned the role based on his previous success at a nearby elementary school. His new school had been identified as a failing school the previous year, and he was tasked with turning it around. The school had a high percentage of students from low-income backgrounds, most of whom had a high level of social and emotional needs and low levels of achievement. Mr. Ellison started the year energized and optimistic. He poured all of

his time and effort into making a difference for the teachers and students in the building. Within a month, however, he realized how daunting the challenge was. Teachers in his building lacked basic classroom management skills, and many teachers, parents, and students were apathetic and disengaged. As a last resort, he called in a behavior consultant to advise him and his staff. As Mr. Ellison described the situation to the consultant in a meeting with his teachers present, he began to cry and had to leave the room. When he returned and started speaking, his tears began to flow again.

Mr. Ellison was experiencing a great deal of stress. He had high expectations and had put a lot pressure on himself. This meeting with the behavior consultant brought all of this pressure to the fore. Using Handout 12.2, write down what you think Mr. Ellison was feeling at that moment (C), specify the event that preceded his feelings (A), and then write down any thoughts (B) that you think he was having about the event that led to the feelings you wrote in C.

You probably guessed that Mr. Ellison was feeling some version of sadness, given that he was crying. That's a safe bet. He felt sad or even very sad, which he labeled *depressed*. When we talked with him, it became clear that he also felt overwhelmed, guilty, and hopeless. When he used the ABC Worksheet (Figure 12.2), he wrote down the event accurately, noting what he said at the moment he started to cry. He then spent some time thinking about his beliefs that were connected to his emotional responses. Note all the thinking errors that were part of his beliefs: see if you can catch the overgeneralizations (implied *never* or *always*), personalizations, moralizing (*should* and *must*), and catastrophizing (*awful* and *terrible*).

Activating Event	**B**eliefs	**C**onsequences (Emotions)
I was describing the problems at our school to the behavior consultants when I started to cry. I had just said how hard we all were working to make a difference for students.	1. We had made no improvements and things are just getting worse.	1. Depressed
	2. This is impossible. No one can help these students. These teachers are useless. I give up.	2. Defeated/hopeless
	3. It's my fault. I should be better. I should do more. I should be able to make this work. I'm a failure.	3. Ashamed
	4. I don't know what to do. I'm stuck. This is a disaster. It is awful.	4. Overwhelmed

FIGURE 12.2. Mr. Ellison's ABC Worksheet.

Using Handout 12.3, take a moment to help Mr. Ellison complete the ABCDE Worksheet. What are some ways that he could dispute the irrational beliefs at Step B and replace them with more adaptive thoughts? Look at each belief and come up with a counter to it that could lead to a new effect. Figure 12.3 provides the ABCDE Worksheet that Mr. Ellison completed.

Mr. Ellison was able to challenge and dispute each of the beliefs that contributed to his emotional distress. He caught each of his thinking errors and rephrased them in ways that were less emotionally charged. In the end, he helped himself arrive at new emotions that were more adaptive and allowed him to perform his job in a more productive way.

Activating Event	**B**eliefs	**C**onsequences (Emotions)
I was describing the problems at our school to the behavior consultants when I started to cry. I had just said how hard we all were working to make a difference for students.	1. We had made no improvements and things are just getting worse. 2. This is impossible. No one can help these students. These teachers are useless. I give up. 3. It's my fault. I should be better. I should do more. I should be able to make this work. I'm a failure. 4. I don't know what to do. I'm stuck. This is a disaster. It is awful.	1. Depressed 2. Defeated/hopeless 3. Ashamed 4. Overwhelmed

Disprove/Dispute/Debate	**E**valuate
1. Just take it one day at a time. We have taken some positive steps, including inviting the consultants here today. 2. This problem took years to create and it will take more than a week to fix. We can do this one step at a time. 3. It takes a village to fix a problem. I can't do this alone. I'm doing the best I can. I want to keep trying and find partners who can help. 4. Take it slow, breathe, it can only get better.	1. Disappointed but open 2. More optimistic 3. Stronger 4. Calmer

FIGURE 12.3. Mr. Ellison's ABCDE Worksheet.

> **IF YOU DO ONLY ONE THING: Plants and Nature**
>
> One simple way to improve the school environment is to incorporate plants and nature into it as much as possible. Adding paintings or pictures of nature, real or artificial plants, and when possible animals (like fish or even dogs) to our environments yields measureable benefits for humans. As described in Chapter 8, research shows that seeing and experiencing nature in almost any way produces measureable changes in our heart rate and blood pressure; in other words, nature helps activate our parasympathetic nervous system and the relaxation response.

SUMMARY

Other school professionals besides teachers experience similar stress and burdens. Finding ways to help all adults in a school manage these burdens in more productive ways can yield benefits for everyone. One way to do this is to establish a culture and environment at school that encourages wellness. Another way is to equip administrators and other professionals in the building with the same coping skills, as we have described in this book.

> **Other school professionals besides teachers experience similar stress and burdens.**

HANDOUT 12.1

Questions to Guide an Effective Problem-Solving Framework

What is the problem?	What are the facts/data as evidence of the problem?
What is causing the problem?	What are the facts/data demonstrating the cause?
What can be done about the problem?	How will we know the solution was employed?
Was the problem resolved?	What facts/data demonstrate the problem has been resolved?

From *Stress Management for Teachers: A Proactive Guide* by Keith C. Herman and Wendy M. Reinke. Copyright 2015 by The Guilford Press. Permission to photocopy this handout is granted to purchasers of this book for personal use only (see copyright page for details). Purchasers can download and print additional copies of this handout from *www.guilford.com/herman-forms*.

HANDOUT 12.2

Complete Mr. Ellison's ABC Worksheet

Activating Event	**B**eliefs	**C**onsequences (Emotions)

From Stress Management for Teachers: A Proactive Guide by Keith C. Herman and Wendy M. Reinke. Copyright 2015 by The Guilford Press. Permission to photocopy this handout is granted to purchasers of this book for personal use only (see copyright page for details). Purchasers can download and print additional copies of this handout from www.guilford.com/herman-forms.

HANDOUT 12.3

Complete Mr. Ellison's ABCDE Worksheet

Activating Event

Beliefs   *Before   After*

Consequences (Emotions)

Disprove/Dispute/Debate

Evaluate

From *Stress Management for Teachers: A Proactive Guide* by Keith C. Herman and Wendy M. Reinke. Copyright 2015 by The Guilford Press. Permission to photocopy this handout is granted to purchasers of this book for personal use only (see copyright page for details). Purchasers can download and print additional copies of this handout from *www.guilford.com/herman-forms*.

CHAPTER 13

Setting Up a TCM Study Group

As a teacher, school psychologist or counselor, or administrator, you may decide to set up a TCM study group. We have found that learning these skills can be enhanced when done as a group. The group process has the benefit of adding social support, which all teachers need from time to time. In addition, teachers can generate more and better solutions to problems when they hear ideas shared by other teachers. Another benefit is that effective groups provide encouragement and even subtle social pressure to complete activities and exercises that we might not do if not for the commitment we make to others. In this chapter we provide guidelines for setting up groups, facilitating them, and making them as effective as possible.

DEVELOPING A PLAN AND TIMELINE

We suggest establishing a schedule of meetings and developing a plan for the total number of sessions you want to complete, as well as the timeline and topics for each session. Ideally, you will meet once a week. Longer intervals between group meetings make it more difficult to have continuity between meetings, and it is easier to get off track if you are not meeting weekly. Depending on the size of the group, you may want to meet for 30 minutes or more. In groups of 10 or more, you probably will want to find an hour to give everyone a chance to participate and be heard. A simple way to do this would be to meet and discuss one chapter of the book each week for a total of 12 to 14 weeks. That way the group could meet for a few months during a single semester of the year. As you divide up the readings each week, you may decide to spend more or less time on some chapters. We have found the adaptive thinking content to be of great interest to teachers, so you may want to split that content over two or more weeks. See Figures 13.1, 13.2, and 13.3 for a sample sequence of readings and meetings for 14-week, 10-week, and 6-week groups, respectively.

> **Establish a schedule of meetings and develop a plan for the total number of sessions, as well as the timeline and topics for each session.**

Week	Focus	Reading
1	Introductions/overview/rules/goal setting	Chapter 1
2	Basics of stress and self-assessment	Chapter 2
3	The TCM	Chapter 3
4	Awareness	Chapter 4
5	Positive/negative thoughts method: *Monitoring thoughts*	Chapter 5
6	Positive/negative thoughts method: *Increasing positive/decreasing negative*	Chapter 5
7	ABC method: *Using ABC Worksheet*	Chapter 6
8	ABC method: *Using ABCDE Worksheet*	Chapter 6
9	Adaptive behaviors: *Pleasant activities and communication*	Chapter 7
10	Adaptive behaviors: *Relaxation skills*	Chapter 7
11	Professional competence	Chapter 8
12	Getting to good: *Mindfulness*	Chapter 9
13	Getting to good: *Values and Virtues*	Chapter 9
14	Summary and next steps	Chapters 10–13

FIGURE 13.1. Sample group schedule for 14-week study group.

Week	Focus	Reading
1	Introductions/overview/rules/goal setting	Chapter 1
2	Basics of stress and self-assessment	Chapter 2
3	The TCM	Chapter 3
4	Awareness	Chapter 4
5	Positive/negative thoughts method	Chapter 5
6	ABC method	Chapter 6
7	Adaptive behaviors	Chapter 7
8	Professional competence	Chapter 8
9	Getting to good	Chapter 9
10	Summary and next steps	Chapters 10–13

FIGURE 13.2. Sample group schedule for 10-week study group.

Week	Focus	Reading
1	Introductions/overview/rules/goal setting Basics of stress and self-assessment	Chapters 1–2
2	The TCM Awareness	Chapters 3–4
3	Positive/negative thoughts method ABC method	Chapters 5–6
4	Adaptive behaviors Professional competence	Chapters 7–8
5	Getting to good	Chapter 9
6	Summary and next steps	Chapters 10–13

FIGURE 13.3. Sample group schedule for 6-week study group.

Regardless of how many sessions you choose, it is a good idea to get all members to commit to attending all sessions and to put a timeline on the total number of sessions rather than leaving the group open ended. At the end, you may decide to continue or reconvene the meetings at a later date. The expectation also would be that each member would complete assigned readings each week and attempt the exercises in that chapter prior to each meeting.

ESTABLISHING GROUP GROUND RULES

If you decide to work as a group, it is important to create a safe environment where everyone feels comfortable expressing their ideas without being judged. A good place to start early in your first meeting is to discuss what the group rules will be and how to enforce them. Come up with four or five group rules and discuss why they are important. Some examples are below:

> **If you decide to work as a group, it is important to create a safe environment where everyone feels comfortable expressing their ideas without being judged.**

- Confidentiality
- One person talks at a time: no side conversations
- Do the readings
- Listen to each other
- Respect each other (no name-calling or judging)
- Be open to learning

If rules are violated, talk about appropriate ways to address it. Write out the group rules on a board or on easel pad paper and post them in the room for each meeting. When people have lapses, a member can point to the list and remind participants about the rule.

GROUP FACILITATION

It is a good idea to select a group facilitator for each meeting. If a school psychologist or other mental health professional is interested in supporting the group, or even is the one who suggested it, he or she can be the facilitator. If the group is composed of all teachers, you might decide to alternate that responsibility by assigning leadership for each chapter. The role of the group facilitator is to come extra-prepared for the meeting on the week he or she leads the discussion, start the group and remind members of the ground rules, and ask questions about the group members' experiences and thoughts while reading the book.

> **It is a good idea to select a group facilitator for each meeting.**

OARS

In Chapter 8, we introduced OARS as strategies for effective communication (OARS = Open-ended questions, Affirmations, Reflections, and Summaries; Miller & Rollnick, 2013). First, ask open-ended questions, or questions that can't be answered with yes/no responses. Your goal as facilitator is to stimulate discussion and reflection among the participants. Asking questions about specific reactions to content or about any surprises or areas of confusion are examples of open-ended questions that can facilitate dialogue among members. Affirmations are verbal or nonverbal communications that convey support and encouragement. Affirmations work best when they are genuine and specific (e.g., "I'm really impressed with how much effort you put into the activities this week"). In addition, affirmations about process rather than outcomes tend to be received better (e.g., "I can see how hard you are thinking about that"). Reflections refer to a listening style of communication where you repeat back to the speaker what you hear him or her saying. This can be as simple as paraphrasing. More advanced reflections try to attend to deeper meanings or feelings the person might be expressing. Reflections are best when they are given as a statement rather than as a question (e.g., "You are proud of yourself and the progress you have made," rather than "Are you feeling proud?"). Finally, it is a good idea to summarize key points that are made along the way. Whenever you get a sense that many ideas have been expressed about a topic or if it feels like you are getting off track as a group, take time to give a brief summary (two or three sentences) of what has been said. Ask whether the summary was accurate and then proceed to the next part of the group.

> 1. Ask open-ended questions.
> 2. Affirmations work best when they are genuine and specific.
> 3. Reflections refer to a listening style of communication where you repeat back to the speaker what you hear them saying.

Structure of the Group

Prepare an agenda prior to each meeting. We provide a sample generic agenda in Figure 13.4. Try to include many of these elements in the agenda you develop.

One useful strategy to start the group is to go around the circle and do a member check-in. Ask each member to report their mood on a scale from 1 to 10, either at that moment or over the day. You can change the type of mood you report on each week (how stressed, anxious, sad, or angry you are feeling). Also ask members to report one or more thoughts that were related to whatever mood they reported. This structured exercise helps cultivate the awareness aspect of the program that is so crucial to its success.

> Prepare an agenda prior to each meeting.

Next, ask people to report any successful experiences they had during the prior week and celebrate these. Discuss any challenges they encountered and spend a few moments brainstorming any solutions. A common discussion might be about finding time to read the

- **Mood Check-In**
  - Ask participants to report their mood right now on a scale from 1 to 10.
  - You can change the mood discussed weekly (positive/negative, happy/sad, anxious/calm).
  - Ask participants to identify one thought or behavior related to their mood rating.
- **Review Homework** from the prior week's chapter.
  - What went well?
  - What was challenging?
  - Brainstorm solutions to any barriers or challenges.
- **Summary of New Chapter**
  - Ask one participant to summarize the big ideas of this week's reading.
- **Group Discussion** about what participants learned from this week's reading
  - What made sense?
  - What did you try or will you try?
  - What was unclear or confusing?
- **Group Exercise(s)** from the current chapter
- **Summary and Goal Setting**
  - Ask a member to summarize the entire meeting.
  - Ask each member to set a goal for the coming week.
    - Ask each member to say why his or her goal is important.
    - Ask each member to rate his or her confidence in meeting that goal.
  - Problem-solve any barriers for members who express low commitment or confidence.

FIGURE 13.4. Sample agenda.

book or to do the exercises. If these issues come up, invite other members to share their experiences in solving these problems and any solutions that have worked for them.

Next, turn to the topic for the week. Have someone summarize the big ideas or take-home messages of the chapter. Walk through each of the skills discussed and ask members to share what they learned and what they will use from the chapter. Do some of the exercises and ask members to describe their answers or experiences.

In the final 5 minutes of the group, take time to summarize what was discussed and ask members to set a goal for the coming week. They can say it aloud or write it down. See Handout 13.1 for a Session Summary Form we use as a way to end each session and to gain commitment for completing assignments and attending future meetings.

TIPS FOR SUCCESSFUL GROUPS

The following is a tip sheet for 15 guidelines we have found useful in ensuring that groups are successful. As facilitator, read these over prior to each group and use them to guide your planning and decision making.

- *Start and end the group on time.* As you know, school professionals are busy people, so respect their time. Decide on when and how long each meeting will last and stick to it. Assign someone to be the time enforcer.

- *Ensure group safety by defining structure and ground rules.* Spend time during the first group talking about the structure and rules that members want to keep the group a safe place for receiving support and sharing ideas. Revisit the rules as needed in subsequent meetings to be sure the group stays a safe place. Assign a member to be in charge of reviewing and monitoring the rules and intervening if and when they are violated.

- *Create an agenda.* Assign one member to develop the agenda for each meeting. See Figure 13.4 for a sample agenda. Invite members to add items to the agenda at the beginning of each group and decide about how much time you want to spend on each item, given the overall allotted time. At a minimum, the agenda should include some time at the beginning to review prior concepts and homework assignments, time to discuss the new readings, practice any of the group exercises, and time at the end to debrief and plan for future groups.

- *Assign and complete homework prior to each meeting.* The group process can be effective for creating subtle social pressure to encourage all members to do the assigned reading and complete the exercises between sessions. Consider giving small rewards each meeting for everyone who completed the assignments.

- *Encourage everyone to participate.* This can be folded into one or more group rules that encourage participation and discourage anyone from dominating the discussions. You might assign one member who is responsible each group for monitoring participation levels and being sure everyone is getting their needs met; or you can have check-in points midway through each session and ask everyone if they have enough opportunities to participate.

- *Assign a group facilitator.* It is helpful to have one group member be in charge of facilitating the discussion. This person's task is to come prepared to the meeting with a set of open-ended questions about the readings, ask questions, and reflect and summarize comments made during the discussion.

- *Minimize lecturing or didactic instruction.* Assume members have read the book, ask them in order to be sure, and then don't feel the need to repeat the entire content. Instead, use the group for discussing ideas in greater detail, sharing ideas with each other, and completing the group activities.

- *Create an atmosphere of trust and encouragement.* Remind members that the goal of the group is to support each other in learning new skills. Set that as a priority for each meeting. Prevent side conversations; these can make people feel judged, as people sometimes assume side comments are about them even when they are not.

- *Avoid interpreting.* Pop psychology sometimes encourages people to over interpret other people's experiences by trying to figure out historic reasons for current maladies (e.g., what was your relationship like with your parents). These historic interpretations usually come with some sort of judgment and usually don't provide any path forward or solutions. Instead, focus on the present and using the skills described in the book. These are proactive and solution-focused approaches to problems.

- *Complete the group activities and add some of your own.* Switch up the format, sometimes doing the exercises as a whole group, and other times doing them as partners and reporting back to the larger group. Consider doing role plays as practice as well, especially for some of the behavior and social skill activities. Role plays can be threatening, but they are one of the best learning tools we have.

- *Make one group rule "Have Fun."* Make a point to use humor and have fun with the activities during the group. Be silly and let your hair down, so to speak. People will keep coming back if the groups are fun.

- *Reinforce participation and success.* Use social encouragement and praise to support each other's progress.

- *Plan breaks for longer meetings.* If you meet for more than an hour, consider adding 5- to 10-minute breaks as needed.

- *Express optimism.* Keep the focus of the group on a hopeful and optimistic note. Express encouragement and the belief that all participants can and will meet their goals.

- *Collect feedback.* Consider gathering feedback about each meeting from group members. This can be accomplished with a simple three- or four-item rating form that asks questions about what went well, what did not go well, and what members would like to happen in the next meeting. You can leave these items open-ended, or you can put them on a 5- to 10-point rating scale.

SUMMARY

We think it is a great idea to use this book as part of a study group. Groups can be fun and they can encourage us in ways that we sometimes can't do alone. When done as part of a broader school effort to promote more effective environments, study groups can contribute to the overall wellness of adults in school. As you know, when adults in schools are doing well, the effects almost always are experienced by students as well.

> **Groups can be fun and they can encourage us in ways that we sometimes can't do alone.**

HANDOUT 13.1

Summary Session Form

- **Summarize Session**
    - The purpose of our meeting today was for us to learn more about _____.
        - Some of your most important lessons are _____.
        - Some of the challenges were _____.
    - Does that sound about right? What else would others like to add?
- **Prepare for Next Meeting**
    - We will meet _____ more times.
    - Our topic next week will be _____.
    - Do you have any questions?
- **Homework Assignment**
    - The homework for the coming week will be to read Chapter _____.
    - In addition, the homework will be to complete the following activity: _____.
- **Rulers**

How **important** is it for you to make this meeting?

1	2	3	4	5	6	7	8	9	10
Not Important At All									Very Important

How **confident** are you that you can make this meeting?

1	2	3	4	5	6	7	8	9	10
Not Confident At All									Very Confident

Is there anything that could get in the way of completing the homework?

What can I do to help make sure this doesn't get in the way?

Can others be helpful to you in helping make sure you complete the assignment?

From *Stress Management for Teachers: A Proactive Guide* by Keith C. Herman and Wendy M. Reinke. Copyright 2015 by The Guilford Press. Permission to photocopy this handout is granted to purchasers of this book for personal use only (see copyright page for details). Purchasers can download and print additional copies of this handout from *www.guilford.com/herman-forms*.

CHAPTER 14

Your Personal Development Plan and Broader Systems Change

You have persisted and made it through to the end of the book. Congratulations! In this final chapter, we want you to reflect on your progress and develop a plan for using any new habits that you would like to continue. We provide some resources for you to assess your progress and to develop a plan for moving forward. We conclude the chapter with some reflection on the broader context of teacher stressors.

PERSONAL DEVELOPMENT PLAN

Take some time to reflect on the progress you have made and any strategies that you especially liked using in this book. One thing we have learned about behavior change is that it takes ongoing reflection and practice to cement new behaviors into our new routines. When we first make positive changes, it takes a lot of energy and focus. As these changes become more familiar and we become more fluent in them, we can devote less time to them. At some point, though, we may encounter new, stressful periods, and we may lose sight of the strategies that worked so well for us earlier. In this regard, it is helpful to come up with a plan for maintaining awareness of your own stress and coping and to think about warning signs that may suggest a need to return to a solid coping routine. Take some time to complete Handout 14.1 and reflect on changes you have made and want to continue.

> **It is helpful to come up with a plan for maintaining awareness of your own stress and coping and to think about warning signs.**

CREATING SYSTEMS CHANGE

Throughout this book, we have put our emphasis on you as an individual and what you can do to manage your stress. On the one hand, this makes sense, because you are the one reading the book and who can make different choices in your own life. On the other hand, we worry that this approach is a bit narrow and ignores the various contexts that surround you and influence your ability to cope with stress. An ecological perspective takes into consideration school environment, district and building policies, community norms, media, federal and state laws, and cultural values as part of the broader systems that have great influence over the teaching profession and how stressful it is. We hope not to send the message with this book that the individual is solely responsible for well-being. It is complicated, however, in thinking through the best way to evoke change in systems and in ourselves. In our view, one way to do this is in a ground-up manner where changes in individuals can create changes in systems that surround them. Grassroots efforts to change public policies and influence popular opinion are examples of this. The other way is more top-down, where we first create change in policies and cultural practices and watch as these changes affect individuals. These are both valid and important ways to change the world. Changing individuals is in some ways easier because it is more accessible. We change ourselves. Changing policy can be more challenging, as it is more distant from our daily experiences, yet it can have the benefit of affecting millions of people at a single stroke. Ideally, we do both. In lieu of public policy changes that make teachers' jobs easier and more valued by society, we wrote this book as a tool for you to manage the inevitable stressors of your job.

Systems change can be more manageable, however, when we focus on the ones that surround us most immediately. For instance, the policies, procedures, and relationships in your school building are much easier for you to influence than state or federal policies. Spend some time thinking about changes that could occur in your surrounding contexts that could make a meaningful difference in helping you and other teachers experience less stress and feel more supported in your daily routines. This may be a worthwhile conversation to have with other teachers and with administrators. Some system-level changes don't require money and may only require minimal effort.

> **Systems change can be more manageable, however, when we focus on the systems that surround us most immediately.**

For instance, some schools we have worked with have taken the principles of Schoolwide Positive Behavior Interventions and Supports (PBIS) and applied it to teachers. PBIS was originally developed to reduce problematic student behavior by increasing rates of positive attention for students when they are meeting expectations (Sugai & Horner, 2002). The same principles can be applied to supporting teacher development.

Big Ideas of PBIS

1. Define expectations.
2. Teach expectations.
3. Monitor and acknowledge desired behavior at higher rates than negative consequences.
4. Provide clear consequences for undesired behavior.
5. Collect information and use it for decision making.

> **GROUP ACTIVITY: Applying PBIS Principles to the Context**
>
> Brainstorm small changes in your work environment that could make a huge difference in helping teachers feel more confident, validated, supported, and less stressed. Think of ways that you can apply these principles not only to yourself but also to creating more nurturing environments at home and at work. Use Handout 14.2 to guide your discussion.

Some schools have developed systems for administrators and teachers to recognize each other in the form of specific praise and tokens that can be exchanged for prizes, privileges, and other low-cost incentives (e.g., dress-down coupons). The goal of these systems is to clearly specify expectations and then deliver high rates of positive attention and reward for those meeting expectations. The benefit of this approach is that it creates a system in line with many of the principles we discussed in this book. If the environment delivers higher rates of positive-to-negative interactions, the people in that environment are more likely to feel positive emotions about themselves, their work, and others. Such environments invite better coping, strengthen social attachments, and encourage positive behaviors. These benefits accrue for both the adults and the students in these buildings.

SUMMARY

As we have established in this book, teachers bear the brunt of stress for an evolving society. While the stressors may change over time, they are ever present. Citizens expect teachers to usher in our most optimistic visions of the future by supporting the youth of the next generation. Sometimes, however, society forgets to provide the tools and resources for such visions to become reality, and teachers are left holding the empty bag of wishes. This can place teachers in the unenviable position of feeling responsible for correcting society's woes. Of course, in reality, teachers are no more or less responsible for contributing to world improvement than other citizens. It is good to remind yourself about that. Moreover, you can only be as helpful to the next generation as you are to yourself. By taking time to read this book and commit to improving your coping strategies, you have taken an important step toward enhancing your wellness and the wellness of those who surround you. We wish you continued positive emotions, engagement, and fulfillment, moments of flow, and months of flourishing as you continue on your journey to *the good life*.

HANDOUT 14.1

Personal Development Plan

I would like to continue to use the following strategies on a daily or weekly basis:

Awareness
- ☐ Mood monitoring
- ☐ Goal setting
- ☐ Problem solving

Adaptive Thinking
- ☐ Positive/negative thoughts method
- ☐ ABC method
- ☐ Coping thoughts
- ☐ Values affirmations
- ☐ Self-disclosure writing

Adaptive Behaviors
- ☐ Increasing pleasant events
- ☐ Communication skills
- ☐ Relaxation
- ☐ Exercise
- ☐ Healthy eating

Getting to Good
- ☐ Values and virtues affirmations
- ☐ Gratitude exercises
- ☐ Mindfulness
- ☐ Personal narratives

To remind myself to use these skills I will do the following: _____
_____
_____

My warning signs that I may need to use these skills more often or try different ones include:

Physical Symptoms
- ☐ Headaches
- ☐ Back aches
- ☐ Stomach pain
- ☐ Chest pain
- ☐ Other muscle tension
- ☐ Frequent illnesses

Behavior Red Flags
- ☐ Poor or restless sleep
- ☐ Lack of exercise
- ☐ Overeating
- ☐ Unhealthy eating
- ☐ Excessive alcohol use
- ☐ Cigarette smoking
- ☐ Other drug use
- ☐ Watching too much TV

Emotional Symptoms
- ☐ Exhausted
- ☐ Sad
- ☐ Anxious
- ☐ Irritable
- ☐ Overwhelmed

Social Red Flags
- ☐ Withdrawing or isolating
- ☐ Arguing with family
- ☐ Conflicts with co-workers

Others
- ☐ _____
- ☐ _____
- ☐ _____
- ☐ _____

(continued)

From *Stress Management for Teachers: A Proactive Guide* by Keith C. Herman and Wendy M. Reinke. Copyright 2015 by The Guilford Press. Permission to photocopy this handout is granted to purchasers of this book for personal use only (see copyright page for details). Purchasers can download and print additional copies of this handout from *www.guilford.com/herman-forms*.

Personal Development Plan *(page 2 of 2)*

When I notice these signs, I will do the following:
- ☐ Reread this book
- ☐ Reread the chapters that are most relevant to my warning signs
- ☐ Increase my use of strategies that worked before
- ☐ Seek social support
- ☐ Set new goals and monitor my progress
- ☐ Work through the problem solving steps
- ☐ Start monitoring my mood again

How **important** is it for me to stick with this plan? (Circle a number and write it in the blank.)

```
    0    1    2    3    4    5    6    7    8    9    10
Not Important                                    Very Important
```

I rated the importance _____. Why did I choose this number and not one number lower? _____

_____

How **confident** am I that I will stick with the plan? (Circle a number and write it in the blank.)

```
    0    1    2    3    4    5    6    7    8    9    10
Not Confident                                    Very Confident
```

I rated my confidence _____. Why did I choose this number and not one number lower? _____

_____
_____
_____

What could I do to help myself become more confident? _____

_____
_____
_____

HANDOUT 14.2

Changing the School Environment

What is one change that would make a difference in creating a more positive school environment for teachers? _____

_____

_____

_____

_____

What are the resources needed to make this change? _____

_____

_____

_____

_____

What do we need to do to make these resources available? _____

_____

_____

_____

_____

What do we want to happen? _____

_____

_____

_____

_____

What are we willing to do? _____

_____

_____

_____

_____

_____

From *Stress Management for Teachers: A Proactive Guide* by Keith C. Herman and Wendy M. Reinke. Copyright 2015 by The Guilford Press. Permission to photocopy this handout is granted to purchasers of this book for personal use only (see copyright page for details). Purchasers can download and print additional copies of this handout from *www.guilford.com/herman-forms*.

References

Antony, M. M. (2000). *The shyness and social anxiety workbook.* New York: New Harbinger.

Armitage, C. J., Harris, P. R., Hepton, G., & Napper, L. (2008). Self-affirmation increases acceptance of health-risk information among UK adult smokers with low socioeconomic status. *Psychology of Addictive Behaviors, 22,* 88–95.

Arroll, B., Goodyear-Smith, F., Crengle, S., Gunn, J., Kerse, N., Fishman, T., et al. (2010). Validation of PHQ-2 and PHQ-9 to screen for major depression in the primary care population. *Annals of Family Medicine, 8*(4), 348–353.

Bandura, A. (1986). *Social foundations of thought and action: A social cognitive theory.* Englewood Cliffs, NJ: Prentice Hall.

Bandura, A. (2004). Health promotion by social cognitive means. *Health Education and Behavior, 31,* 143–164.

Barlow, D., & Craske, M. (2006). *Mastery of anxiety and panic: Workbook.* New York: Oxford University Press.

Beck, A. T., Rush, A. J., Shaw, B. F., & Emery, G. (1979). *Cognitive therapy of depression.* New York: Guilford Press.

Burns, D. D. (1999). *Feeling good: The new mood therapy* (rev. and updated). New York: New American Library.

Bushman, B. J. (2002). Does venting anger feed or extinguish the flame?: Catharsis, rumination, distraction, anger, and aggressive responding. *Personality and Social Psychology Bulletin, 28*(6), 724–731.

Butler, A. C., Chapman, J. E., Forman, E. M., & Beck, A. T. (2006). The empirical status of cognitive-behavioral therapy: A review of meta-analyses. *Clinical Psychology Review, 26*(1), 17–31.

Clark, D. A., & Beck, A. T. (2010). Cognitive theory and therapy of anxiety and depression: Convergence with neurobiological findings. *Trends in Cognitive Sciences, 14*(9), 418–424.

Clum, G. (1990). *Coping with panic: A drug-free guide to coping with dealing with anxiety attacks.* New York: Thomsen/Cole.

Cohen, S., & Janicki-Deverts, D. (2012). Who's stressed?: Distributions of psychological stress in the United States in probability samples from 1983, 2006, and 2009. *Journal of Applied Social Psychology, 42*(6), 1320–1334.

Cohen, S., Kamarck, T., & Mermelstein, R. (1983). A global measure of perceived stress. *Journal of Health and Social Behavior, 24,* 385–396.

Cohen, S., Mermelstein, R., Kamarck, T., & Hoberman, H. (1985). Measuring the functional components of social support. In I. G. Sarason & B. R. Sarason (Eds.), *Social support: Theory, research and application* (pp. 73–94). The Hague: Martinus Nijhoff.

Colvin, G., Sugai, G., Good, R. H., & Lee, Y. (1997). Using active supervision and precorrection to improve transition behaviors in an elementary school. *School Psychology Quarterly, 12,* 344–363.

Crone, D., Hawken, L., & Horner, R. (2010). *Responding to problem behavior in schools: The Behavior Education Program* (2nd ed.). New York: Guilford Press.

Crone, D., & Horner, R. (2003). *Building positive behavior support systems in schools: Functional behavioral assessment.* New York: Guilford Press.

Cuijpers, P. (1997). Bibliotherapy in unipolar depression: A meta-analysis. *Journal of Behavior Therapy and Experimental Psychiatry, 28*(2), 139–147.

Cuijpers, P. (1998). A psychoeducational approach to the treatment of depression: A meta-analysis of Lewinsohn's "Coping With Depression" course. *Behavior Therapy, 29,* 521–533.

Cuijpers, P., Donker, T., van Straten, A., Li, J., & Andersson, G. (2010). Is guided self-help as effective as face-to-face psychotherapy for depression and anxiety disorders?: A systematic review and meta-analysis of comparative outcome studies. *Psychological Medicine, 40,* 1943–1957.

Csikszentmihalyi, M. (1990). *Flow: The psychology of optimal experience.* New York: Harper & Row.

Dansinger, M. L., Gleason, J., Griffith, J. L., Selker, H. P., & Schaefer, E. J. (2005). Comparison of the Atkins, Ornish, Weight Watchers, and Zone diets for weight loss and heart disease risk reduction: A randomized trial. *Journal of the American Medical Association, 293*(1), 43–53.

De Pry, R. L., & Sugai, G. (2002). The effects of active supervision and pre-correction on minor behavioral incidents in a sixth grade general education classroom. *Journal of Behavioral Education, 11,* 155–267.

Dhabhar, F. S., Malarkey, W. B., Neri, E., & McEwen, B. S. (2012). Stress-induced redistribution of immune cells—From barracks to boulevards to battlefields: A tale of three hormones–Curt Richter Award Winner. *Psychoneuroendocrinology, 37*(9), 1345–1368.

Dhabhar, F. S., Saul, A. N., Daugherty, C., Holmes, T. H., Bouley, D. M., & Oberyszyn, T. M. (2010). Short-term stress enhances cellular immunity and increases early resistance to squamous cell carcinoma. *Brain, Behavior, and Immunity, 24*(1), 127–137.

D'Zurilla, T. J., & Nezu, A. M. (2007). *Problem-solving therapy: A positive approach to clinical intervention.* New York: Springer.

Doll, B., Brehm, K., & Zucker, S. (2014). *Resilient classrooms: Creating healthy environments for learning* (2nd ed.). New York: Guilford Press.

Eaton, W., Anthony, J. C., Mandel, W., & Garrison, R. (1990). Occupations and the prevalence of major depressive disorder. *Journal of Occupational Medicine, 32,* 1079–87.

Eisenberger, R., Pierce, D., & Cameron, J. (1999). Effects of reward on intrinsic motivation—negative, neutral, and positive: Comment on Deci, Koestner, and Ryan. *Psychological Bulletin, 125,* 677–691.

Ellis, A. (1997). *A guide to rational living* (3rd ed.). New York: Wilshire books.

Ellis, A. (2004). *Rational emotive behavior therapy: It works for me—It can work for you.* Amherst, NY: Prometheus Books.

Embry, D. (2002). The Good Behavior Game: A best practice candidate as a universal behavioral vaccine. *Clinical Child and Family Psychology Review, 5,* 273–297.

Evans, G. W. (2003). A multimethodological analysis of cumulative risk and allostatic load among rural children. *Developmental Psychology, 39*(5), 924.

Fischer, J., & Corcoran, K. J. (1994). *Measures for clinical practice: A Sourcebook: Adults* (Vol. 2). New York: Simon & Schuster.

Fixen, D., Naoom, S., Blase, K., Friedman, R., & Wallace, F. (2005). *Implementation research: A synthesis of the literature.* Tampa, FL: University of South Florida, Louis de la Parte Florida Mental Health Institute, The National Implementation Research Network.

Foa, E. B. (2001). *Stop obsessing!* New York: Bantam Books.

Frumkin, H. (2001). Beyond toxicity: Human health and the natural environment. *American Journal of Preventive Medicine, 20*, 234–240.

Good, T., & Brophy, J. (2003). *Looking in classrooms* (9th ed.). New York: Allyn & Bacon.

Hanh, T. N. (1992). *Peace is every step: The path of mindfulness in everyday life*. New York: Bantam Books.

Hanh, T. N. (1995). *The miracle of mindfulness*. New York: Harper Audio.

Hickmon, J. A., Reinke, W. M., & Herman, K. C. (2013). *Empirically derived profiles of teacher stress, burnout, self-efficacy, and coping and associated student outcomes.* Manuscript submitted for publication.

Hirai, M., & Clum, G. (2006). A meta-analytic study of self-help interventions for anxiety problems. *Behavior Therapy, 37*, 99–111.

Holmes, T. H., & Rahe R. H. (1967). The Social Readjustment Rating Scale. *Journal of Psychosomatic Research, 11*, 213–218.

Huan, M., Hamazaki, K., Sun, Y., Itomura, M., Liu, H., Kang, W., et al. (2004). Suicide attempt and n-3 fatty acid levels in red blood cells: A case control study in China. *Biological Psychiatry, 56*, 490–496.

Hyman, B. M. (1999). *The OCD workbook*. New York: New Harbinger.

Ingersoll, R. M. (2002). High turnover plagues schools. *USA Today*, 13A.

Kabat-Zinn, J. (1994). *Wherever you go, there you are: Mindfulness meditation in everyday life*. New York: Hyperion.

Kabat-Zinn, J. (2013). *Full catastrophe living: Using the wisdom of your body and mind to face stress, pain, and illness* (rev. ed.). New York: Bantam Books.

Keller, A., Litzelman, K., Wisk, L. E., Maddox, T., Cheng, E. R., Creswell, P. D., et al. (2012). Does the perception that stress affects health matter?: The association with health and mortality. *Health Psychology, 31*(5), 677.

Kessler, R. C., Chiu, W. T., Demler, O., & Walters, E. E. (2005). Prevalence, severity, and comorbidity of twelve-month DSM-IV disorders in the National Comorbidity Survey Replication (NCS-R). *Archives of General Psychiatry, 62*, 617–627.

Kroenke, K. (2007). The 2-item Generalized Anxiety Disorder scale had high sensitivity and specificity in a primary care setting. *Evidence-Based Medicine, 12*, 149.

Kroenke, K., Spitzer, R. L., Williams, J. B., & Löwe, B. (2009). An ultra-brief screening scale for anxiety and depression: The PHQ–4. *Psychosomatics, 50*(6), 613–621.

Lewinsohn, P. M., Muñoz, R. F., Youngren, M. A., & Zeiss, A. M. (1992). *Control your Depression*. New York: Simon & Schuster.

Lewis, T. J., Colvin, G., & Sugai, G. (2000). The effects of precorrection and active supervision on the recess behavior of elementary students. *Education and Treatment of Children, 23*, 109–121.

Lochman, J. (2004). *The Life Events Questionnaire*. Unpublished scale, University of Alabama.

Lyubomirsky, S. (2008). *The how of happiness*. New York: Penguin Books.

Lyubomirsky, S., & Lepper, H. (1999). A measure of subjective happiness: Preliminary reliability and construct validation. *Social Indicators Research, 46*, 137–155.

Maslach, C., Schaufeli, W. B., & Leiter, M. P. (2001). Job burnout. *Annual Review of Psychology, 52*, 397–422.

Markway, B. (1992). *Dying of embarrassment: Help for social anxiety and phobia*. New York: New Harbinger.

MacPhillamy, D. J., & Lewinsohn, P. M. (1972). *The Pleasant Events Schedule*. Unpublished manuscript, University of Oregon, Eugene, OR.

Miller, W. M., & Rollnick, S. (2013). *Motivational interviewing* (3rd ed.). New York: Guilford Press.

Miller, W. R., & Muñoz, R. F. (1982). *How to control your drinking*. Albuquerque: University of New Mexico Press.

Mischoulon, D., Papakostas, G. I., Dording, C. M., Farabaugh, A. H., Sonawalla, S. B., Agoston, A. M., et al. (2009). A double-blind, randomized controlled trial of ethyl-eicosapentaenoate for major depressive disorder. *Journal of Clinical Psychiatry, 70,* 1636–1644.

Pennebaker, J. (1997). Writing about emotional experiences as a therapeutic process. *Psychological Science, 8,* 162–166.

Poulin, M. J., Brown, S. L., Dillard, A. J., & Smith, D. M. (2013). Giving to others and the association between stress and mortality. *American Journal of Public Health, 103,* 1649–1655.

Radloff, L. S. (1977). CES-D scale: A self-report depression scale for research in the general populations. *Applied Psychological Measurement, 1,* 385–401.

Radloff, L. S. (1991). The use of the center for epidemiological studies of depression scale in adolescents and young adults. *Journal of Youth and Adolescence, 20,* 149–166.

Rathvon, N. (2008). *Effective school interventions: Evidence-based strategies for improving student outcomes.* New York: Guilford Press.

Reed, M. B., & Aspinwall, L. G. (1998), Self-affirmation reduces biased processing of health-risk information. *Motivation and Emotion, 22,* 99–132.

Reinke, W. M., Herman, K. C., & Sprick, R. (2011). *Motivational interviewing for effective classroom management: The classroom check-up.* New York: Guilford Press.

Reinke, W. M., Lewis-Palmer, T., & Merrell, K. (2008). The classroom check-up: A class wide teacher consultation model for increasing praise and decreasing disruptive behavior. *School Psychology Review, 37,* 315–332.

Sanchez-Craig, M. (1993). *Saying when: How to quit drinking or cut down.* Toronto: Addiction Research Foundation.

Sapolsky, R. M. (2004). *Why zebras don't get ulcers* (3rd ed.). New York: Freeman.

Sarris, J., Kavanagh, C. J., & Newton, R. (May/June, 2008). Depression and exercise. *Complementary Medicine,* 48–62.

Scheier, M. F., Carver, C. S., & Bridges, M. W. (1994). Distinguishing optimism from neuroticism (and trait anxiety, self-mastery, and self-esteem): A re-evaluation of the Life Orientation Test. *Journal of Personality and Social Psychology, 67,* 1063–1078.

Seligman, M. E. P. (2002). *Authentic happiness.* New York: Free Press.

Seligman, M. E. P. (2011). *Flourish.* New York: Free Press.

Selye, H. (1974). *Stress without distress.* New York: Lippincott.

Sobell, M. B., & Sobell, L. C. (1993). *Problem drinkers: Guided self-change treatment.* New York: Guilford Press.

Spitzer, R. L., Kroenke, K., Williams, J. B., and the Patient Health Questionnaire Primary Care Study Group (1999). Validation and utility of a self-report version of PRIME-MD: The PHQ primary care study. *Journal of the American Medical Association, 282,* 1737–1744.

Sprick, R. (2006). *Discipline in the secondary classroom: A positive approach to behavior management* (2nd ed.). Eugene, OR: Pacific Northwest.

Sprick, R. (2008). *CHAMPS: A proactive and positive approach to classroom management* (2nd ed.). Eugene, OR: Pacific Northwest.

Sprick, R., Booher, M., & Garrison, M. (2009). *Behavioral response to intervention: Creating a continuum of problem solving and support.* Eugene, OR: Pacific Northwest.

Sprick, R., & Garrison, M. (2008). *Interventions: Evidence-based Behavioral Strategies for Individual Students.* (2nd ed.). Eugene, OR: Pacific Northwest.

Sprick, R., Knight, J., Reinke, W., Skyles, T., & Barnes, L. (2010). *Coaching classroom management: Strategies and tools for administrators and coaches.* Eugene, OR: Pacific Northwest.

Stormont, M., Herman, K. C., Reinke, W. M., David, K. B., & Goel, N. (2013). Latent profile analysis of teacher perceptions of parent contact and comfort. *School Psychology Quarterly, 28*(3), 195.

Stormont, M., Reinke, W. M., Herman, K. C., & Lemke, E. (2012). *Academic and behavior supports for at-risk students: Tier 2 Interventions.* New York: Guilford Press.

Sugai, G., & Horner, R. (2002). The evolution of discipline practices: School-wide positive behavior supports. *Child and Family Behavior Therapy, 24*(1–2), 23–50.

Teychenne, M., Ball, K., & Salmon, J. (2008). Physical activity and likelihood of depression in adults: A review. *Preventive Medicine, 46,* 397–411.

Tschannen-Moran, M., & Hoy, A. W. (2001). Teacher efficacy: Capturing an elusive construct. *Teaching and Teacher Education, 17,* 783–805.

Üstün, T. B., Ayuso-Mateos, J. L., Chatterji, S., Mathers, C., & Murray, C. J. L. (2004). Global burden of depressive disorders in the year 2000. *British Journal of Psychiatry, 184,* 386.

Webster-Stratton, C. (1999). *How to promote children's social and emotional competence.* Los Angeles: Sage.

Weissman, A. (1979). *Dysfunctional Attitude Scale: A validation study.* Unpublished doctoral dissertation, University of Pennsylvania, Philadelphia.

Weissman, A. N. (1980). *Assessing depressionogenic attitudes: A validation study.* Paper presented at the 51st Annual Meeting of the Eastern Psychological Association, Hartford, CT.

Yuen, E. Y., Liu, W., Karatsoreos, I. N., Feng, J., McEwen, B. S., & Yan, Z. (2009). Acute stress enhances glutamatergic transmission in prefrontal cortex and facilitates working memory. *Proceedings of the National Academy of Sciences, 106*(33), 14075–14079.

Index

ABCDE method
    for administrative pressure, 191–192
    overview of, 95–96
    for parent challenges, 197–198
    practicing, 98
    sample completed worksheets, 99–100
    worksheets for, 96–98, 107, 108
ABC method
    beliefs, identifying, 87–90
    case examples, 85–86
    core beliefs, identifying, 94
    funnel technique, 91
    goals of, 83–84
    overview of, 62, 83
    self-assessment, 84, 101
    self-monitoring, 84–86, 102–103
    thinking errors, 91–94
    worksheets for, 102, 103
Academic performance of students, 9, 154
Acceptance, 180
Accountability era, 3–4
Achievement, as aspect of flourishing, 177
Activating events in ABC method, 83
Acute stress, benefits of, 14–15
Adaptive behaviors
    for administrative pressure, 190
    for administrators, 218–219
    communication and problem solving, 114–119
    developing, 39
    healthy eating and exercise, 123–124
    increasing positive-to-negative ratio, 110–112
    minimal interventions, 124–126
    overview of, 109–110
    pleasant activities, 112–114
    relaxation skills, 119–123
Adaptive core beliefs, 94

Adaptive thoughts
    for administrative pressure, 190–191
    becoming expert on thoughts, 62–63
    developing, 38
    positive/negative thoughts method, 65–72
    rose-colored glasses compared to, 64
    self-assessment, 64–65
    using method, 72
    See also ABC method
Adding Fun to My Classroom form, 137
Administrators
    awareness, cultivating, 215–223
    positive coping culture and, 215
    pressures from, 189–192
    professional development and, 164–166
    support from and expectations of, 17
    talking about stress and coping, 223–225
    TCM for, 225–227, 230, 231
Affirmations, 118, 235
Agenda for study group, 235–236, 237
Aggressive communication, 116
Alcohol use, 42–43, 212–213
All-or-none thinking, 91–92
Allostasis, 13
Altruism, 183
Anger, thoughts that bring about, 87, 212
Anxiety disorders, 207–210
Applications of strategies
    administrative pressures, 189–192
    peer conflicts, 192–195
    working with parents, 195–201
    work-life balance, 201–202
Assertive communication, 116–118, 194
Assessments, 169–170, 216–217. *See also* Self-assessments; Surveys
Attention of students, gaining, 145–146

Index

Authentic happiness, 177
Autogenic relaxation, 121–122
Automatic thoughts, 94
Awareness skills
    for administrators, 215–223
    deep breathing, 52–53
    developing, 37–38, 39
    feelings journal, 51
    goal setting, 53–54
    mood monitoring, 49–51
    problem solving, 54–57

Baseline data, collecting, 72
Basic Mood Monitoring Form, 49–50, 58
Beginner's mind, 180
Behaviors
    control over, 35–36
    defined, 31
    inappropriate, 152–159
    of students, dealing with, 159–163, 173–174
    thoughts, feelings, and, 32–33
    See also Adaptive behaviors; Proactive classroom management strategies
Behavior-specific praise, 148–149
Behaviors Related to Stress and Coping Screening, 41–42, 45
Beliefs, 83, 85, 87–90, 94, 102–103
Bibliotherapy, 9–10, 211
Blowing things out of proportion, 72
Body language, 222
Books, self-help, 7, 209–210, 211, 213, 223
Breathing, 52–53, 119–120, 179
Bullying, 193–195
Burnout, 223–224

Care of self, 202, 206
Catastrophizing, 92–93
Cathartic release as coping strategy, 22–23
Central nervous system (CNS), 14–15
Challenges for teachers, 4–5
Changing
    building commitment to, 25
    negative cycles, 34–35
    school environment, 240–242, 245
Chronic stress and illness, 12–13
Classroom and Teaching Screening, 46
Classrooms
    effective management of, 4, 141–142, 167–168
    having fun in, 113, 137
    positive-to-negative ratio in, 43, 111, 148
    See also Proactive classroom management strategies
Coaching and professional development, 164
Cognitive therapy, 211
Collaborative spirit, 221
Colleagues, relationships with, 18, 115–116, 192–195
Common Negative Thoughts and Their Positive Replacements, 77
Communication, effective, 116–119, 194
Competence, sense of, 39, 164–166
Complete Mr. Ellison's ABCDE Worksheet, 231

Complete Mr. Ellison's ABC Worksheet, 230
Consequences, 83, 152–153
Constructive feedback, 221
Consultation and professional development, 164
Coping, 8–9, 22–25
Coping thoughts, 68–69, 82, 156, 158, 222–223
Core beliefs, identifying, 94
Counseling, benefits of, 208
Credit, giving self, 70
Cuing positive thoughts, 69–70

Deep breathing, 52–53, 119–120
Defensive reactions, 222–223
Depression, 39, 42, 210–211
Diet, healthy, 123–124
Diversity of student needs, 19
Dysfunctional Attitude Scale, 64–65, 74–76

Eating, 123–124, 177–178
Ecological perspective, 241
Education, climate of, 3–6
Efficacy, 140. *See also* Self-efficacy
Embarrassment, thoughts related to, 88
Engagement, as aspect of flourishing, 177
Errors in thinking, 91–94
Escape, as coping strategy, 22
Events, emotional reactions to, 4, 5–6
Exaggeration, 72
Exercise, 90, 123–124, 126, 211
Expectations, 142–146, 199
Explicit reprimands, 152
Exposure in treatment for anxiety disorders, 209
Extinction, 155
Extinction bursts, 217

Facilitation of study group, 234–236, 237, 239
Faculty meetings, 218–219
Failure, perceptions of, 21
Feedback, negative, delivery of, 220–223
Feedback form for conferences, 199–201, 204
Feelings
    control over, 35
    defined, 31
    expressing, 114–115, 116–118
    mood monitoring, 49–51
    thoughts, behaviors, and, 32–33
Feelings journal, 51
Flooding, 209
Flourishing, 177
Flow, 176
Fortunetelling, 93
Friendships, 111
Function-based plans for behaviors, 159–163, 173–174
Funnel technique, 91, 105

Generalized anxiety disorder (GAD), 207, 208
Generosity, 183
Getting to good, 37, 175–177
Goal setting, 53–54, 72, 82, 165–166, 167
Goal-Setting Sheet, 53–54, 60

Good Behavior Game, 151
Good life, getting to, 175–177
Gossip, 111, 193
Gratitude, 183
Gratitude journal, 73
Gratitude note, 99
Ground rules for study group, 234, 236–237
Group contingencies, 150–151
Guided imagery, 69, 122

Healthy eating, 123–124
Home, positive-to-negative ratio at, 111–112
Homeostatic regulation of stress, 13

Ignoring behavior, planned, 154–155, 156, 158
Illness and stress, 12–13
Immune system and stress, 12–13, 14–15
Inappropriate behavior, handling, 152–159
Incentives, 113–114, 149–150
Incentives for Me form, 138
Inspiring quotes, 69
Instruction, differentiating, 19
Interactions. *See* Positive-to-negative ratio
Interpersonal Support Evaluation List, 115, 139
Irony of experiences of teachers, 4

Journaling, 51, 73, 124–125

Letting go, 180
Life events, 4, 5–6, 14, 20
Life Events Questionnaire, 23, 27
Life stories, 183–184
Life stress, 22
Listening skills, 118–119, 225
List of Common Challenging Areas form, 101

Maladaptive core beliefs, 94
Meaning, as aspect of flourishing, 177
Mental health disorders, 207–214. *See also* Depression
Menu of options, developing, 221–222
Michigan State University Counseling Center, 209
Mindfulness, 177–180
Mind reading, 93
Minimal interventions, benefits of, 124–126
Mini-muscle relaxations, 121
Modeling positive examples of rules, 143–146
Mood monitoring, 49–51, 57, 59
Moralization, 92
Motivational interviewing, 212
My Coping Thoughts form, 69, 81
My Life Pie, 201–202, 205

Narratives, 183–184
Nature, incorporating into daily life, 125–126, 228
Negative cycles of thoughts, feelings, and behaviors, 32–33
Negative feedback, delivering, 220–223
Nonjudging, 179–180
Nonstriving, 180

Normalization of stress and coping, 223–224
Nutrition, 123–124

OARS, 118–119, 235
Open-ended questions, 118, 235
Overgeneralization, 91–92
Overreaction to situation, 84

Paradox of mindful being, 178
Parasympathetic nervous system, 14
Parents, relationships with, 22, 195–201
Parent-teacher conferences, 199–201, 204
Passion for teaching, recalling, 66–67
Passive communication, 116
Patience, 180
Patient Health Questionnaire (PHQ-2), 42, 208, 210
Peer coaching, 164–165, 166
Peer conflicts, 192–195
Perceived Stress Scale, 23–24, 28
Perceptions of administration, assessing, 216–217
Performance feedback, 165
Peripheral nervous system (PNS), 14–15
Personal development plan, 240, 243–244
Personalization, 93
Physiology of stress, 14–15
Plan for Teaching Classroom Routines and Tasks, 172
Plan for Teaching Classroom Rules, 171
Planned ignoring, 154–155, 156, 158
Plants, adding to environment, 125–126, 228
Pleasant activities, 112–114
Pleasant Events Goals and Weekly Schedule, 136
Pleasant Events I Want to Try form, 135
Pleasant Events Schedule, 127–134
Positive and Negative Method Goal Setting, 72, 82
Positive Behavior Interventions and Supports (PBIS), 241–242
Positive cycles of thoughts, feelings, and behaviors, 34–35
Positive emotion, 177
Positive/negative thoughts method, 62, 65–72
Positive psychology, 176–177
Positive teaching, 4
Positive-to-negative ratio, 43, 110–112, 148, 199, 219–220
Practicing positive examples of rules, 143–146
Practicing strategies
  ABCDE method, 99, 191–192
  identifying thoughts, 88–90, 104, 105
  importance of, 10
  mindfulness, 180
  mood monitoring, 50
  planned ignoring, 158
Praise, behavior-specific, 148–149
Precorrection, 146–148
Priming and cues, 69–70
Proactive classroom management strategies
  behavior-specific praise, 148–149
  explicit reprimands, 152
  group contingencies and token economies, 150–151